IMAM HUSSAIN (A)
LIFE AND LEGACY

SAYYID ALI AL-HAKEEM

THE MAINSTAY FOUNDATION

Author: Sayyid Ali Al-Hakeem

Translated and Edited by: The Mainstay Foundation

© 2019 The Mainstay Foundation

Printed in the United States.

ISBN: 978-1943393701

To our guide. To our hope. To our salvation.

To our Prophet (s).

CONTENTS

ABOUT THE AUTHOR

Sayyid Ali Al-Hakeem is an esteemed Muslim scholar, lecturer, and researcher residing in Dubai, UAE. Sayyid Al-Hakeem spent ten years studying at the Islamic seminaries of Qum, Iran. There, he completed his Advanced Seminars (a Ph.D. equivalent in Islamic seminaries) in Islamic Jurisprudence and Thought. He also received a Master's degree in Islamic Thought from the Islamic University of Lebanon. Sayyid Al-Hakeem has dedicated the past twenty-two years of his life to service of the Muslim community in different capacities. He serves as a resident scholar in the Imam Hassan Mosque, Dubai. He is the Chair of the Religious Committee and the religious supervisor of the Charitable Deeds Committee of the Ja'afariya Endowment Charitable Council of Dubai.

TRANSLATOR'S PREFACE

The task of translating Sayyid Ali Al-Hakeem's book was gratifying and enlightening. The book delivered precious nuggets of knowledge and polished pearls of wisdom in a style that is conversational and pleasant. This book is our attempt to pass these nuggets and pearls on to you in a style that is similarly conversational and pleasant. We thank the Sayyid for allowing us to benefit from this endeavor. We wish for him a life filled with scholarly attainment, in hopes that he will continue to pass along his treasures.

Here, we must humbly admit some of our biggest limitations. First, we must admit the great difficulty that comes with the attempting to translate the Holy Quran. Muslim scholars have pondered on the meanings of the holy text for centuries, and the meanings of its verses only grow deeper as time passes. The process of translation always begs us to find precise meanings for the passages that we translate. But when we encounter the majesty of the Holy Quran, we find ourselves incapable of understanding, let alone translating, its true and deep meanings. We turned to the works of translators who have attempted to do this before. Although no translation can do justice to the Holy Quran, we found that the translation of Ali Quli Qarai to be the most proper in understanding when compared to the understanding of the text as derived by our grand scholars. As such, we decided to rely on Qarai's translations throughout this book, with some adaptations that allowed us to weave the verses more properly with the rest of the work.

A second great limitation came with translation of the narrations of the Grand Prophet Muhammad (s) and his Holy Household. Their words are ever so deep and ever so powerful. We attempted to convey these passages to the reader in a tone that is understandable without deviating from the essence of the words of these immaculate personalities. We pray that we were successful in this endeavor.

Finally, we want to take this opportunity to thank you for your support. As students of Islam and as translators of this text, our greatest purpose is to please God by passing along these teachings to others. By picking up this book, you've lent your crucial support in this endeavor. We hope that you will continue your support throughout the rest of this book, and we ask that you keep us in prayers whenever you pick it up.

The Editorial and Translation Team,

The Mainstay Foundation

INTRODUCTION

In the Name of God, the Most Compassionate, the Most Merciful

إِنَّ اللَّهَ اصْطَفَى آدَمَ وَنُوحًا وَآلَ إِبْرَاهِيمَ وَآلَ عِمْرَانَ عَلَى الْعَالَمِينَ

﴿٣٣﴾ ذُرِّيَّةً بَعْضُهَا مِن بَعْضٍ ۗ وَاللَّهُ سَمِيعٌ عَلِيمٌ ﴿٣٤﴾

Indeed Allah chose Adam and Noah, and the progeny of Abraham and the progeny of Imran above all the nations; some of them are descendants of the others, and Allah is all-hearing, all-knowing.[1]

God Almighty sent the Holy Prophet Muhammad (s) as a mercy to all creation and the final messenger to humanity. The Holy Prophet (s) was promised that the message he delivered would be safeguarded and would remain until the Day of Judgment. This is to the contrary of the history of all other pervious messages which were at some point distorted by individuals who wanted to safeguard their own interests and ambitions.

God promised that the message of Islam would not be distorted like the pervious messages. Yet, the Muslim nation was

---

[1] The Holy Quran, 3:33-34.

1

no different than previous nations. Desire, greed, deviance, ignorance, oppression, and all the other vices can be observed in the Muslim nation as in all other nations. So how is it that this message has been safeguarded?

God Almighty protected the message of Islam on both intellectual and practical levels. On an intellectual level God ensured that the message would be encompassed in the Holy Quran – a book which is immune to addition, subtraction, or alteration of any kind. God says,

$$\text{إِنَّا نَحْنُ نَزَّلْنَا الذِّكْرَ وَإِنَّا لَهُ لَحَافِظُونَ}$$

Indeed We have sent down the Reminder, and indeed We will preserve it.[2]

But the Holy Book by itself is not enough to protect the message from distortion. The Quran – by its own acknowledgement – includes verses that are definitive and others that are metaphorical. It contains general and specific verses. Some verses are abrogated and others are abrogating. This means that although the text of the Holy Quran is immune from alteration, its verses can be misunderstood and misappropriated. God says,

$$\text{هُوَ الَّذِي أَنزَلَ عَلَيْكَ الْكِتَابَ مِنْهُ آيَاتٌ مُحْكَمَاتٌ هُنَّ أُمُّ}$$
$$\text{الْكِتَابِ وَأُخَرُ مُتَشَابِهَاتٌ ۖ فَأَمَّا الَّذِينَ فِي قُلُوبِهِمْ زَيْغٌ فَيَتَّبِعُونَ مَا}$$
$$\text{تَشَابَهَ مِنْهُ ابْتِغَاءَ الْفِتْنَةِ وَابْتِغَاءَ تَأْوِيلِهِ ۗ وَمَا يَعْلَمُ تَأْوِيلَهُ إِلَّا اللَّهُ ۗ}$$

---

[2] The Holy Quran, 15:9.

وَالرَّاسِخُونَ فِي الْعِلْمِ يَقُولُونَ آمَنَّا بِهِ كُلٌّ مِّنْ عِندِ رَبِّنَا وَمَا يَذَّكَّرُ
إِلَّا أُولُو الْأَلْبَابِ

It is He who has sent down to you the Book. Parts of it are definitive verses, which are the mother of the Book, while others are metaphorical. As for those in whose hearts is deviance, they pursue what is metaphorical in it, courting temptation, and seeking its interpretation. But no one knows its interpretation except Allah and those firmly grounded in knowledge; they say, 'We believe in it; all of it is from our Lord.' And none takes admonition except those who possess intellect.[3]

Therefore, there had to be something in addition to the Book of God to preserve the message of Islam on a practical level. There needed to be something equal to the Quran which preserved the true understanding of its teachings and verses. The Holy Prophet (s) pointed us toward this second safeguard when he declared,

إني تارك فيكم ما إن تمسكتم بهما لن تضلوا بعدي كتاب الله
وعترتي أهل بيتي لن يفترقا حتى يردا علي الحوض

Verily, I am leaving among you [two weighty things,] if you hold to them you will never stray after me: the Book of God and my kindred, my household. Indeed, the two will never separate until they come back to me by the Pond [of al-Kawthar on the Day of Judgment].[4]

---

[3] The Holy Quran, 3:7.

[4] Al-Nisa'i, *al-Sunan al-Kubra*, 5:45; al-Majlisi, *Bihar al-Anwar*, 23:155.

The Holy Quran in turn spoke of the importance of this second 'weighty thing.' It said,

Say [O' Prophet Muhammad], 'I do not ask you any reward for it except the love of [my] relatives.[5]

When we study the history of this second 'weighty thing' – the history of the Holy Household of the Messenger of God (s) – we find that they stood with absolute devotion and determination in protection of God's message. They stood against any attempt to misrepresent the teachings of the Holy Quran and the tradition of the Holy Prophet (s).

The members of this Holy Household devoted themselves to the protection of this divine message. They dedicated themselves to the promotion of its true teachings. They sacrificed everything they had, even their own lives, in pursuit of this mission.

The stance of Imam Hussain (a) is the clearest example of the Holy Household's great sacrifices. He gave everything he had, including his own life, for the sake of reforming the nation of his grandfather and correcting the path of the nation after its deviance. He declared when he set out for the sake of this reform,

إِنِّى لَمْ أَخْرُجْ أَشِرًا وَلا بَطَرًا ، وَلا مُفْسِدًا وَلا ظَالِمًا ، وَإِنَّمَا خَرَجْتُ لِطَلَبِ الإِصْلاحِ فِي أُمَّةِ جَدِّي ، أُرِيدُ أَنْ آمُرَ بِالْمَعْرُوفِ وَأَنْهى عَنِ الْمُنْكَرِ ، وَأَسِيرَ بِسِيرَةِ جَدِّي وَأَبِي عَلِيِّ بْنِ أَبِي طَالِبٍ فمن قبلني بقبول الحق فالله أولى بالحق ومن رد

---

[5] The Holy Quran, 42:23.

علي أصبر حتى يقضي الله بيني وبين القوم بالحق وهو خير
الحاكمين

I do not revolt due to discontent [with God's blessings], nor out of arrogance. I did not rise as a corruptor, nor as an oppressor. Rather, I wish to call for reform in the nation of my grandfather. I wish to call for what is good, and to forbid what is evil. [I wish to] follow the tradition of my grandfather [the Prophet] and my father....[6]

Imam Hussain (a) could not have achieved his goal without the support of that blessed group of individuals who rode with him towards the inevitable sacrifice. They understood the Imams (a) mission and supported him every step of the way. For that, Imam Hussain (a) praised them and said,

أما بعد، فإني لا أعلم أصحابا أولى ولا خيرا من أصحابي، ولا
أهل بيت أبرّ ولا أوصل من أهل بيتي

Surely, I don't know of any companions more worthy than my companions, nor a family more pure and rooted than my own.

In this book, we will study some of the characteristics and achievements of this great man and his movement. We will look at Imam Hussain's (a) life and death. We will study the stance that he took and how the remainder of the Holy Household (a) contributed to that stance. We will examine the great triumph that his stance achieved despite the tragedy.

---

[6] Ibn Shahrashoob, *al-Manaqib*, 3:241.

Dear reader, this book is based on a compilation of Friday sermons that I have delivered over the years, as well as lectures I have given at a number of commemorations and celebrations. Throughout such gatherings, I have been able to address and speak on a wide array of issues relevant to the Muslim community.

At the insistence of a number of dear brothers, I compiled my notes to publish a series of books with the hopes that God will accept the work and that the benefit will spread to the believers. I tried to maintain the conversational tone of the original sermons in order to make the books more reader friendly. After a series of these books were printed in the original Arabic, a group of believers then insisted to have the work translated into English so that English-speaking audiences may benefit as well.

I thank God, the Exalted, for His infinite support and favor. I must also thank everyone who participated in making this book a reality.

I ask God, the Almighty, to take this work as an act of devotion for His sake and to accept it by His grace, He is surely the All-Kind and Magnanimous.

Ali Al-Hakeem,
Dubai, United Arab Emirates

Nurture

In the Name of God, the Most Compassionate, the Most Merciful

إِنَّمَا يُرِيدُ اللَّهُ لِيُذْهِبَ عَنكُمُ الرِّجْسَ أَهْلَ الْبَيْتِ وَيُطَهِّرَكُمْ تَطْهِيرًا

Indeed Allah desires to repel all impurity from you, O People of the Household, and purify you with a thorough purification.[1]

On the third of the lunar month of Sha'ban in the fourth year after the Hijra, a newborn entered the immaculate household of divine guidance. The Holy Prophet Muhammad (s) received glad tidings of the birth of his grandson, Al-Hussain ibn Ali ibn Abi Talib (a). Al-Hussain (a), the third Immaculate Imam[2] of Shia Islam, along with his grandfather the Prophet (s), his father Imam Ali (a), his mother Lady Fatima (a), and his older brother Imam Hassan (a), were the core of that

---

[1] The Holy Quran, 33:33.

[2] Twelver Shia Muslims believe that prophets and Imams are granted a 'blessing such that they have no occasion to disobey a command or commit a sin, despite their ability to do so.' (See: Allama al-Hili, *al-Bab al-Hadi 'Ashar*). They are capable of sinning, but they choose not to. This quality is what we refer to as their 'Immaculate nature.'

household which God Almighty 'purified a thorough purification.' They were the ones destined to give everything they had for the sake of advancing a message dictated by the Almighty.

THE CHARACTER OF IMAM HUSSAIN (A)

It should be clear that the nurturing of a child is underway even in the early days after his birth. He begins to experience the world around him and his character begins to form. The world around him begins to leave its marks on him even at that early stage. In fact, Islam clarifies that the process of nurturing a child starts well before that. As the Holy Prophet (s) is reported to have said,

الشقي من شقي في بطن أمه والسعيد من سعد في بطن أمه

The [truly] blessed is blessed in the womb of his mother. The [truly] wretched is wretched in the womb of his mother.[3]

There were doubtlessly a multitude of factors that helped shape the character of an individual like Imam Hussain (a), who was willing to make the greatest of sacrifices for the sake of God and His message. The Imam's (a) family and community, his nature and nurture, are all variables that left a clear impact on his character, ultimately allowing him to produce the grand legacy which we celebrate to this day.

It is important to note that when we discuss the nurturing of Imam Hussain (a) we are pursuing two distinct goals. Firstly, we are trying to understand how this immaculate household,

---

[3] Al-Sadouq, *al-Tawheed*, 356.

headed by the Holy Prophet (s), was able to nurture Imam Hassan (a) and Imam Hussain (a) to prepare them to take on the responsibilities of being the Imam. Secondly, we seek to understand how the Holy Prophet (s) nurtured his loved ones so we can take him as a role model in our lives and implement his teachings with our own children – after all, he is a messenger who does not speak of whim and whose whole existence is tied to the pleasure of God Almighty.

In this regard, it is important to note the social environment in which the Holy Prophet (s) was nurturing his grandsons. At that time, the Arab community took pride in concealing their emotions and not expressing any love for their children. They saw any form of emotional expression as weak and petty. An individual once saw the Holy Prophet (s) kissing and playing with his grandsons in the mosque. The man was horrified and chastised the Holy Prophet (s), proudly exclaiming that he has ten sons and not once did he ever kiss any of them. The Holy Prophet (s) tells the man that he has a heart of stone that is as distant as can be from human nature.

The Holy Prophet (s) teaches us the importance of the emotional aspect of childrearing. He teaches us that we must make sure to satisfy our children's emotional needs at that stage so that we can establish a healthy relationship and build the rest of our nurturing on that firm basis. We must not neglect our children or be overly stringent with them, especially at the earliest stages of development.

The Holy Prophet (s) broke the social norms of the time and taught his followers – through both words and actions – how to properly raise their children with love and care.

NURTURING AN IMMACULATE LEADER

The nurture of Imam Hussain (a) was built on a number of important factors that developed the majestic character that shines brighter and brighter every day. Even as time passes, the followers of Imam Hussain (a) only grow in love and admiration for his character and sacrifice. The factors that shaped this grand character can be summarized in the following:

A Divine Connection

Since his birth, Imam Hussain (a) was raised on the basis of being ever connected to God Almighty. The first words that hit his ears were words of glorification and praise to the Almighty in the form of the *adhan* and *iqama*, recited by the Holy Prophet (s) himself into his newborn ears. These words were thus molded into his very existence and became his calling and mission.

Imam Hussain (a) would grow up with the constant remembrance and mentioning of God surrounding him. His grandfather the Prophet (s) would mention the Almighty Lord with every one of his actions. His father would do nothing but with a clear intent of pleasing God. His mother would not act except in seeking closeness to God. Imam Hussain (a) lived in an environment filled with divine purpose.

Through all this, Imam Hussain (a) learned what it meant to be a servant of Almighty God. Even at a young age, he would fulfill the oath he made to God alongside his parents. When the young Hassan (a) and Hussain (a) fell ill, Imam Ali (a) and Lady Fatima (a) made an oath that they would fast for three days if their children were cured. When the young Imams (a) recovered, their parents kept their promise. Hassan (a) and Hussain (a) would fast alongside their mother and father as a form of dedication to the Almighty who granted them health. When it came time to break their fast at the end of the day, a destitute man knocked on their door and asked for food. Out of sheer dedication to God, they gave whatever little food they had as charity and remained hungry until the next day. The following day they again fasted in fulfillment of their oath, and again they gave away their meal to an orphan who asked for help. The third day would again be like the previous two, with the family giving their meal to a hungry prisoner.

Can we imagine any young child that would bear being hungry for three consecutive days without a single bite to eat? Yet, Imam Hassan (a) and Imam Hussain (a) did just that. Why? Because they truly understood the meaning of service to God Almighty and the burden of an oath made to Him. That is why they were deserving of the highest honors described in the Holy Quran. God Almighty says,

فَوَقَاهُمُ اللَّهُ شَرَّ ذَٰلِكَ الْيَوْمِ وَلَقَّاهُمْ نَضْرَةً وَسُرُورًا ﴿١١﴾ وَجَزَاهُم بِمَا صَبَرُوا جَنَّةً وَحَرِيرًا ﴿١٢﴾ مُّتَّكِئِينَ فِيهَا عَلَى الْأَرَائِكِ ۖ لَا يَرَوْنَ فِيهَا شَمْسًا وَلَا زَمْهَرِيرًا ﴿١٣﴾

So Allah saved them from [Judgment] Day's ills and graced them with freshness [on this faces] and joy [in their hearts]. He rewarded them for their patience with a garden and [garments of] silk, reclining therein on couches, without facing any [scorching] sun, or [biting] cold.[4]

This true knowledge of and dedication to God was an essential building block of Imam Hussain's (a) character. He would continue to live his life with those principles guiding his every move and inspiring his every thought.

Innate Guidance

God Almighty imbued within mankind an innate method of guidance towards the truth. An individual's environment can play a disruptive role in that process which can drive the individual away from that innate guidance that God gifted to us all. That is why the Holy Prophet (s) says,

كل مولود يولد على الفطرة حتى يكون أبواه يهودانه أو ينصرانه
أو يمجسانه

Every newborn is born with a fitra. It is his parents that teach him Judaism, Christianity, or Zoroastrianism.[5]

Weakness in an individual's character can be attributed back to this fact. When an individual is raised to believe in things that contradict his innate nature, contradiction and doubt begin to tear his character apart.

---

[4] The Holy Quran, 76:11-13.

[5] Al-Nu'man, *Sharh al-Akhbar*, 1:190.

The exact opposite effect can be seen in the nurturing of Imam Hussain (a). Everything he was taught by his parents and grandfather was aligned perfectly with the innate guidance that God imbued in us all. Of course, we cannot expect differently when the Imam (a) was born in the household of the Messenger of God (s) whose message was completely in line with the guidance He gifted us with. How could there be any contradiction in Imam Hussain's (a) character when the teachings of his family did not in any way conflict with human nature?

The Nurturers

One reason for the undermining of a child's character comes from the incompatibility between the parents and their disagreements over how to raise the child. Many times, we find that each parent has his or her own method of raising the child. While the mother may say 'no' to the child's particular request, the father might say 'yes.' The child sees two conflicting role models in the home and is not able to distinguish between the two. The internal contradiction within the home creates an atmosphere not well suited for childrearing.

This problem did not exist in the household of the message. Whatever principle was taught by the Holy Prophet (s) was reaffirmed by the Commander of the Faithful (a) and Lady Fatima (a). There was absolutely no conflict in terms of both words and actions. An immaculate role model was present for the Imam (a), manifested in the form of his parents and grandfather. That is why his character and the character of his brother were perfect reflections of their Immaculate nurturers. They were therefore the continuation of that divine line, not just by blood but by character, words, and deeds.

Honesty

Honesty is a defining character in the process of childrearing. When the nurturer is honest and well intentioned in all his actions, the child learns that crucial trait. And when the nurturer is a liar and a hypocrite, the child will take after him as well.

Imam Hussain (a) was raised in the household of truth. His grandfather was known even by his enemies as the most honest and trustworthy. His parents were same in their private and public lives. Imam Hussain (a) was raised to be honest with himself, with others, and with God Almighty. That is why he made that glorious stance and ultimate sacrifice for the sake of God's true religion.

LESSONS

Any household that claims to follow that Immaculate Household must look at their actions and make sure they conform to those of their role models. We study how the Holy Prophet (s), Imam Ali (a), and Lady Fatima (a) raised Imam Hassan (a) and Imam Hussain (a) not only to better understand their lives and character, but to find in them the model behavior we can emulate. We must learn to raise our children as the Immaculate Household raised theirs, so that we can bring up a generation that can carry forward the principles and values of our faith.

We must also mention here that these are not the only factors that shaped Imam Hussain's (a) character. If we were to put any other child in his position, would he form that same Immaculate character?

There is a metaphysical aspect to the nurturing of this divinely chosen household – an aspect not easily dissected and studied. They hold a position which no prophet or angel could attain. As the blessed traditions tell us, God Almighty created them two thousand years before the creation of Adam. In fact, they were the means of Adam's salvation. God Almighty says,

$$\text{فَتَلَقَّىٰ آدَمُ مِن رَّبِّهِ كَلِمَاتٍ فَتَابَ عَلَيْهِ ۚ إِنَّهُ هُوَ التَّوَّابُ الرَّحِيمُ}$$

Then Adam received certain words from his Lord, and He turned to him clemently. Indeed He is the All-clement, the All-merciful.[6]

The metaphysical aspects of Imam Hussain's (a) upbringing was doubtlessly present and effective. Yet, just because we cannot expect our children to reach his high stature does not mean that we cannot benefit from the model put in place by the Holy Prophet (s). Indeed God says,

$$\text{لَّقَدْ كَانَ لَكُمْ فِي رَسُولِ اللَّهِ أُسْوَةٌ حَسَنَةٌ لِّمَن كَانَ يَرْجُو اللَّهَ وَالْيَوْمَ الْآخِرَ وَذَكَرَ اللَّهَ كَثِيرًا}$$

---

[6] The Holy Quran, 2:37.

> *There is certainly a good exemplar for you in the Apostle of*
> *Allah — for those who look forward to Allah and the Last*
> *Day, and remember Allah much.*[7]

We must learn from our beloved Prophet Muhammad (s) so
we can raise a generation that will carry his teachings and
message into the future.

---

[7] The Holy Quran, 33:21.

QUESTIONS

In the Name of God, the Most Compassionate, the Most Merciful

إِنَّ اللَّهَ اشْتَرَىٰ مِنَ الْمُؤْمِنِينَ أَنفُسَهُمْ وَأَمْوَالَهُم بِأَنَّ لَهُمُ الْجَنَّةَ ۚ
يُقَاتِلُونَ فِي سَبِيلِ اللَّهِ فَيَقْتُلُونَ وَيُقْتَلُونَ ۖ وَعْدًا عَلَيْهِ حَقًّا فِي
التَّوْرَاةِ وَالْإِنجِيلِ وَالْقُرْآنِ ۚ وَمَنْ أَوْفَىٰ بِعَهْدِهِ مِنَ اللَّهِ ۚ
فَاسْتَبْشِرُوا بِبَيْعِكُمُ الَّذِي بَايَعْتُم بِهِ ۚ وَذَٰلِكَ هُوَ الْفَوْزُ الْعَظِيمُ

*Indeed Allah has bought from the faithful their souls and
their possessions for paradise to be theirs: they fight in the way
of Allah, kill, and are killed. A promise binding upon Him
in the Torah and the Evangel and the Quran. And who is
truer to his promise than Allah? So rejoice in the bargain you
have made with Him, and that is the great success.*[1]

MARTYRDOM

God Almighty is the true owner of all things. When a human
being is said to own something, the word generally means

---

[1] The Holy Quran, 9:111.

that the individual has the right to use and dispose of whatever he owns. God owns all things because He created all things and may do whatever He wills with His creatures. So in reality, He owns all things while we own nothing. God gave us the ability to use and dispose of some of the things He created for the duration of our lives and within set rules and regulations. Still, out of His unending kindness and mercy, He deals with His creatures as if they truly own what they have been given limited authority over. So for example, he asks us to lend Him some of our wealth. He says in the verse,

مَّن ذَا الَّذِي يُقْرِضُ اللَّهَ قَرْضًا حَسَنًا فَيُضَاعِفَهُ لَهُ أَضْعَافًا كَثِيرَةً
وَاللَّهُ يَقْبِضُ وَيَبْسُطُ وَإِلَيْهِ تُرْجَعُونَ

Who is it that will lend Allah a good loan that He may multiply it for him severalfold? Allah tightens and expands [the means of life], and to Him you shall be brought back.[2]

Not only does God Almighty ask us to lend Him what He owns, He even asks to buy it from us. He says,

إِنَّ اللَّهَ اشْتَرَىٰ مِنَ الْمُؤْمِنِينَ أَنفُسَهُمْ وَأَمْوَالَهُم بِأَنَّ لَهُمُ الْجَنَّةَ

Indeed Allah has bought from the faithful their souls and their possessions for paradise to be theirs.[3]

Is there any better bargain than this? Is there a better bargain than one where you give up what you never really owned to its true owner, in exchange for eternal bliss and happiness?

---

[2] The Holy Quran, 2:245.

[3] The Holy Quran, 9:111.

That is indeed the greatest bargain.

Of course, God does not act haphazardly or make meaningless promises. He only promises so much in exchange for the believers to devote their souls to Him because of the great value and importance of the soul. God outlined the importance of the soul in a number of verses and put great penalties on anyone taking a soul without due right. He says,

مِنْ أَجْلِ ذَلِكَ كَتَبْنَا عَلَى بَنِي إِسْرَائِيلَ أَنَّهُ مَن قَتَلَ نَفْسًا بِغَيْرِ
نَفْسٍ أَوْ فَسَادٍ فِي الْأَرْضِ فَكَأَنَّمَا قَتَلَ النَّاسَ جَمِيعًا وَمَنْ أَحْيَاهَا
فَكَأَنَّمَا أَحْيَا النَّاسَ جَمِيعًا

That is why We decreed for the Children of Israel that whoever kills a soul, without [its being guilty of] manslaughter or corruption on the earth, is as though he had killed all mankind, and whoever saves a life is as though he had saved all mankind.[4]

To transgress against one soul is to transgress against all humanity. To save one soul is to save all humanity. This is the great value that God places on the human soul. Even the individual human being, after being granted ownership over his own self, does not have the authority to transgress over his soul. No one has the authority to take his own life. God gave us bodies and souls not to do with as we please, but for us to safeguard and to use in line with our ultimate purpose. God says,

---

[4] The Holy Quran, 5:32.

وَأَنفِقُوا فِي سَبِيلِ اللَّهِ وَلَا تُلْقُوا بِأَيْدِيكُمْ إِلَى التَّهْلُكَةِ ۛ وَأَحْسِنُوا ۛ
إِنَّ اللَّهَ يُحِبُّ الْمُحْسِنِينَ

Spend in the way of Allah, and do not cast yourselves with your own hands into destruction; and be virtuous. Indeed Allah loves the virtuous.[5]

THE VALUE OF THE SOUL

In light of all this, we should also recognize that the value of the human soul differs from one individual to another. Again God does not act haphazardly and would not favor some individuals over others without reason. Similarly, God does not equate a wretched soul immersed in the filth of sin and deviation, with the souls of His most righteous servants. So the souls of the pious and the virtuous are given greater value because they are more obedient of God's commands and more reflective of the qualities that He wishes to see in His servants.

We see this concept in play when we look at a number of the martyrs in the different battles fought at the time of the Holy Prophet (s). There were many martyrs in the battle of Uhud, but Hamza, the uncle of the Holy Prophet (s), received special praise from the Holy Prophet (s). He was even called the "Master of Martyrs." Why? Hamza was an individual of great piety, virtue, and dedication to the message of God – thus his status was raised above other martyrs. The same can be seen with Ja'far ibn Abi Talib who was martyred in the battle of

---

[5] The Holy Quran, 2:195.

Mu'tah, he also received special praise due to his great struggle in the way of the message of God.

As we discussed before, the human soul has great value in the eyes of God and should not be treated lightly. It should be maintained and protected. As the blessed verse directs, a person should not 'cast himself into destruction.' This doubtlessly applies more pertinently when it comes to individuals of more pure souls. Thus, for prophets, messengers, and the righteous servants of God, whose souls are more valuable in the eyes of God, there needs to be a higher level of consciousness about maintaining and protecting their own lives.

All this being said, a person may begin to wonder about the situation which Imam Hussain (a) was in. Before setting out towards Kufa, Imam Hussain (a) was advised by a number of individuals, including his half-brother Muhammad ibn al-Hanafiyya, that he should not set out or else he will be murdered. The general atmosphere at the time all hinted towards an imminent tragedy. In fact, we see that many of the words of Imam Hussain (a) actually foreshadowed, or even explicitly spoke of the forthcoming tragedy.

While on his journey from Mecca towards Kufa, Imam Hussain (a) met a poet by the name of Farazdaq and asked him about the people of Iraq. Farazdaq replied, "Their hearts are with you, but their swords are with the Umayyad clan. Judgment will come from the heavens. God will do what He wills." Imam Hussain (a) replied,

صدقت . لله الأمر يفعل ما يشاء ، وكلّ يوم ربّنا في شأن . إنْ نزل القضاء بما نحبّ فنحمد الله على نعمائه ، وهو المستعان

على أداء الشكر ، وإنْ حال القضاء دون الرجاء فلم يعتدِ مَنْ

كان الحقّ نيّته ، والتقوى سريرته

True. But it is the will of God, and He does as He pleases. Every day our Lord is engaged in some work. If He were to dictate things that please us, we praise Him, thank Him, and ask His support in our thankfulness. And if His dictates are to stand in the way of our hopes, it would not affect anyone whose intention is righteous and who is pious at heart.[6]

So why did Imam Hussain (a) undertake the journey towards Kufa, despite knowing of the great tragedy that was to come? Did he not have an obligation to safeguard his own life and the lives of his followers? Did he 'cast himself into destruction' by stepping outside Mecca and Medina? Could he not have preserved his life and dedicated it to teaching and advising the Muslim nation?

These doubts were presented by some historians and authors in their books, either due to their lack of understanding of the Imam's purpose or in order to cast doubt into the legitimacy of his movement. We must therefore tackle a few points in order to answer these questions and dispel any doubts on this topic..

CAST INTO DESTRUCTION?

We cannot say that the holy verse which prohibits 'casting oneself into destruction' is so broad as to cover the actions

---

[6] Al-Tabari, *Tareekh Al-Tabari*, 4:290.

of Imam Hussain (a). We can list a number of reasons in this regard.

First, to understand the verse in such broad terms would go against a number of other verses which allow for circumstances in which war may be acceptable. In fact, we find that many prophets and righteous servants engaged in some type of warfare, such as Moses, David, Solomon, and our Holy Prophet Muhammad (s). Therefore, the verse cannot mean that engaging in an activity where there will certainly be some loss of life, such as war, is never justified. God says in the Holy Quran,

وَكَأَيِّن مِّن نَّبِيٍّ قَاتَلَ مَعَهُ رِبِّيُّونَ كَثِيرٌ فَمَا وَهَنُوا لِمَا أَصَابَهُمْ فِي سَبِيلِ اللَّهِ وَمَا ضَعُفُوا وَمَا اسْتَكَانُوا ۗ وَاللَّهُ يُحِبُّ الصَّابِرِينَ ﴿١٤٦﴾ وَمَا كَانَ قَوْلَهُمْ إِلَّا أَن قَالُوا رَبَّنَا اغْفِرْ لَنَا ذُنُوبَنَا وَإِسْرَافَنَا فِي أَمْرِنَا وَثَبِّتْ أَقْدَامَنَا وَانصُرْنَا عَلَى الْقَوْمِ الْكَافِرِينَ ﴿١٤٧﴾ فَآتَاهُمُ اللَّهُ ثَوَابَ الدُّنْيَا وَحُسْنَ ثَوَابِ الْآخِرَةِ ۗ وَاللَّهُ يُحِبُّ الْمُحْسِنِينَ ﴿١٤٨﴾

How many a prophet there has been with whom a multitude of godly men fought. They did not falter for what befell them in the way of Allah, neither did they weaken, nor did they abase themselves; and Allah loves the steadfast. All that they said was, 'Our Lord, forgive us our sins and our excesses in our affairs, make our feet steady, and help us against the faithless lot.' So Allah gave them the reward of this world and the fair reward of the Hereafter; and Allah loves the virtuous.[7]

The Holy Quran not only praises the prophets and godly men who fought alongside the prophets, but also explains some of the circumstances where war may be justified. God says,

$$وَمَا لَكُمْ لَا تُقَاتِلُونَ فِي سَبِيلِ اللَّهِ وَالْمُسْتَضْعَفِينَ مِنَ الرِّجَالِ وَالنِّسَاءِ وَالْوِلْدَانِ الَّذِينَ يَقُولُونَ رَبَّنَا أَخْرِجْنَا مِنْ هَٰذِهِ الْقَرْيَةِ الظَّالِمِ أَهْلُهَا وَاجْعَل لَّنَا مِن لَّدُنكَ وَلِيًّا وَاجْعَل لَّنَا مِن لَّدُنكَ نَصِيرًا$$

Why should you not fight in the way of Allah and the oppressed men, women, and children, who say, 'Our Lord, bring us out of this town whose people are oppressors, and appoint for us a guardian from Yourself, and appoint for us a helper from Yourself'?[8]

God also disparaged those who are unwilling to make such a sacrifice due to their excessive attachment to this world.

$$يَا أَيُّهَا الَّذِينَ آمَنُوا مَا لَكُمْ إِذَا قِيلَ لَكُمُ انفِرُوا فِي سَبِيلِ اللَّهِ اثَّاقَلْتُمْ إِلَى الْأَرْضِ ۚ أَرَضِيتُم بِالْحَيَاةِ الدُّنْيَا مِنَ الْآخِرَةِ ۚ فَمَا مَتَاعُ الْحَيَاةِ الدُّنْيَا فِي الْآخِرَةِ إِلَّا قَلِيلٌ ﴿٣٨﴾ إِلَّا تَنفِرُوا يُعَذِّبْكُمْ عَذَابًا أَلِيمًا وَيَسْتَبْدِلْ قَوْمًا غَيْرَكُمْ وَلَا تَضُرُّوهُ شَيْئًا ۚ وَاللَّهُ عَلَىٰ كُلِّ شَيْءٍ قَدِيرٌ ﴿٣٩﴾$$

---

[7] The Holy Quran, 3:146-48.

[8] The Holy Quran, 4:75.

O you who have faith! What is the matter with you that when you are told: 'Go forth in the way of Allah,' you sink heavily to the ground? Are you pleased with the life of this world instead of the Hereafter? But the wares of the life of this world compared with the Hereafter are but insignificant. If you do not go forth, He will punish you with a painful punishment, and replace you with another people, and you will not hurt Him in the least, and Allah has power over all things.[9]

So to fight in the way of God is a great thing. Of course, this means that engaging in battle be done in line with the rules and dictates of God. God has set guidelines as to who can declare war, for what reasons, and how to engage in warfare. It is when these rules are ignored that a person who engages in battle casts himself into destruction. The Commander of the Faithful (a) says,

إن الجهاد باب فتحه الله لخاصة أوليائه، وسوغهم كرامة منه لهم ونعمة ذخرها، والجهاد لباس التقوى، ودرع الله الحصينة وحصنه الوثيقة

Jihad is a gate which God opened to his select servants. He made it appealing to them as an honor and safeguarded it for them as a blessing. Jihad is the cloak of piety, and it is God's sturdy shield and His impenetrable fortress.[10]

So was Imam Hussain (a) aware of all these rules? Or was he merely suicidal when he set out towards Karbala?

---

[9] The Holy Quran, 9:38, 39.

[10] Al-Tousi, *Tahtheeb al-Ahkaam*, 6:123.

IMAM HUSSAIN (A)

History makes it clear that Imam Hussain (a) knew exactly what he was doing and what the end result would be. But if he was merely suicidal, there would be no reason for him to take the women and children with him on the journey. Why would he have them endure the pain and humiliation of captivity if he was on a suicide mission? Why would he do so when history makes it clear that he was the most honorable, proud, and protective of his family? There would be no meaning to any of this if his goal was simply a suicide.

Second, Imam Hussain's (a) movement was clearly legitimate. After all, he is one of the Immaculate leaders who God Almighty appointed to safeguard the religion. There is no doubt that Imam Hussain (a) is one of the members of the household whom God 'purified a thorough purification.'[11] He is known by all Muslims as the master of the youth of Paradise. As the Holy Prophet (s) once said,

الحسن والحسين سيدا شباب أهل الجنة وأبوهما خير منهما

Hassan and Hussain are the masters of the youth of Paradise, and their father is greater than them.[12]

We cannot reconcile these laurels with the claim that he cast himself into destruction or that he was 'killed with a sword which he unsheathed,' as some have claimed. Ibn Khaldoun responds to these claims in his Muqaddima, writing,

Judge Abu Bakr ibn al-Arabi al-Maliki erred in writing in his book al-'Awasim wa al-Qawasim that Hussain was

---

[11] The Holy Quran, 33:33.

[12] Al-Sadouq, *O'youn Akhbar al-Rida (a)*, 1:36.

killed with a sword which he unsheathed. This was due to his oversight of the fact that justice is a requisite of Islamic caliphate. And who is more just than Hussain during his time?[13]

In fact, Imam Hussain's (a) movement became a precedent which Muslim jurists cited when discussing the legitimacy of revolution against an unjust ruler. Ibn Muflih al-Hanbali says, "Ibn 'Aqeel and Ibn al-Jawzi ruled in favor of the legitimacy of revolution against an unjust leader, citing the just revolution of al-Hussain against Yazid."[14]

So who would have the audacity to question Imam Hussain's (a) movement after this?

This is in addition to the fact that Imam Hussain's (a) movement was explicitly mentioned and blessed by the Holy Prophet Muhammad (s). There are many accounts where the Holy Prophet (s) mentions Imam Hussain (a) and his movement and martyrdom, and cries for what would happen to his grandson. If Imam Hussain's (a) movement was not legitimate, the Holy Prophet (s) would surely have forbidden him from setting out, or at least advised against it. This means that, at the very least, the Holy Prophet (s) did not oppose Imam Hussain's (a) movement. In fact, it is our belief that the Holy Prophet (s) blessed his movement as a divinely chosen path for a divinely chosen Imam.

All this can be seen in the multitude of narration from the Holy Prophet (s) where he tells of what would happen to his

---

[13] Al-Muqarram, *Maqtal al-Hussain (a)*, 31.

[14] Ibid.

grandson. One of the more famous narration is from the home of the Holy Prophet's (s) wife Um Salama.

أن رسول الله (ص) كان في بيت أم سلمة وعنده جبرئيل (ع) فدخل عليه الحسين (ع) فقال له جبرئيل: إن أمتك تقتل ابنك هذا، ألا أريك من تربة الأرض التي يقتل فيها؟ فقال رسول الله (ص): نعم. فأهوى جبرئيل (ع) بيده وقبض قبضة منها فأراها النبي (ص)

The Messenger of God (s) was at the house of Um Salama and Gabriel was present when Hussain (a) walked in. Gabriel said to [the Prophet (s)], 'Your nation will kill this son of yours. Do you wish me to show you the dust of the land where he will be killed?' The Messenger of God (s) said, 'Yes.' Gabriel stretched his hand and grabbed a handful of its dust and showed it to the Prophet (s).[15]

In fact, the narrations of the Holy Household show that Imam Hussain (a) was always acting in accordance to the dictates of his grandfather the Holy Prophet (s). This can be seen in the Imam's discussion with his half-brother Muhammad ibn al-Hanafiyya who had advised him not to leave Medina. Imam Hussain (a) promised him to think about his concern. The next day the Imam organized his caravan and was heading out when Muhammad ibn al-Hanafiyya asked him about their discussion the night before, Imam Hussain (a) replied,

---

[15] Al-Majlisi, *Bihar al-Anwar*, 44:236.

بلى ولكن بعد أن فارقتك أتاني رسول الله ص وقال: يا حسين
اخرج فان الله تعالى شاء أن يراك قتيلا

*The Messenger of God came to me [i.e. in a vision] after I
left you. He said to me, 'O Hussain. Set out [on your jour-
ney], for God has surely willed to see you as a martyr.'*[16]

Third, the scope of the blessed verse forbidding that an individual cast himself into destruction is clearly limited. If we
look at the verse in its context, we see that its proper application is in seeking retribution. The blessed verses read,

الشَّهْرُ الْحَرَامُ بِالشَّهْرِ الْحَرَامِ وَالْحُرُمَاتُ قِصَاصٌ ۚ فَمَنِ اعْتَدَىٰ
عَلَيْكُمْ فَاعْتَدُوا عَلَيْهِ بِمِثْلِ مَا اعْتَدَىٰ عَلَيْكُمْ ۚ وَاتَّقُوا اللَّهَ وَاعْلَمُوا
أَنَّ اللَّهَ مَعَ الْمُتَّقِينَ

*A sacred month for a sacred month, and all sanctities require
retribution. So should anyone aggress against you, assail him
in the manner he assailed you, and be wary of Allah, and
know that Allah is with the Godwary. Spend in the way of
Allah, and do not cast yourselves with your own hands into
destruction; and be virtuous. Indeed Allah loves the virtuous.*[17]

If we study the movement of Imam Hussain (a), we see that
retribution was never the driving factor behind his actions.
He always had more sublime goals in mind, and was able to

---

[16] Al-Majlisi, *Bihar al-Anwar*, 44:251.

[17] The Holy Quran, 2:194.

achieve the greatest of goals through his movement. Thus, the blessed verse clearly does not apply to his movement.

WHY NOT SEEK PROTECTION?

Some people may wonder, why did Imam Hussain (a) not do more to protect his own life? Is the life of a believer not sacred in the eyes of God? Could he not have been a great benefit to the Muslim nation through his knowledge and teachings had he only lived longer? Why did he not seek protection against Yazid and his armies?

Imam Hussain (a) knew exactly what he was doing. He knew where he was heading, what would happen to him, and the outcome of that tragedy. Some people take a shallow look at history and claim that Imam Hussain (a) was duped by the people of Kufa, who promised him aid and betrayed him. But a deep and true look at Imam Hussain's (a) words and actions reveals to us the exact opposite.

Let us put aside for a moment the fact that Imam Hussain (a) was an Immaculate, a divinely chosen leader. Let us objectively assess his words and actions without a theological reference. Imam Hussain (a) was a man of knowledge, wisdom and experience. On countless occasion, he would foretell of what would happen to him. He knew that there were individuals in Kufa who would sell him out – much like they sold out his father and brother before. He received news of their betrayal on his way to Kufa. Many along the way advised him to turn back or to seek refuge anywhere but Kufa.

Imam Hussain (a) knew exactly what was going on around him. His attachment to the letters and promises of the people of Kufa was only so that he can show clear evidence and proof of how he was betrayed. But the question remains, why did he set out for Kufa in the first place, and why would he not change course after receiving news of the treachery that happened in the city?

It is easy to draw conclusions and create theories in retrospect. Yet, theories often fall short when they do not rely on a full understanding of the history and its actors. To provide a precise and accurate answer to this question, we must therefore look at Imam Hussain's (a) character and understand his circumstances.

Imam Hussain (a) was never regarded as an ordinary individual. Even during his lifetime, people disagreed whether or not he was an Immaculate leader chosen by God Almighty. Yet everyone agreed that he was the last living grandson of the Holy Prophet (s) and that he was the natural continuation of the Prophet's (s) message. Everyone agreed that he was the last living member of the People of the Cloak and that he was of the Holy Household which God Almighty 'purified a thorough purification.'[18] Everyone agreed that he was the 'master of the youth of paradise'[19] and an 'Imam whether he sits or stands.'[20] He was respected and loved throughout the Muslim nation. He was doubtlessly the most legitimate religious authority at the time. His actions were therefore of special significance to the entire nation.

---

[18] The Holy Quran, 33:33.

[19] Al-Sadouq, *O'youn Akhbar al-Rida (a)*, 1:36.

[20] Al-Majlisi, Bihar al-Anwar, 43:278.

Imam Hussain's (a) circumstances were also special. The circumstances surrounding his movement were doubtlessly different than any circumstance which his father Imam Ali (a) and his brother Imam Hassan (a) faced. Those circumstances meant that the nation was at a watershed moment, and his actions at that moment affect us to this day. They even affect our future, as we see in the link constantly drawn by our Immaculate Imams between him and Imam Mahdi (a).

Imam Hussain (a) faced a seminal moment in the history of Islam – namely, the hereditary transfer of power from Muawiya to his son Yazid. Yazid was well-known for his impiety and lack of respect for any value or principle. The nation was about to be subjugated under the miscreant Yazid. Because of his status amongst Muslims, Imam Hussain (a) was the first to be asked to pledge allegiance since it would lend great legitimacy to Yazid.

This can be clearly seen in the actions of al-Walid ibn 'Utba, the governor of Medina. When news of Muawiya's death reach Medina, al-Walid could not wait until the next morning to demand Imam Hussain's (a) allegiance to Yazid. He called the Imam to his house that very night and demanded the oath of fealty. Imam Hussain (a) first asked the governor to give him until sun rise to make a decision, but his request was refused and he was threatened with a public execution. When the Imam saw that there was no way to evade, he made his well-known declaration, refusing to pay allegiance to Yazid. He said,

أيها الأمير إنا أهل بيت النبوة ومعدن الرسالة ومختلف الملائكة
بنا فتح الله وبنا يختم، ويزيد رجل شارب الخمور قاتل النفس
المحرمة معلن بالفسق ومثلي لا يبايع مثله

*Governor! We are the household of the Prophet (s), the core
of the message, and the harbor of Angels. By us, God has
introduced [His message], and to us He will return it. Yazid
is a deviant, a miscreant, a drunkard, and a murderer. He
has publically professed his impiety. Someone like me will
never pay allegiance to the likes of him.[21]*

When Marwan ibn al-Hakam, a confidant of Muawiya, suggested that Imam Hussain (a) should pay allegiance to Yazid, the Imam replied,

على الإسلام السلام إذا بليت الأمة براع مثل يزيد

*Say goodbye to Islam if the nation is tried with a caretaker
like Yazid....[22]*

Imam Hussain's (a) Options

Thus, it is clear that Islam was at a crossroad at that moment in its history. Imam Hussain (a), a unique individual who was loved and respected by all Muslims, was about to make a decision. He was facing a circumstance unlike anything his predecessors had to endure. So what were the options available to Imam Hussain (a) at that point? Let us consider some of the possibilities one by one.

---

[21] Al-Muqarram, *Maqtal al-Hussein (a)*, 131.

[22] Al-Muqarram, *Maqtal al-Hussein (a)*, 133.

Allegiance. Imam Hussain's (a) first possible option was to give allegiance to Yazid. This was the option that the Umayyad governor acted quickly to ensure, and was clearly in the best interest of the ruling class. Allegiance from Imam Hussain (a) would have given Yazid the greatest vindication he could ask for and would lend great legitimacy to his rule. Imam Hussain (a) doubtlessly understood the implications of this, especially in light of Yazid's character as a deviant who brazenly professes his impiety.

Paying allegiance to Yazid would therefore destroy every value and principle the Holy Prophet (s) worked so hard to instill in the Muslim nation. What would remain of Islam if the deviant in the nation is followed as a legitimate leader and a role model? And what would remain of Imam Hussain's (a) status and legitimacy? Surely, he would have lost the great status which God Almighty elevated him to, as well as losing all respect in the eyes of the people. No one could possible rise and lead a movement of reform in the Muslim nation after its greatest religious role model publicly affirmed the actions of the greatest deviant. The true teachings of Islam would surely have been lost.

This first option was out of the question.

Silence. Could Imam Hussain (a) have simply remained silent, neither paying allegiance to Yazid nor taking any move against him? This was not an option that the ruling class would allow. They knew well that if Imam Hussain (a) did not pay allegiance, many other notable Muslims would be encouraged to refrain from giving an oath of fealty and defy Yazid's rule. That is why the governor of Medina acted so hastily in seeking Imam Hussain's pledge of allegiance. He knew that the key to Yazid's legitimacy laid in Imam Hussain's (a) hands.

Historical accounts clearly support this conclusion. We see that Marwan ibn al-Hakam would advise al-Walid ibn 'Utba, the governor of Medina, not to agree to anything but allegiance. When Imam Hussain (a) requested that he be given the night to think, Marwan advised al-Walid,

> *If he were to leave right now without swearing allegiance, you would not be able to put him in a similar situation again. There would be bloodshed between you and him. Detain him until he swears allegiance, or else strike off his head.*[23]

Simply remaining silent would put Imam Hussain (a) in a weak position. The Umayyad propaganda machine would begin to systematically tarnish his reputation. In the end, he would probably be assassinated in his own home, most likely by poison. His movement and message would end right there and we would not have that same legacy that resulted from the greatest of tragedies.

Retreat to Mecca. What if Imam Hussain (a) retreated to the Grand Mosque in Mecca and sought refuge and protection there? Does the Holy Quran not command that "whoever enters [the Grand Mosque] shall be secure"?[24] This option was in fact suggested by a number of prominent Muslim figures at the time, including Imam Hussain's (a) half-brother Muhammad ibn al-Hanafiyya. But the Imam knew well the

---

[23] Al-Muqarram, *Maqtal al-Hussein (a)*, 130.

[24] The Holy Quran, 3:97.

extent of the Umayyad audacity in transgressing against God's divinely drawn boundaries. He knew that Yazid would murder him inside the Great Mosque without hesitation. When ibn al-Zubayr suggested this option to him, he replied,

والله لأن أقتل خارجا منه بشبر أحب إلي أن أقتل داخلا منه بشبر

By God, to be killed outside [the Grand Mosque] by an inch is more preferable to me than to be killed inside it by an inch.[25]

History has recorded the degree of the Umayyad Dynasty's brazenness in this regard. Early in his rule, Yazid gave command of his army to Amr ibn Sa'eed ibn al-'Aas. He also gave him authority over the Hajj and the mandate to "kill Hussain wherever you find him."[26] Shortly after Imam Hussain's martyrdom, Abdullah ibn al-Zubayr's revolution was able to take control of Mecca. The Umayyad army did not hesitate to set siege to the city. During the siege, Umayyad's catapults destroyed parts of the Grand Mosque.

Therefore, there would be no clear benefit for Imam Hussain (a) to retreat to Mecca. Moreover, his murder in the Grand Mosque would only tear at the sanctity of that blessed place.

A Stronghold Elsewhere. Another option suggested to Imam Hussain (a) was to find any area within the Muslim nation – outside Hijaz and Iraq – and establish a foothold and take refuge there. One of the suggestions at the time was

---

[25] Al-Tabari, Tareekh al-Tabari, 4:289.

[26] Al-Turaihi, *al-Muntakhab*, 304.

for the Imam (a) to go to Yemen and establish a stronghold in its mountains. The Imam (a) also had a multitude of supporters in that region who would have aided him against the Umayyad armies.

While this option may have meant safety for Imam Hussain (a), it is not without its drawbacks. Hijaz and Iraq – both having served as capital to the Muslim nation at that time – were the most important Muslim provinces. The Imam (a) would have moved out of the heart of the Muslim nation and left a void to be filled by Umayyad falsehoods and deviance. The ruling authorities could easily cast him as a heretic who fled their righteous grasp. Imam Hussain (a) would therefore be undermining his own legitimacy and character by evading confrontation.

And who is to say that this option would ensure the Imam's (a) safety? Yazid would not hesitate to muster his entire army against Imam Hussain (a). If the armies fail, Yazid could have reverted to his father's strategies and assassinated the Imam with poison. Again, this would mean that the Imam (a) would pass away without leaving that undeniable legacy.

The option of establishing a stronghold somewhere on the fringes of the Muslim nation was untenable. It would have undermined Imam Hussain's (a) character and legitimacy without providing any guarantee of success for his movement.

Confrontation. Confrontation was Imam Hussain's (a) best option to achieve his goal.

First, he would safeguard his own character and legitimacy in the eyes of the Muslim nation. After all, he was headed towards Kufa only after receiving an abundance of letters calling him to implement reform in that city. He clearly was not a criminal on the run. No one could say that he lacked legitimacy in his movement. He maintained the moral upper hand, and made sure that it was clear for everyone to see.

Second, everyone at the time knew that Yazid was going to murder Imam Hussain (a) if he refused to pay allegiance. Since paying allegiance was not an option, the Imam's martyrdom was inevitable. He therefore had to be proactive and dictate the terms of his martyrdom so that he can reap the greatest benefits from his movement – namely to safeguard the message of Islam and reform the nation of his grandfather.

Finally, the grand tragedy had to take place in the heart of the Muslim nation. It could not have occurred in an uninhabited and easily forgotten mountain or valley on the outskirts of the nation. That would have meant that his sacrifice would easily be forgotten. Imam Hussain (a) chose to make his stand in the heart of Muslim civilization so that his tomb would continue to stand as a beacon for the values he stood for. As Lady Zaynab so eloquently stated in the court of Yazid,

فكد كيدك واسع سعيك وناصب جهدك فوالله لا تمحو ذكرنا

ولا تميت وحينا

Plot as you wish. Continue with your undertakings. Exert all your efforts. But, by God, you will never erase our remembrance. You will never kill our inspiration.[27]

THE PROGENY

There is one last question that presents itself at this point. Why did the remainder of the Imams (a) after Imam Hussain (a) not rise just as he did, especially in light of the fact that the rulers of the time were also corrupt deviants?

We know that the Imams (a) are Immaculate leaders chosen by God to carry His message after the Holy Prophet (s). His choices cannot be arbitrary. There must be a reason for any of their actions or omissions. When it comes to this issue in particular, we see a number of reasons that could have stopped them from taking on the same role as Imam Hussain (a).

First, the Imams (a) did not face the same circumstances that Imam Hussain (a) faced. If they did, they would have revolted liked Imam Hussain (a). Even Imam Hussain (a) lived for years under the rule of Muawiya and did not revolt during that time. It wasn't until the change of circumstances with the rise of Yazid that the Imam (a) made his stance.

Second, Imam Hussain's (a) mission was to safeguard the message of Islam. That mission was accomplished by his stance in Karbala. A similar sacrifice was not necessary for the Imams (a) after Imam Hussain (a).

---

[27] Al-Muqarram, *Maqtal al-Hussein (a)*, 359.

Third, life is a sacred trust given to mankind by God Almighty. It cannot be treated trivially or risked haphazardly. There must therefore be a great deal to be achieved by engaging in battle. When Imam Hussain (a) achieved his great triumph in Karbala, the remainder of the Imams (a) could not make additional significant triumphs through battle. There was not enough to warrant the shedding of their blood or the blood of others.

Finally, there is no doubt that multiple successive revolts against the ruling powers meant the weakening of the state. This meant the weakening of the Muslim nation against the neighboring empires which saw Muslims as enemies. The Imams were careful not to go down this road. So long as Islam was safe, they were content. As Imam Ali (a) once said,

لأسلمن ما سلمت أمور المسلمين ولو لم يكن به جور إلا علي
خاصة

By God, I will accede so long as the matters of the Muslims are secure, and so long as this transgression remains against me alone [as an individual].[28]

The Immaculate Imams (a) from the Household of the Holy Prophet (s) experienced many trials and tribulations during their time. They were patient and persevered for the sake of protecting the message of Islam. Without their continued struggle and persistence in pursuit of their mission, we would not see the pure message of Islam continue to this day. Despite the continued persecution, our beloved Imams (a) were

---

[28] Al-Radi, *Nahj al-Balagha*, Sermon 73.

able to build a righteous community that lived by the words of God and safeguarded them.

THE MASTER OF MARTYRS

THE REWARDS OF MARTYRS

The fire of Imam Hussain's (a) love is experienced every year by his followers and admirers. Despite more than a thousand years passing since the tragedy, we still remember that event every year and weep for them as if we lost a loved ones yesterday. This love makes Imam Hussain's (a) name eternal, even after his martyrdom. Indeed, God Almighty promised the martyrs an eternal life. God says,

$$\text{وَلَا تَقُولُوا لِمَن يُقْتَلُ فِي سَبِيلِ اللَّهِ أَمْوَاتٌ ۚ بَلْ أَحْيَاءٌ وَلَكِن لَّا تَشْعُرُونَ}$$

Do not call those who were slain in Allah's way 'dead.' No, they are living, but you are not aware.[1]

Imam Hussain (a) is the Master of Martyrs and doubtlessly embodies the greatest manifestation of that verse's meaning.

---

[1] The Holy Quran, 2:154.

There are multiple verses that speak of martyrs as 'living.' So what does that mean? Is it a metaphorical statement or is there a real life which they are living after their martyrdom?

There are several reasons which leads us to believe that the life described in these verses is not merely metaphorical.

First, if the verses were only speaking in a metaphorical sense the description would be a fiction and illusion. We cannot adopt the view of the materialists and say that there is no real life after death. While it may seem plausible that the life being described in the verse is only a reference to the continuation of a martyr's memory and legacy, that cannot be an accurate understanding of God's words. After all, memory and heritage cannot be felt, understood, and enjoyed by the dead. It cannot be a real reward for someone who sacrifices everything he has for the sake of his Lord. Thus, the promised life after martyrdom must be real and tangible, and not merely a metaphor and fiction.

Second, the verse itself refutes the claim that the promised life is metaphorical. God says, "They are living, but you are not aware."[2] We are certainly aware of their continued memory and legacy. If this was the only reward, then the verse would be inaccurate in its description.

Third, the other verses that describe this life add further proof in their descriptions. God says,

وَلَا تَحْسَبَنَّ الَّذِينَ قُتِلُوا فِي سَبِيلِ اللَّهِ أَمْوَاتًا ۚ بَلْ أَحْيَاءٌ عِندَ رَبِّهِمْ يُرْزَقُونَ ﴿١٦٩﴾ فَرِحِينَ بِمَا آتَاهُمُ اللَّهُ مِن فَضْلِهِ

---

[2] The Holy Quran, 2:154.

وَيَسْتَبْشِرُونَ بِالَّذِينَ لَمْ يَلْحَقُوا بِهِم مِّنْ خَلْفِهِمْ أَلَّا خَوْفٌ عَلَيْهِمْ
وَلَا هُمْ يَحْزَنُونَ ﴿١٧٠﴾ يَسْتَبْشِرُونَ بِنِعْمَةٍ مِّنَ اللَّهِ وَفَضْلٍ
وَأَنَّ اللَّهَ لَا يُضِيعُ أَجْرَ الْمُؤْمِنِينَ ﴿١٧١﴾

*Do not suppose those who were slain in the way of Allah to
be dead; no, they are living and provided for near their Lord,
exulting in what Allah has given them out of His grace, and
rejoicing for those who have not yet joined them from [those
left] behind them, that they will have no fear, nor will they
grieve. They rejoice in Allah's blessing and grace, and that
Allah does not waste the reward of the faithful.*[3]

Thus we know that the life given as a reward to the martyrs
is not merely metaphorical. It is a real life that allows them to
experience and enjoy the blessings of their Lord. Their death
is not as we commonly understand death - a transition to a
state of insentience and non-existence. They are living near
their Lord and being provided for and blessed. That is why
the noble traditions state that these martyrs do not wish to
return again to this temporal world, except for an opportunity
to be martyred again. The Holy Prophet (s) said,

ما من نفس تموت لها عند الله خير يسرها أن ترجع الى الدنيا
وأن لها الدنيا وما فيها، إلا الشهيد فإنه يتمنى أن يرجع الى الدنيا
فيقتل مرة أخرى لما يرى من فضل الشهادة.

*There is no dying soul — [having achieved a] good status with
God — that would be pleased to return back to the [temporal]*

---

world, even if it were given the entire world and what is in it. That is except for the martyr who wishes to be returned to this world to be killed again, due to what he knows of the value of martyrdom.[4]

In addition, the martyr is forgiven any and all sins and transgressions. Imam al-Sadiq (a) said,

من قتل في سبيل الله لم يعرفه الله شيئا من سيئاته

Whoever dies for the sake of God, God will not [have him carry the burden of] any of his misdeeds.[5]

THE MEANING OF MARTYRDOM

So there is an immense reward for the martyrs characterized by a new life given to them after their martyrdom. But what does it mean to be a martyr in the first place?

The Arabic word for martyrdom is *shahada*, which is described by our scholars as "the attainment of a thing itself, either by the senses as in what is observable, or through internal processes as in the *wijdaniyyat* like knowledge, love, and hatred."[6] Shahada is therefore an experience higher than imagination and theoretical knowledge. That is why a witness shares the same name with a martyr - *shaheed*. That very same word was used in the Holy Quran to describe the Holy Prophet (s) as the witness to all nations.

---

[4] Al-Hindi, *Kanz al-'Ommal*, 4:290.

[5] Al-Kulayni, *al-Kafi*, 5:54.

[6] Al-Tabatabaei, *al-Mizan*, 3:349.

It is said that the martyrs will be witnesses to all nations alongside the Holy Prophet (s). God says in the Holy Quran,

$$وَكَذَلِكَ جَعَلْنَاكُمْ أُمَّةً وَسَطًا لِتَكُونُوا شُهَدَاءَ عَلَى النَّاسِ وَيَكُونَ الرَّسُولُ عَلَيْكُمْ شَهِيدًا$$

Thus We have made you a middle nation that you may be witnesses to the people, and that the Apostle may be a witness to you.[7]

These witnesses will testify to the truthfulness of God's prophets and messengers and to how their people rejected the message which God sent them with. The Holy Prophet (s) will then testify to the truthfulness of these witnesses testimony. And because testimony requires an honorable and trustworthy witness, the most honored of Muslims will be chosen for this role. This is a status suitable to those who sacrificed all they had for the sake of God.

There are also numerous other reasons which are cited in describing how the martyrs got that name. Some say that it is because God Almighty and the angels all testify that they are deserving of paradise. Others say it is because they are attended to by the angels who witness their status and guide them to paradise. Still others say that it is because the martyrs testify to the truthfulness of the Holy Prophet (s) and make their sacrifices for the sake of that testimony. There is also the possibility that it is because they are living and witnessing all that happens after their death and to the bounties of their Lord.

---

[7] The Holy Quran, 2:143.

short, there are numerous possibilities for why the martyrs may have received this name, all of which are plausible. In fact, if we reflect on these possibilities, we find that they are all likely descriptions of the status of martyrs. They are given this high status and these sublime honors as a reward for their ultimate sacrifice for the sake of the Almighty and His message.

THE VALUE OF MARTYRDOM

Every member of society has his or her own value relative to what they offer to their community. Physicians, academicians, police officers, and all other professions bring value to society based on how they contribute to the advancement of humankind. Martyrs have a special value that rises above all other members of society. As the Holy Prophet (s) said,

فوق كل بر بر حتى يقتل الرجل في سبيل الله فإذا قتل في سبيل الله عز وجل فليس فوقه بر

For every virtue there is a higher virtue. That is until a person is killed for the sake of God, for if he is killed for the sake of God – the Most Honored and Majestic – there is no virtue above that.[8]

That is why communities give such great attention to their fallen heroes. We see communities across the globe venerating individuals who lose their lives for the sake of a greater ideal – whether it is police officers keeping peace in their neighborhoods, troops protecting their homeland against a

[8] Al-Kulayni, *al-Kafi*, 5:53.

foreign enemy, or revolutionaries seeking to reform their nation. We venerate such individuals because they give their lives, the most valuable thing they possess, for the sake of the ideals of justice, freedom, and prosperity for their communities. This veneration is even greater when the martyrs represent the value system revealed to us by the Almighty.

There is no doubt that an individual which sacrifices in order to instill these values in his community should be remembered and venerated. The pure blood of a martyr illuminates the path ahead for his nation towards a better manifestation of its ideals.

This special value and distinction is given to a martyr for a number of reasons, including:

Firstly, a martyr sacrifices the most valuable thing in his possession – his own life. Many individuals sacrifice for the betterment of their communities, giving up time, effort, and wealth for the sake of others. But life is the greatest thing that God has granted us. Sacrificing this great treasure is surely the greatest sacrifice that can be made.

Secondly, a martyr immortalizes his memory when he makes this ultimate sacrifice. It is true that we see the memory of other individuals like philosophers and philanthropists continue on, but there is an important distinction to be made. A philosopher offers his ideas and thought to the world, and so we see that it is only his ideas that are immortalized. A philanthropist that sacrifices his wealth for his community immortalizes his wealth and not his character. But a martyr who sacrifices his life for the sake of humanity immortalizes exactly what he gave – his own life and character.

Thirdly, martyrs provide a guiding light for their communities. By making their sacrifices they teach their nations about freedom and making a principled stance. They are shining role models for all to follow.

Fourthly, a martyr sacrifices for the sake of all while others cannot make their sacrifices had it not been for the martyrs. Philosophers and philanthropists cannot make their contributions if it were not for the martyrs who secured the requisite freedom and security for them and their communities. Thus the martyrs share in the achievements of all others, while no one can lay claim to the great sacrifice that they made.

That is why martyrdom gives life to a nation. It is a sacrifice based on principle, an act appreciated and venerated in communities across the world.

Yet, martyrdom takes new and greater meaning when it is for the sake of the greatest of values. When we look at the history of revelation and the sacrifices that were made by the followers of God's prophets, we see the greatest examples of martyrdom. We see it especially in the great sacrifice of our beloved Imam Hussain (a), who truly understood the deep meanings of martyrdom. That is why he declared,

إني لا أرى الموت إلا سعادة والحياة مع الظالمين إلا برما

I do not see anything in death but satisfaction, while living with the oppressors is nothing but weariness.[9]

---

[9] Al-Hilli, *Mutheer al-Ahzan*, 32.

HONOR

يَقُولُونَ لَئِن رَّجَعْنَا إِلَى الْمَدِينَةِ لَيُخْرِجَنَّ الْأَعَزُّ مِنْهَا الْأَذَلَّ ۚ وَلِلَّهِ الْعِزَّةُ وَلِرَسُولِهِ وَلِلْمُؤْمِنِينَ وَلَٰكِنَّ الْمُنَافِقِينَ لَا يَعْلَمُونَ

They say, 'When we return to the city, the honorable will surely expel the meek from it.' Yet all honor belongs to God and His Apostle and the faithful, but the hypocrites do not know.[1]

Imam Hussain's (a) movement was not like any ordinary political movement. It was a movement that embodied and championed all the virtues which set mankind apart from all other creatures. After all, it was a movement entirely devoted to God Almighty and undertaken for His sake. It was a movement for the sake of God's divine commands. It was a revolution against all vices which He forbade.

Anyone who studies Imam Hussain's (a) movement will see that it embodied all aspects of virtue. Imam Hussain (a), his

---

[1] The Holy Quran, 63:8.

51

family, and companions embodied the ideals of patience, resolve, and bravery. They showcased humility, dignity, and magnanimity. They exemplified the highest of ideals throughout their journey towards the inevitable massacre. The most sublime of human ideals which our beloved Imam (a) embodied was the virtue of honor. Let us take a closer look at this virtue, its importance, and the role it played in Imam Hussain's (a) movement.

HONOR TO HUMANITY

God Almighty created humanity and made it the greatest of His creations. He says in the Holy Quran,

$$وَلَقَدْ كَرَّمْنَا بَنِي آدَمَ وَحَمَلْنَاهُمْ فِي الْبَرِّ وَالْبَحْرِ وَرَزَقْنَاهُم مِّنَ الطَّيِّبَاتِ وَفَضَّلْنَاهُمْ عَلَىٰ كَثِيرٍ مِّمَّنْ خَلَقْنَا تَفْضِيلًا$$

Certainly We have honored the Children of Adam, and carried them over land and sea, and provided them with all the good things, and preferred them with a complete preference over many of those We have created.[2]

God even took mankind as His representatives on earth. He says,

$$هُوَ الَّذِي جَعَلَكُمْ خَلَائِفَ فِي الْأَرْضِ ۚ فَمَن كَفَرَ فَعَلَيْهِ كُفْرُهُ ۖ وَلَا يَزِيدُ الْكَافِرِينَ كُفْرُهُمْ عِندَ رَبِّهِمْ إِلَّا مَقْتًا ۖ وَلَا يَزِيدُ الْكَافِرِينَ كُفْرُهُمْ إِلَّا خَسَارًا$$

---

[2] The Holy Quran, 17:70.

It is He who made you [His] representatives on the earth. So whoever is faithless, his unfaith is to his own detriment. The unfaith of the faithless does not increase them with their Lord [in anything] except disfavor, and their unfaith increases the faithless in nothing except loss.[3]

As God's most favored creatures and His representatives on earth, humanity has great value over all other creatures. Human life is given great sanctity – murder is one of the most heinous crimes a person can commit. In fact, God equates the taking of one innocent life to the murder of humanity in its entirety. God says,

مِنْ أَجْلِ ذَٰلِكَ كَتَبْنَا عَلَىٰ بَنِي إِسْرَائِيلَ أَنَّهُ مَن قَتَلَ نَفْسًا بِغَيْرِ نَفْسٍ أَوْ فَسَادٍ فِي الْأَرْضِ فَكَأَنَّمَا قَتَلَ النَّاسَ جَمِيعًا وَمَنْ أَحْيَاهَا فَكَأَنَّمَا أَحْيَا النَّاسَ جَمِيعًا ۚ وَلَقَدْ جَاءَتْهُمْ رُسُلُنَا بِالْبَيِّنَاتِ ثُمَّ إِنَّ كَثِيرًا مِّنْهُم بَعْدَ ذَٰلِكَ فِي الْأَرْضِ لَمُسْرِفُونَ

That is why We decreed for the Children of Israel that whoever kills a soul, without [its being guilty of] manslaughter or corruption on the earth, is as though he had killed all mankind, and whoever saves a life is as though he had saved all mankind. Our apostles certainly brought them manifest signs, yet even after that, many of them commit excesses on the earth.[4]

God Almighty endowed mankind with many great gifts – one of the greatest being the gift of honor and dignity. If we read

---

[3] The Holy Quran, 35:39.

[4] The Holy Quran, 5:32.

into the verses of the Holy Quran, we see that God made this gift contingent on an individual's proximity to Him. The closer an individual is to God and His divine attributes, the greater that individual's honor and dignity. It is narrated that the Holy Prophet (s) looked towards the Ka'ba one day and said,

مرحبا بالبيت مل أعظمك وأعظم حرمتك على الله، والله للمؤمن أعظم حرمة منك لأن الله حرم منك واحدة ومن المؤمن ثلاثة: ماله ودمه وأن يظن به ظن السوء

Greetings unto the House [of God]! O' how great you are and how great is your sanctity in eyes of God! Yet by God, a believer has greater sanctity than you. Surely, God has granted you one sanctity and three to the believer – in his wealth, his blood, and that he shall not be thought ill of.[5]

In another narration the Holy Prophet (s) said,

المؤمن أكرم على الله من ملائكته المقربين

A believer is more honorable in the eyes of God than His closest angels.[6]

A believer is an individual of flesh and blood like any other human, but is distinguished by his relationship to the Almighty. It is this relationship that dictates honor for a believer. God is the most honorable and mighty, so by association to God the believer also becomes honorable and mighty. That is the truth which the Holy Quran spoke about in the

---

[5] Al-Nisabouri, *Rawdat al-Wa'edhin*, 293.

[6] Al-Hindi, *Kanz al-'Ommal*, 1:164.

verse – "All honor belongs to God and His Apostle and the faithful, but the hypocrites do not know."[7] The hypocrites are ignorant of this connection and the honor that God gives to the believers by their relationship to Him and His Messenger (s).

The great honor that God gives to the believers also comes with responsibilities. God declared for the faithful to be honorable, so they cannot dishonor themselves after God's decree. Imam al-Sadiq (a) is narrated to have said,

إن الله فوض الى المؤمن أمره كله ولم يفوض إليه أن يكون ذليلا أما سمعت الله تعالى يقول (ولله العزة ولرسوله وللمؤمنين) فالمؤمن يكون عزيزا ولا يكون ذليلا، إن المؤمن أعز من الجبل لأن الجبل يستقل منه بالمعاول والمؤمن لا يستقل من دينه بشيء.

Surely God empowered the believers in everything, except that they be dishonorable [or dishonored]. Have you not heard that God Almighty said, 'Yet all honor belongs to God and His Apostle and the faithful'? The believer is honorable and is not dishonorable. A believer is more honorable than a mountain. A mountain can be chipped away with pickaxes, but a believer's faith cannot be chipped away.[8]

It is also narrated that Imam al-Baqir (a) said,

---

[7] The Holy Quran, 63:8.

[8] Al-Tousi, *Tahtheeb al-Ahkam*, 6:179.

إن الله تبارك وتعالى أعطى المؤمن ثلاث خصال: العز في الدنيا
والآخرة والفلح في الدنيا والآخرة والمهابة في صدور الظالمين.

Surely God, the Most Blessed and Almighty, gave the believer
three traits — honor in this worldly life and the hereafter, suc-
cess in this worldly life and the hereafter, and grandeur in the
eyes of the oppressors.[9]

We can see examples of the honor that God willed for the
faithful in some of the religious rulings of Islam. For example, God does not allow for the believers to prostrate to anyone but Him. Our faith also does not allow us to kiss the
hands of anyone except our parents, the Holy Prophet (s),
and whoever represents the Holy Prophet (s) such as the Immaculate Imams (a) and our grand scholars. Imam al-Sadiq
(a) is narrated to have said that a believer should not kiss the
head or hand of anyone except a prophet or his vicegerents.
He said,

لا يقبل رأس أحد ولايده إلا رسول الله صلى الله عليه وآله أو
من اريد به رسول الله صلى الله عليه وآله

Do not kiss the head or hand of anyone except the Messenger
of God (s) or whoever [represents] the Messenger of God (s).[10]

So we see that God wants the believer to always be dignified
and honorable.

---

[9] Al-Kulayni, *al-Kafi*, 8:234.

[10] Al-Kulayni, *al-Kafi*, 2:185.

We must also realize that the only true and lasting honor is the one that comes from our relationship to God. Honor derived from wealth can quickly turn into the humiliation of poverty. Honor gained by power and influence is also as fleeting. Thus, a person's relationship to the Almighty and Eternal God is the only source of everlasting honor and dignity.

We also see that an individual who grows further away from God also distances himself from honor and humanity. This distance can make the individual much like the beasts of the wild, or even worse. God Almighty says in the Holy Quran,

أَرَأَيْتَ مَنِ اتَّخَذَ إِلَهَهُ هَوَاهُ أَفَأَنْتَ تَكُونُ عَلَيْهِ وَكِيلًا ﴿٤٣﴾ أَمْ
تَحْسَبُ أَنَّ أَكْثَرَهُمْ يَسْمَعُونَ أَوْ يَعْقِلُونَ ۚ إِنْ هُمْ إِلَّا كَالْأَنْعَامِ ۖ بَلْ
هُمْ أَضَلُّ سَبِيلًا ﴿٤٤﴾

Have you seen him who has taken his desire to be his god? Is it your duty to watch over him? Do you suppose that most of them listen or exercise their reason? They are just like cattle; indeed, they are further astray from the way.[11]

We practically see all of this in our lives. We see the faithful holding on to a set of principles that ensure their honor and dignity. The believer is always honest in everything he does. He never asks his needs from anyone but God. He treats everyone with respect and receives the same. These are some examples of the attributes that ensure a believer's honor is maintained within his community.

---

[11] The Holy Quran, 25:43-44.

On the other hand, a deviant who has distanced himself from God is willing to let go of all the principles that ensure his honor. He is willing to lie, cheat, and commit any crime to satisfy his desires. This deviance destroys any honor that the individual may have had.

HUSSAIN'S (A) HONOR

After the passing of our Holy Prophet Muhammad (s), the Muslim nation faced a set of circumstances that ultimately led to the rise of the Umayyad clan as the ruling authority. One of the main goals of this newly established dynasty was to solidify its power by stripping the nation of any honor or dignity it had. They were not satisfied to strip the honor of one person or group – that alone being a crime of greater sanctity than destroying the venerable Ka'ba – but they wanted to subjugate the entire nation. Muwaiya ibn Abu Sufyan made this clear directly after his pact with Imam Hassan (a). Historians say the Muawiya entered the Grand Mosque of Kufa and told the masses,

> O' people of Kufa! Do you think that I fought you for the sake of preserving the prayers, the alms, or the pilgrimage? No. I knew that you prayed, paid alms, and performed the pilgrimage. I fought you to gain power over you and control your fates. God has given me this desire despite your opposition. All blood that you have spilt in this battle has been lost for naught.[12]

---

[12] Al-Mu'tazili, *Sharh Nahj al-Balagha*, 16:93.

The policy of the Umayyad clan was to gain power over the nation no matter the cost and without head to any principle. The tragedy reached its peak when Yazid ibn Muawiya – widely known for his deviance and lack of respect for any ideals or sanctity – inherited the throne after his father. What honor would the Muslims have after that?

This was the background from which Imam Hussain (a) launched his eternal movement. He was the true heir of the Holy Prophet (s) and the one tasked with guarding this nation after the passing of his grandfather, father, and brother. It was up to him to restore the nation's lost honor. It was his responsibility to remind mankind that they should not will-fully sell themselves into slavery. As his father the Commander of the Faithful once said,

ولا تكن عبد غيرك وقد جعلك الله حرا

Do not be a slave to others when God created you free![13]

The grandeur of Imam Hussain's (a) stance was that it was not about the honor of one individual or group. It was a movement to restore honor to an entire nation.

Let us here mention a few anecdotes from Imam Hussain's (a) movement to restore the nation's honor.

Refusal to Pledge Allegiance

When Muawiya ibn Abu Sufyan passed away, the Umayyad governor over the city of Medina, al-Waleed ibn 'Utba ibn Abu Sufyan, called Imam Hussain (a) to the palace that very

---

[13] Al-Radi, *Nahj al-Balagha*, 3:51.

night. He demanded that the Imam (a) give allegiance to Yazid that very night. Imam Hussain (a) replied,

مثلي لا يبايع سرا فإذا دعوت الناس الى البيعة دعوتنا معهم

Someone like me does not pay allegiance in secret. When you call the people to pay allegiance, call us alongside them.[14]

When Imam Hussain (a) wanted to leave the palace, Marwan ibn al-Hakam warned al-Waleed that if Hussain (a) leaves the palace now they will never be able to extract a pledge of allegiance out of him. That was the night in which Imam Hussain (a) famously declared,

أيها الأمير إنا أهل بيت النبوة ومعدن الرسالة ومختلف الملائكة
بنا فتح الله وبنا يختم، ويزيد رجل شارب الخمور قاتل النفس
المحرمة معلن بالفسق ومثلي لا يبايع مثله

Governor! We are the household of the Prophet (s), the core of the message, and the harbor of Angels. By us, God has introduced [His message], and to us He will return it. Yazid is a deviant, a miscreant, a drunkard, and a murderer. He has publically professed his impiety. Someone like me will never pay allegiance to the likes of him.[15]

Imam Hussain (a) lays out a clear equation. He is the only surviving grandson of the Holy Prophet (s) and the head of the household of revelation. The opposing side is Yazid – a drunken miscreant who cannot be called a 'believer' let alone

---

[14] Al-Muqarram, *Maqtal al-Hussein (a)*, 130.

[15] Al-Muqarram, *Maqtal al-Hussein (a)*, 131.

the 'prince of the believers.' The obvious result of this equation is that an individual like Imam Hussain (a) would never pay allegiance to an individual like Yazid.

This honorable and courageous stance is one unlike any stance taken by Imam Hussain's (a) contemporaries. Many of the sons of the Holy Prophet's (a) companions quickly leapt to give their allegiance to Yazid so as to avoid Umayyad wrath.

Declaring his Stance

We see another of Imam Hussain's (a) honorable stances when he declared the purpose of his movement in a letter he wrote to his half-brother Muhammad ibn al-Hanafiyya. The Imam (a) said,

إِنِّي لَمْ أَخْرُجْ أَشِرًا وَلا بَطَرًا ، وَلا مُفْسِدًا وَلا ظَالِمًا ، وَإِنَّمَا خَرَجْتُ لِطَلَبِ الإِصْلاحِ في أُمَّةِ جَدِّي ، أُرِيدُ أَنْ آمُرَ بِالْمَعْرُوفِ وَأَنْهى عَنِ الْمُنْكَرِ ، وَأَسِيرَ بِسِيرَةِ جَدِّي وَأَبي عَلِيّ بْنِ أَبي طَالِب

I do not revolt due to discontent [with God's blessings], nor out of arrogance. I did not rise as a corruptor, nor as an oppressor. Rather, I wish to call for reform in the nation of my grandfather. I wish to call for what is good, and to forbid what is evil. [I wish to] follow the tradition of my grandfather [the Prophet] and my father Imam Ali ibn Abu Talib.

فمن قبلني بقبول الحق فالله أولى بالحق ومن رد علي أصبر حتى يقضي الله بيني وبين القوم بالحق وهو خير الحاكمين

Whoever accepts me because I carry the truth, then God is the refuge of the honest. As for whoever rejects this call, I will be patient until God judges between me and the rejecters with His justice. Surely, He is the best of judges.[16]

Imam Hussain (a) clearly laid out the principles for which he was setting out. He made this declaration with the honor and dignity of an individual who is confident of his relationship to the Almighty. He set out with the purpose of calling to what is good and forbidding evil. He foresaw the opposition he would face but declared his determination to continue on the path that God prescribed for him. He did not waver in his mission, but professed his confidence in God's justice and judgment. This is the greatest example of an honorable stance taken in support of God's divine message.

Facing an Army

Imam Hussain (a) faced an army hundreds of times larger than his own camp, yet he continued to stand with honor and dignity in support of his principles. When an enemy commander suggested that Imam Hussain (a) give in to Yazid's demands, he declared,

لا والله لا أعطيهم بيدي إعطاء الذليل ولا أقرّ فرار العبيد. يا عباد الله إنّي عُذْتُ بِرَبّي وَرَبِّكُمْ أَنْ تَرْجُمُونِ. أعوذ بربي وربكم من كل متكبر لا يؤمن بيوم الحساب.

By God! I will not give them my allegiance in disgrace. I will not flee like a slave. O' servants of God! I seek the protection

---

[16] Ibn Shahrashoob, *al-Manaqib*, 3:241.

of my Lord and your Lord, if you would [dare murder] me.'
I seek the protection of my Lord and your Lord from the
tyrant that does not believe in Judgment Day.[17]

He declared that he will not bend to Yazid's forces in humiliation. Neither will he flee in disgrace. He was ready to face the fate that was dictated by his circumstances so long as it meant that he can deliver his message and fulfill his goal.

Although the Umayyad army seemed bent on massacring him, his family, and his companions, Imam Hussain (a) did not falter in his stance. He stood and gave another sermon to the opposing army in which advised them then said,

أَلا وإِنّ الدّعيّ ابن الدّعيّ قد ركز بين اثنتين: بين السلّة و

الذلّة، وهيهات منا الذلّة. يأبى الله لنا ذلك ورسوله والمؤمنون،

وحجور طابت وطهرت، وأنوف حميّة، ونفوس أبيّة، من أن

نؤثر طاعة اللّئام على مصارع الكرام.

Surely, the imposter — a son of an imposter — has [given us a choice] between death and disgrace. Surely, far from us is disgrace. God refuses that for us. So do his Messenger (s), the believers, noble and purified households, zealous souls, and proud spirits. All refuse that we accept obedience to the wicked over a noble death.[18]

Imam Hussain (a) made a stance that showed humanity how to stand with honor and dignity in support of the most sublime of values and divine teachings. It is his indubitable and

---

[17] Al-Tabari, *Tareekh al-Tabari*, 4:323.

[18] Al-Hilli, *Mutheer al-Ahzaan*, 40.

unshakable relationship with God Almighty that gave our beloved Imam the great honor that he held and continues to hold. We must learn from his stance how to live a life of honor rooted in our relationship with God.

BROTHER IMAMS

In the Name of God, the Most Compassionate, the Most Merciful

وَاتْلُ عَلَيْهِمْ نَبَأَ ابْنَيْ آدَمَ بِالْحَقِّ إِذْ قَرَّبَا قُرْبَانًا فَتُقُبِّلَ مِنْ أَحَدِهِمَا وَلَمْ يُتَقَبَّلْ مِنَ الْآخَرِ قَالَ لَأَقْتُلَنَّكَ ۖ قَالَ إِنَّمَا يَتَقَبَّلُ اللَّهُ مِنَ الْمُتَّقِينَ ﴿٢٧﴾ لَئِن بَسَطتَ إِلَيَّ يَدَكَ لِتَقْتُلَنِي مَا أَنَا بِبَاسِطٍ يَدِيَ إِلَيْكَ لِأَقْتُلَكَ ۖ إِنِّي أَخَافُ اللَّهَ رَبَّ الْعَالَمِينَ ﴿٢٨﴾

Relate to them truly the account of Adam's two sons. When the two of them offered an offering, it was accepted from one of them and not accepted from the other. [One of them] said, 'Surely I will kill you.' [The other one] said, 'Allah accepts only from the Godwary. Even if you extend your hand toward me to kill me, I will not extend my hand toward you to kill you. Indeed, I fear Allah, the Lord of all the worlds.' [1]

As we read and learn about Imam Hussain (a), we must not forget about the remainder of the Holy Household who played an essential role in safeguarding the message of our Holy Prophet Muhammad (s). These individuals were

---

[1] The Holy Quran, 5:27-28.

granted the position of leadership over the nation and guardianship over the faith due to their Immaculate character and absolute devotion to God. As God says in the Holy Quran,

وَجَعَلْنَا مِنْهُمْ أَئِمَّةً يَهْدُونَ بِأَمْرِنَا لَمَّا صَبَرُوا ۖ وَكَانُوا بِآيَاتِنَا يُوقِنُونَ

When they had been patient and had conviction in Our signs, We appointed amongst them Imams to guide [the people] by Our command.[2]

The head of this Holy Household sacrificed all he had to deliver the message and mission which his Lord entrusted to him. He devoted himself to building a community that embodies God's teachings and devotes itself to His pleasure. Yet he faced extreme hardship and made great sacrifices along that path. As he himself said,

ما أوذي نبي مثلما أوذيت

No prophet has been mistreated like I have been.[3]

The mistreatment of the Holy Prophet (s) did not stop at his person. The greatest injury that the Messenger of God (s) suffered came with how the Muslim nation treated his family after his passing. The height of the tragedy came with the martyrdom of the grandsons who he had so adored during his lifetime – individuals which he did not only love due to their kinship, but because God Almighty had commanded him to love them.

---

[2] The Holy Quran, 32:24.

[3] Al-Majlisi, *Bihar al-Anwar*, 39:86.

As we read about Imam Hussain's (a) life and learn from his stance, we would be amiss to ignore the life and stance of his brother Imam Hassan (a). After all, the two brother Imams are the masters of the youth of Paradise and are Imams whether they sit or rise. If we study the stance of Imam Hassan (a), we find that he dedicated his life to the service of the sublime goals of the Holy Household. He endured patiently and sacrificed sincerely despite all the tribulations that he faced. His patience and sacrifices laid the groundwork that allowed his brother to make that eternal stance in the land of Karbala.

As we are study the life and stance of Imam Hussain (a), we must turn back and give justice to Imam Hassan (a) and how he laid the groundworks for the triumph at Karbala.

About Imam Hassan (a)

Let us first take a look at the character of Imam Hassan (a) through some of the narrations of the Holy Prophet (s). Upon reading these narrations, we will not only realize the greatness of this personality and the great love that the Holy Prophet (s) had for him, but also the fact that he was a divinely appointed heir to the Prophet (s) and guardian of the faith.

The Holy Prophet (s) once said to one of his companions,

إن لكل شيء موقعا في القلب وما وقع موقع هذين الغلامين من قلبي شيء قط

Everything has a place within the heart. Surely, nothing has ever taken a place in my heart like these two boys.

When the companion exclaimed his surprise at these words the Holy Prophet (s) said,

وما خفي عليك أكثر إن الله أمرني بحبهما

What you do not know is greater. Surely, God commanded me to love them.[4]

It is also narrated that the Holy Prophet (s) said,

من أراد أن يتمسك بعروة الله الوثقى التي قال الله في كتابه،
فليوال علي بن أبي طالب والحسن والحسين فإن الله يحبهما من
فوق عرشه

Whoever wishes to hold on to God's firm rope which He mentions in His book, let him follow Ali ibn Abu Talib (a), Hassan (a), and Hussain (a). Surely, God loves them from atop His throne.[5]

The Holy Prophet (s) is also reported to have said,

ابناي هذان إمامان قاما أو قعدا

These two sons of mine are Imams whether they sit or stand.[6]

There are many other narrations to this effect emphasizing the need for us to love and follow these personalities. More-

---

[4] Al-Qummi, *Kamil al-Ziyarat*, 113.

[5] Al-Qummi, *Kamil al-Ziyarat*, 114.

[6] Al-Majlisi, *Bihar al-Anwar*, 43:278.

over, we see that the command to love him is not just a request made by the Holy Prophet (s), but a direct command from God. We must realize that the Holy Prophet (s) would not command the nation to love an individual so unless the individual is someone who has attained God's love and pleasure. Because the Holy Prophet (s) commanded us to love and follow Imam Hassan (a), we know that the Imam's life and actions were in complete devotion to God and absolute reflections of His divine teachings.

All this leads us to certainty that Imam Hassan's (a) actions were in the best interest of the religion of Islam and the Muslim nation, regardless of whether or not we understand the reasoning. Our inability to recognize the wisdom in his stance or understand the depth of his vision should not lead us to doubt in his Immaculate character.

THE TREATY

A couple of misconceptions are sometimes raised regarding the peace treaty that Imam Hassan (a) signed with Muawiya. Some say that Imam Hassan (a) pledge allegiance to Muawiya, which would mean that Muawiya's accession to the caliphate was legitimate and must be accepted. They also say that if the position of Imam is by divine appointment as the Shia claim, then Imam Hassan's (a) pledge of allegiance to Muawiya contradicts that view.

These misconceptions can be answered as follows:

First, there are many misconceptions that are widely circulated by people even though they have no basis in historical facts. Imam Hassan (a) never pledged allegiance to Muawiya.

He did not abdicate the position of Imam or successorship to the Holy Prophet (s) to Muawiya. The position is in fact one of divine appointment and cannot be simply assigned or delegated without God's divine command.

Second, if we go back to the historical accounts of the peace treaty and the terms of the pact, we see that these claims have no basis in Imam Hassan's (a) actions. It was only the Umayyad propaganda machine that spread these lies and misconceptions as means of legitimizing Muawiya's rule over the Muslim nation.

Anyone who looks carefully into the historical record will realize that Muawiya's caliphate did not have an iota of legitimacy. All the historical facts point to the conclusion that Imam Hassan (a) did not legitimize Muawiya's rule in any way.

Imam Hassan (a) did not pledge allegiance to Muawiya. Even though some historians may have erroneously labeled the agreement as a pledge, the historical record is clear that it was a treaty between two parties and not a concession from one to the other.

If we go back to the provisions of the agreement, we see that Imam Hassan (a) placed as a condition that he would not be obliged to call Muawiya the 'prince of the believers.' This in itself shows us that Imam Hassan (a) never paid allegiance to Muawiya. How? The Imam (a) is doubtlessly one of the believers which Muawiya claimed command and authority over. By rejecting to give this title to Muawiya, Imam Hassan (a) is implicitly saying, 'Muawiya is not my prince.' By imbedding this seemingly simple term in the agreement, Imam Hassan

(a) was able to show that he did not intend to lend legitimacy to Muawiya through the treaty.

Similarly, Imam Hassan (a) also included in the pact a condition that he is not obliged to be a witness or party to any case in an Umayyad court. This provision also strips Muawiya of any claim to legitimacy, as the Imam (a) refused to recognize the authority of the Umayyad legal system.

So we see that Imam Hassan (a) never abdicated the position of Imam to Muawiya. Rather, he agreed to a peace accord in which political authority would be given to Muawiya without any legitimacy given from the Imam. Thus, it should be clear that Imam Hassan (a) never pledge allegiance to Muawiya or legitimized his government in any way.

Unfortunately, many historians did not grasp the wisdoms behind our Imams' stances and did not realize the great role played by the Household of the Prophet (s) in safeguarding the Muslim nation. When Imam Hassan (a) entered into a peace accord with Muawiya, he did not give up his role as a divinely appointed leader and guardian of the faith. He did not lose his position as Imam simply because political power was usurped by others. In fact, he continued to lead the nation by providing guidance, spreading knowledge, and warning of the dangers that threatened its wellbeing.

IMMACULATE WISDOM

One of Imam Hassan's (a) greatest struggles was the fact that his position was misunderstood. These problems arise when a nation attempts to impose its own fallible and lacking judgment against its Immaculate and divinely appointed leaders.

This is a dilemma which was experienced by many of the prophets and messengers of old. The Immaculate leader is often misunderstood, which in turn leads to doubt in the minds of his followers. This eventually leads to insurrection against God and His messengers and appointed leaders.

It seems that the wisdom in Imam Hassan's (a) stance was not apparent to many in the Muslim nation, even the closest and most devout followers of the Holy Household. His position was not understood and the depth of his vision was not realized. History tells us that many Muslims objected to his peace accord and made arguments similar to the ones made against the Holy Prophet (s) after he entered the peace accord of Hudaibiya.

Take, for example, Imam Hassan's (a) conversation with a companion by the name of Abu Sa'eed who asked about the reasons behind the peace accord. Imam Hassan (a) said,

يا أبا سعيد ألستُ حجة الله تعالى ذكرُه على خلقه وإماماً عليهم بعد أبي عليه السلام.

O' Abu Sa'eed! Am I not the proof of God, glorified be His name, over His creatures and an Imam after my father peace be upon him?

I said, "Yes." He said,

ألست الذي قال رسول الله صلى الله عليه وآله وسلم لي ولأخي، الحسن والحسين إمامان قاما أو قعدا

Am I not him, along with my brother, of whom the Messenger of God (s) said 'Hassan and Hussain are two Imams whether they rise or sit.'

I said, "Yes." Then he said,

فأنا إذن إمام لو قمت وأنا إمام إذا قعدت، يا أبا سعيد علة
مصالحتي لمعاوية هي علة مصالحة رسول الله صلى الله عليه وآله
وسلم لبني ضمرة وبني أشجع ولأهل مكة حين انصرف من
الحديبية أولئك كفّار بالتنزيل ومعاوية وأصحابه كفّار بالتأويل.

Then I am an Imam if I rise and an Imam if I sit. O' Abu Sa'eed, the reason for my peace accord with Muawiya is the same as the reason for the peace accord of the Messenger of God (s) with the Banu Dumra, Banu Ashja', and the people of Mecca when leaving Hudaibiya. Those were polytheists by tanzeel [i.e. the explicit word of revelation]. Muawiya and his ilk are polytheists by the ta'weel [i.e. the implicit application of revelation].

يا أبا سعيد إذا كنت إماما من قبل الله تعالى ذكره لم يجب أن
يسفه رأيي فيما أتيته من مهادنة. وإن كان وجه الحكمة فيما أتيته
ملتبساً.

O' Abu Sa'eed, if I am an Imam by the appointment of God, glorified be His name, then my views in regards to this peace accord I entered into should not be derided. This is even if the reasoning behind my actions is not clear.

ألا ترى الخضر لما خرق السفينة وقتل الغلام واقام الجدار

سخط موسى فعله لاشتباه وجه الحكمة عليه حتى أخبره فرضي

فهكذا أنا سخطتم علي بجهلكم وجه الحكمة فيه ولولا ما أتيت لما

ترك من شيعتنا على وجه الأرض أحد إلا قتل

Do you not see that when al-Khidr tore the boat, killed the boy, and built the wall, Moses grew angry towards him due to a misunderstanding of the reasoning behind these actions? And that when [al-Khidr] informed [Moses] of the reasons, [Moses] was satisfied? Similarly, I have made you angry at me due to your ignorance of the reasoning [behind the treaty]. Yet if it were not for my actions, none of our Shia would be left on the face of the earth as all would be murdered.[7]

The Imam (a) explains that a true devotee should not doubt the actions of an Immaculate leader appointed by God Almighty. Any doubt in the Imam's actions is a doubt in the Holy Prophet (s) and, consequently, doubt in God who appointed these individuals as leaders and guardians of the faith. Of course, this does not mean that we cannot seek to understand the reasons behind our Imams actions, and Imam Hassan (a) would on multiple occasions explain his reasoning to his followers. In fact, if we study Imam Hassan's (a) words, we see two main reasons for his acceptance of peace with Muawiya.

First, Imam Hassan (a) sought to protect the righteous community of devotees who followed the path of the Holy

---

[7] Al-Sadouq, *'Ilal al-Sharae'*, 1:211.

Prophet (s) and his Household. This is actually a consideration that we see drove many of the actions of our Imams (a)
– they were always concerned with the safety and wellbeing
of their followers. After all, virtue and piety cannot spread
without the virtuous and pious to be role models to others.
A religion and school of thought is only ink on paper if it
does not have followers. So Imam Hassan (a) entered into
the accord to protect this righteous community. As he told
some of his followers who urged him to battle Muawiya,

أنتم شيعتنا وأهل مودّتنا، فلو كنت بالحزم في أمر الدنيا أعمل

ولسلطانها أربض وأنصب ما كان معاوية بأبأس منّي بأساً ولا

أشدّ شكيمة ولا أمضى عزيمة، ولكنّي أرى غير ما رأيتم وما

أردت فيما فعلت إلاّ حقن الدم. فارضوا بقضاء الله وسلّموا

لأمره والزموا بيوتكم وأمسكوا

You are our followers and admirers. You know that if I were
working to achieve worldly goals, or if I were to work and
scheme to gain power, I would be no less powerful, generous,
or resolute than Muawiya. But I am of a different opinion
than yours. I did not do what I did for any reason other than
averting bloodshed. So accept God's judgment and submit to
Him. Remain at home. Refrain [from revolution]. Sheathe
your blades...[8]

It was clear to Imam Hassan (a) that a battle with Muawiya
was doomed for failure and would result in nothing but loss
for the Holy Household and its followers. He was able to cut

---

[8] Al-Balathiri, *Ansab Al-Ashraaf*, 3:290-91.

the losses and preserve his community by entering into the peace accord with Muawiya.

Second, the Imam (a) made his decision in accordance to what is in the best interest of the Muslim nation. To our Imams (a), protecting the nation is a top priority even if it meant great losses for the Holy Household and its followers. Imam Hassan (a) made it clear that this was one of his considerations when he said,

أن معاوية نازعني حقا هو لي دونه فنظرت لصلاح الأمة وقطع
الفتنة... فرأيت أن أسالم معاوية واضع الحرب بيني وبينه...
ورأيت حقن الدماء خير من سفكها ولم أرد بذلك إلا صلاحكم
وبقاءكم وان أدرى لعله فتنة لكم ومتاع إلى حين

Surely, Muawiya has fought me over a right that is mine and not his. Yet I looked at the best interest of the nation and ending sedition... I saw that I should enter into peace with Muawiya and end the war between us... I saw that protecting lives was better than bloodshed. I did not want anything by this other than your best interest and survival. I knew that it would be a trial upon you and a sustenance for a [limited] time.[9]

Through stances such as this, Immaculate Imams (a) embody the greatest teachings of the Holy Quran. They gladly welcome a hand stretched out to hurt them so long as their own hands are not implicated in hurting anyone. They embody the blessed verse,

---

[9] Al-Majlisi, *Bihar al-Anwar*, 44:30.

لَئِن بَسَطتَ إِلَيَّ يَدَكَ لِتَقْتُلَنِي مَا أَنَا بِبَاسِطٍ يَدِيَ إِلَيْكَ لِأَقْتُلَكَ

إِنِّي أَخَافُ اللَّهَ رَبَّ الْعَالَمِينَ

*Even if you extend your hand toward me to kill me, I will
not extend my hand toward you to kill you. Indeed, I fear
Allah, the Lord of all the worlds.*[10]

A DIFFERENT STANCE

So we know that there was great wisdom behind Imam Hassan's (a) actions. Yet the fact remains that Imam Hassan (a) chose peace with Muawiya while Imam Hussain (a) chose to rise up against Yazid. It is clear that our Imams each took a different stance. The question we must ask is, 'were the differences in the Imams' actions and stances based on differences in their personalities and character? If not, how can we explain the differences in their actions?'

There is no significant difference in the character and personalities of our Imams. They all represent an extension of the character of the Holy Prophet (s). They were all products of an upbringing in the Holy Household. They shared the same purpose, goals, abilities, and qualities. They were at all times connected to God Almighty and working for His pleasure in accordance to His commands.

The differences we see in our Imams' (a) stances and actions go back to what their circumstances dictated. Their singular goal was to lead humanity closer to their Lord. Yet the circumstances facing each Imam dictated that they pursue this

---

[10] The Holy Quran, 5:28.

goal in different ways. That is why we see one of our Imams took the helm of political authority, while another signed a peace treaty with his enemies, a third revolted against the authorities of the time, and a fourth taught the message through supplication, and so on.

We can therefore be certain that had Imam Hassan (a) lived at the time of Imam al-Sadiq (a), he would have used the same methods as Imam al-Sadiq (a). If Imam al-Rida (a) lived at the time of Imam al-Sajjad (a), his actions would be those of Imam al-Sajjad (a).

We must acquiesce that the difference in the stances of Imam Hassan (a) and Imam Hussain (a) is the most seemingly contradictory. On the one hand, Imam Hassan (a) chose to end his war with Muawiya and sign a treaty that allowed the Umayyad clan to tighten its political grasp over the Muslim nation. On the other hand, Imam Hussain (a) chose to lead a rebellion against Yazid and sacrifice everything in his battle against the Umayyad army. This seeming contradiction led to many flawed analyses of our Imams' (a) actions.

We see that some historians interpreted Imam Hassan's (a) stance as a reflection of a more peace-loving and agreeable character. They therefore praise him for his supposed acquiescence to Umayyad rule. In fact, it is highly possible that the individuals who made this claim were actually attempting to tarnish the image of Imam Ali (a) and Imam Hussain (a), casting them as belligerent and blood-thirsty in contrast to Imam Hassan (a). Other historians claimed that Imam Hassan's (a) stance was due to cowardice and weak character. This is doubtlessly an attempt to tarnish Imam Hassan's (a) image, and has all the marks of Umayyad propaganda.

We cannot accept any of these erroneous assessments of our Imams' (a) stances. So how can we correctly reconcile the great differences in their choices?

There is no doubt that Imam Hassan (a) and Imam Hussain (a) are both divinely chosen guardians of the faith. This is evident in many narrations of the Holy Prophet (s). He said:

الحسن والحسين سيدا شباب أهل الجنة

Hassan (a) and Hussain (a) are the masters of the youth of Paradise.[11]

الحسن والحسين إمامان قاما أو قعدا

Hassan (a) and Hussain (a) are Imams whether they rise or sit.[12]

أنتما الإمامان ولأمكما الشفاعة

You [O' Hassan (a) and Hussain (a)] are Imams and your mother [Lady Fatima (a)] is an intercessor [on the Day of Judgment].[13]

There are numerous other narrations which speak of the two grandsons of the Holy Prophet (s) in absolutely equal terms. Therefore, there cannot be any difference amongst them in terms of their divinely appointed roles as Imams. Each of

---

[11] Al-Qummi, *Qurb al-Isnad*, 111.

[12] Al-Sadouq, *'Ilal al-Sharae'*, 211..

[13] Al-Arbali, *Kashf al-Ghumma*, 2:129.

them undoubtedly acted in accordance to what the duties of his role dictated.

In fact, if we look at the historical record we see that the individual who most devotedly and unwaveringly supported Imam Hassan (a) in his decision was none other than Imam Hussain (a). We see many of the Shia of the time, including the most loyal and devoted companions, expressing doubt and unease with Imam Hassan's (a) actions. Yet Imam Hussain (a) did not utter a single word of doubt or opposition to his brother. This was not simply out of respect for his elder brother, but out of conviction that entering into the treaty was the best course of action. The historical record is clear that Imam Hussain (a) did not waver in his conviction that the two different roles played by him and his brother were part of a greater strategy to achieve one sublime goal. It was clear that without the role that Imam Hassan (a) played, Imam Hussain (a) could not fulfill his own.

We see all this in Imam Hussain's (a) replies to the individuals who approached him asking him to revolt during the life time of Imam Hassan (a). He would say,

صدق ابو محمد، فليكن كل رجل منكم حلسا من احلاس بيته، ما دام هذا الإنسان حيا.

Abu Muhammad [i.e. Imam Hassan] (a) is right. Let every one of you [remain in his home] so long as this man [i.e. Muawiya] remains alive.[14]

---

[14] Al-Daynouri, *Al-Akhbar Al-Tiwal*, 221.

Even after the passing of his brother, Imam Hussain (a) would remain steadfast in his support of the peace signed with Muawiya. In fact, he would tell his followers that so long as Muawiya remains alive, the peace will continue. He would say,

اما أخي فأرجو ان يكون الله قد وفقه، وسدده فيا يأتى، واما
انا فليس رأيي اليوم ذلك، فالصقوا رحمكم الله بالأرض، واكمنوا
في البيوت، واحترسوا من الظنه ما دام معاويه حيا،

As for my brother, I pray that God has blessed him and supported him [in the hereafter]. As for me, I do not see that the day has come. Stand your ground, may God have mercy on you. Remain in your homes. Take caution against the suspicions [of the Umayyad state] so long as Muawiya remains alive....[15]

---

[15] Al-Daynouri, *Al-Akhbar Al-Tiwal*, 222.

A CALL TO LIFE

In the Name of God, the Most Compassionate, the Most Merciful

يَا أَيُّهَا الَّذِينَ آمَنُوا اسْتَجِيبُوا لِلَّهِ وَلِلرَّسُولِ إِذَا دَعَاكُمْ لِمَا يُحْيِيكُمْ

وَاعْلَمُوا أَنَّ اللَّهَ يَحُولُ بَيْنَ الْمَرْءِ وَقَلْبِهِ وَأَنَّهُ إِلَيْهِ تُحْشَرُونَ

﴿٢٤﴾ وَاتَّقُوا فِتْنَةً لَا تُصِيبَنَّ الَّذِينَ ظَلَمُوا مِنكُمْ خَاصَّةً وَاعْلَمُوا

أَنَّ اللَّهَ شَدِيدُ الْعِقَابِ ﴿٢٥﴾

*O you who have faith! Answer Allah and the Apostle when
he summons you to that which will give you life. Know that
Allah intervenes between a man and his heart and that toward Him you will be mustered. And beware of a punishment, which shall not visit the wrongdoers among you exclusively, and know that Allah is severe in retribution.[1]*

God Almighty created mankind in order to live honorably
and virtuously in this world. Yet the life which we have been
given as human being is different than the life we observe in
other creatures. Life for a human being is more than just the
physical, material life. It is a life of the mind and spirit which

---

[1] The Holy Quran, 8:24-25.

God commanded us to live. Through the quality of this life, mankind may either rise above all of God's creatures or sink to their lowest nadir.

Thus, God tells us that we must follow His commands and follow His Messenger (s) so we may live – not a physical life, but the life of intellectual and spiritual growth and movement. God says,

أَوَمَن كَانَ مَيْتًا فَأَحْيَيْنَاهُ وَجَعَلْنَا لَهُ نُورًا يَمْشِي بِهِ فِي النَّاسِ كَمَن مَّثَلُهُ فِي الظُّلُمَاتِ لَيْسَ بِخَارِجٍ مِّنْهَا ۚ كَذَٰلِكَ زُيِّنَ لِلْكَافِرِينَ مَا كَانُوا يَعْمَلُونَ

Is he who was lifeless, then We gave him life and provided him with a light by which he walks among the people, like one who dwells in a manifold darkness which he cannot leave? To the faithless is thus presented as decorous what they have been doing.[2]

Thus, an individual who is truly alive is the individual who carries the light of guidance, knowledge, and obedience to God in his heart.

God has sent us prophets and messengers as a blessing in order to take us from darkness into light, from ignorance into knowledge, and from death into life. God's messengers are His means of returning life to human nations. That is why the Holy Quran emphasizes the need to follow the example of God's chosen servants. It is only then that we can live a

[2] The Holy Quran, 6:122.

true life – one of happiness, honor, benevolence, and guidance.

Yet despite this call towards life, we see that many individuals ignore God's call and choose to live in a state of death, with a dead mind and a dead spirit. Why is it that so many people ignore the call towards life?

We ask this question here because when we study the movement of Imam Hussain (a) we find that it was truly a call for life. Imam Hussain (a) set out from Medina to Kufa in order to call the nation of his grandfather toward the life that the Messenger of God (s) called them towards before. Yet the Muslims did not answer his call and chose to forgo true life. Let us discuss this call, the nation's failure to answer, and the repercussions of that failure.

A CALL TO LIFE

Imam Hussain (a) declared that his movement was in fact a call towards true life. It was a call towards honor, dignity, and guidance. It is a call to life because it was in absolute conformity to the call of God and His Messenger (s). It was a call to free ourselves from all forms of slavery and servitude that does not fall in line with service to our Lord. A call for us to live a life of knowledge and dignity that God wanted for us.

Imam Hussain (a) set out to reform the nation of his grandfather. He set out in order to call for what is good and forbid every evil. He set out to free the nation from the chains that the Umayyad used to enslave it. Imam Hussain (a) clearly indicated to all of this in his sermons throughout his journey from Medina to Karbala and even amid that battle. Before leaving Medina, he would tell his kinsmen,

إنه من لحق بي استشهد معي ومن تخلف لم يبلغ الفتح

Surely, whoever follows me will be martyred alongside me. Whoever does not follow me will not witness the triumph.[3]

Indeed, all the calls and movements of the prophets and messengers were calls to life. If mankind had answered these calls, it would not have faced the struggles that it did. If mankind answers this call now, it would free itself from all trials, tribulations, oppression, and wretchedness.

If the Muslim nation had answered the call of Imam Hussain (a) and supported his movement, it would not have had to face the great repercussions of abandoning the Immaculate Imam.

A Call Unanswered

We must wonder how it was that Imam Hussain's (a) call was left unanswered. When Imam Hussain (a) stood in the lands of Karbala, he had less than a hundred individuals stand alongside him and his family members. He was the grandson and closest living individual to the Holy Prophet (s). His grandfather had praised him and his brother Imam Hassan (a) on numerous occasions. All Muslims agree that Imam Hassan (a) and Imam Hussain (a) are the masters of the youth of Paradise. Therefore, there is no doubt that these two

---

[3] Al-Saffar, *Basa'er al-Darajat*, 501.

Imams' movements were sound and legitimate. So why was the call left unanswered?

The fact that so few individuals supported Imam Hussain (a) and answered his call does not take away from the legitimacy of his movement. After all, many of God's chosen messengers were abandoned by their people. Prophet Noah called his people to God for nine hundred and fifty years. All prophets suffered at the hands of their people. Our beloved Holy Prophet Muhammad (s) would even say,

No prophet has been mistreated like I have been.[4]

Thus, the fact that Imam Hussain's (a) call was left unanswered is not an anomaly historically speaking. It is a continuation of mankind's historical rejection of God's prophets, messengers, and chosen servants. Still, we are attempting to understand why mankind has continuously rejected these calls. We can list a few reasons as follows:

Lethargy

One reason behind people's repeated rejection of God's call is lethargy. People become too accustomed to their way of life and do not wish to make any changes. Sometimes, it is because people fear that a change will actually have a negative effect on them in some way. Other times, people reject change because it is difficult and requires effort. This is especially true when answering the call requires a stance against oppression or a sacrifice for the sake of truth.

---

[4] Al-Majlisi, *Bihar al-Anwar*, 39:86.

We see that the Holy Prophet (s) was able to rally the people of the Arabian Peninsula to answer the call towards Islam. They embraced the message he delivered and adopted the teachings of Islam. In answering this call, many early Muslims faced the tribulations of being driven out of their homes, disowned by their families, and fought by their kinsmen. They endured all of this for the sake of truth. This strength that the Holy Prophet's (s) call gave the nation allowed it to grow and become a leader scientifically, culturally, and economically.

Yet after the passing of the Holy Prophet (a) and under the leadership of individual's like the Banu Umayya, that torch quickly flickered and died. With the conquests and expansions of that era, the Muslim nation soon saw rapid economic growth that allowed many Muslims to live in a state of luxury relative to the poverty of the near past. At the same time, Umayyad policies of discrimination and favoritism drove further division within the Muslim nation. Thus, a nation that had rallied willingly under the banner of the Holy Prophet (s) began to cling to this material world and forget about his message and teachings.

When any individual clings to the life of this world, he will find it very difficult to make any change. It is very difficult to forgo a luxury and willingly embrace hardship of any kind. This is true whether the change in question is a small and simple aspect of our daily lives, or a sacrifice to be made for the sake of the hereafter. It is especially true because we often lack an understanding of the consequences of our actions and the repercussions that our inaction could lead to.

This is why we find that when Imam Hussain (a) first set out from Medina, he was surrounded by a large group of followers and devotees. Yet people quickly began to disperse when they realized that there was no worldly reward to be gained from this movement. As the Imam (a) continued to declare that the only reward will be reaped in the hereafter, the lethargic and materialistic began to abandon him.

Unclarity

When Muawiya died and left Yazid as his heir, many in the Muslim nation did not realize the dire repercussions that would ensue if someone like Yazid held power. Social change is often a slow process. It cannot be detected immediately, but can only be seen across long spans of time. As such, the people of the time did not see the immense change in the Muslim nation when Yazid was made its ruler. Only the individuals of foresight whom God had endowed with the light of guidance could see the true repercussions of such an event.

Imam Hussain (a) recognized the problem from the first day. When the governor of Medina demanded that Imam Hussain (a) give allegiance to Yazid, the Imam (a) responded,

أيها الأمير إنا أهل بيت النبوة ومعدن الرسالة ومختلف الملائكة بنا فتح الله وبنا يختم، ويزيد رجل شارب الخمور قاتل النفس المحرمة معلن بالفسق ومثلي لا يبايع مثله

Governor! We are the household of the Prophet (s), the core of the message, and the harbor of Angels. By us, God has introduced [His message], and to us He will return it. Yazid is a deviant, a miscreant, a drunkard, and a murderer. He

*has publicly professed his impiety. Someone like me will never
pay allegiance to the likes of him.[5]*

When Marwan ibn al-Hakam, a confidant of Muawiya, suggested that Imam Hussain (a) should pay allegiance to Yazid,
the Imam replied,

على الإسلام السلام إذا بليت الأمة براع مثل يزيد

*Say goodbye to Islam if the nation is tried with a caretaker
like Yazid….[6]*

It is because of this shortsightedness that many people are
lenient with the cultural, philosophical, ethical, and spiritual
devolution that they see in their society. Such individuals are
in fact allowing the nation to fall prey to the greatest ills without truly understanding the nature of the circumstance.

Self Interest

Banu Umayya were known for their bribery and discrimina-
tory economic policies. They used the public treasury to buy
the support and quiet enemies. It was through these tactics
that Muawiya was able to install Yazid as his heir, buying the
support of tribal chieftains with massive gifts of wealth and
property.

Yazid continued the policies of his father. When he first ac-
ceded to the Umayyad throne, he spoke to the people of the
Levant and said,

---

[5] Al-Muqarram, *Maqtal al-Hussein (a)*, 131.

[6] Al-Muqarram, *Maqtal al-Hussein (a)*, 133.

Glad tidings of people of the Levant! Good is still in your midst! There will be a massacre between me and the people of Iraq, as I have seen in a dream three nights ago a river between me and the people of Iraq a river of blood flowing rapidly.

He then distributed large amounts of wealth to the Levantines.[7] The same policy was implemented by Ubaydullah ibn Ziyad, who paid off many tribal chieftains and people of influence to side with Yazid. In the end, many were willing to side with deviance and corruption in protection of their own material interests.

There were also numerous individuals who did not side with Yazid but abandoned Imam Hussain (a) out of sheer self-interest as well. These were the men who were adversaries of Yazid and had ambitions of leadership. They saw Imam Hussain (a) as a thorn in their side because of the great reverence he held in the hearts of people.

Repercussions

Rejecting the divine call leads society down the path of great trials and tribulations. This does not stop with those who rejected the call, but affect even the pious. That is because the effects of social ills and moral degeneration do not differentiate between the pious and impious. They afflict entire communities and nations indiscriminately.

The Muslim nation's refusal to heed Imam Hussain's (a) call had severe consequences in the short and long term. In fact,

---

[7] Al-Muqarram, *Maqtal al-Hussein (a)*, 128.

we continue to live these repercussions to this day. It will only be through our Twelfth Holy Imam (a) that the social ills that were cultivated in those days will be cured. We will not detail the great long-term consequences of this issue. Instead, let us focus on two of the short-term consequences that immediately followed the massacre at Karbala.

Al-Harra. Tragedy of Karbala shook the nation to its core and awakened its slumbering conscience. After the tragedy, the people of Medina realized who Yazid was and understood the gravity of having someone like him lead the Muslim nation. The people of Medina rose against Yazid and prepared themselves to battle his army. The situation grew so dire that Marwan ibn al-Hakam, Yazid's cousin and future Umayyad caliph, entrusted his family to Imam al-Sajjad (a) and fled the city.

Yazid prepared an army and placed Muslim ibn 'Uqba, a known brute, as its general. His commands were to kill the rebels and leave no sanctity undefiled in the city. Muslim did just that. The event of al-Harra became a black page in the history of Islam. Historians say that,

> On the day of al-Harra, seven hundred reciters of the Holy Quran were killed, including three companions of the Messenger of God (s)... They attacked the women so that they say that a thousand unmarried women were impregnated on those days.[8]

Muslim ibn 'Uqba then took allegiance by forcing the people of Medina to submit themselves as slaves to Yazid. All of this

---

[8] Ibn Katheer, *al-Bidaya*, 6:262, 8:241.

would not have occurred had the Muslims answered Imam Hussain's (a) call from the outset and supported him in his movement.

Burning the Ka'ba. When the Umayyad army finished with Medina, it was led by al-Husayn ibn Numair towards Mecca where Abdullah ibn al-Zubayr was leading his own revolt against Yazid. The Umayyad army besieged Mecca and pelted it with catapults. Flaming projectiles would hit the Grand Mosque and burn a part of the Ka'ba.

This is how the Umayyad clan took power over the Muslim nation. They took its people as slaves and spent its treasuries on their own wretched desires. Their appointed clergymen would lead prayers in their name every day. As the supposed successors of the Holy Prophet (s), their names would be coupled with the name of God and His Messenger (s).

Thus, the nation's rejection of the call to life lead to its own misery. As God says,

$$
\text{يَا أَيُّهَا الَّذِينَ آمَنُوا اسْتَجِيبُوا لِلَّهِ وَلِلرَّسُولِ إِذَا دَعَاكُمْ لِمَا يُحْيِيكُمْ}
$$
$$
\text{وَاعْلَمُوا أَنَّ اللَّهَ يَحُولُ بَيْنَ الْمَرْءِ وَقَلْبِهِ وَأَنَّهُ إِلَيْهِ تُحْشَرُونَ}
$$
$$
\text{﴿٢٤﴾ وَاتَّقُوا فِتْنَةً لَا تُصِيبَنَّ الَّذِينَ ظَلَمُوا مِنكُمْ خَاصَّةً وَاعْلَمُوا}
$$
$$
\text{أَنَّ اللَّهَ شَدِيدُ الْعِقَابِ ﴿٢٥﴾}
$$

Answer Allah and the Apostle when he summons you to that which will give you life. Know that Allah intervenes between a man and his heart and that toward Him you will be mustered. And beware of a punishment, which shall not visit the wrongdoers among you exclusively, and know that Allah is severe in retribution.[9]

---

[9] The Holy Quran, 8:24-25.

THE AUDACITY OF THE CRIME

In the Name of God, the Most Compassionate, the Most Merciful

أَمْ يَحْسُدُونَ النَّاسَ عَلَىٰ مَا آتَاهُمُ اللَّهُ مِن فَضْلِهِ ۖ فَقَدْ آتَيْنَا آلَ
إِبْرَاهِيمَ الْكِتَابَ وَالْحِكْمَةَ وَآتَيْنَاهُم مُّلْكًا عَظِيمًا

Do they envy those people for what Allah has given them out of His bounty? We have certainly given the progeny of Abraham the Book and wisdom, and We have given them a great sovereignty.[1]

We have taken some time thus far to speak about the great status of Imam Hussain (a) and his closeness to the Holy Prophet (s). We have mentioned some of the narrations in which the Messenger of God (s) praised his Holy Household and commanded the people to love and follow them.

As we remember and learn about Imam Hussain (a) an important question poses itself. How could the Muslims of the time murder their prophet's grandson in such a cruel way?

---

[1] The Holy Quran, 4:54.

How could they take their prophet's family captive and treat them as they did? They did all this while claiming that they were followers of the Holy Prophet Muhammad (s) and his message. They claimed to love the Prophet (s) and knew that he commanded them to love his Holy Household.

All that occurred during that period would be very easily understandable had the nation simply rejected the message and returned to their old ways after the passing of the Holy Prophet (s). Instead, they attached themselves to him and even claimed to act in his name while brutally murdering his family. These questions are truly mindboggling.

The answer to these questions can be found in the greatest moral corruptions of the time. We can list these causes as follows:

ENVY

Envy is one of the most lethal illnesses to strike mankind. It fills hearts with hatred and leads individuals to commit crimes just to get at another person or principle. We see this plainly not only in the parables of ancient nations, but even before the history of mankind on earth.

Envy is the cause of one of the first instances of disobedience of God's divine commands. The Holy Quran relays to us the story of Satan who was a jinni but was elevated to the ranks of the angels because of his worship and obedience to the Almighty. Yet when God commanded all to bow down before Adam, Satan refused God's command claiming that he

was worthier than Adam. Satan threw his high rank and proximity to God away and became the vilest of beings simply
because of his envy.

Envy is also the motive behind the first known human crime.
Soon following the creation of mankind, Adam's son Cain
grew envious of his brother Abel. This envy gave rise to humanity's first murder. God says,

وَاتْلُ عَلَيْهِمْ نَبَأَ ابْنَيْ آدَمَ بِالْحَقِّ إِذْ قَرَّبَا قُرْبَانًا فَتُقُبِّلَ مِنْ أَحَدِهِمَا
وَلَمْ يُتَقَبَّلْ مِنَ الْآخَرِ قَالَ لَأَقْتُلَنَّكَ قَالَ إِنَّمَا يَتَقَبَّلُ اللَّهُ مِنَ
الْمُتَّقِينَ ﴿٢٧﴾ لَئِنْ بَسَطتَ إِلَيَّ يَدَكَ لِتَقْتُلَنِي مَا أَنَا بِبَاسِطٍ
يَدِيَ إِلَيْكَ لِأَقْتُلَكَ إِنِّي أَخَافُ اللَّهَ رَبَّ الْعَالَمِينَ ﴿٢٨﴾

*Relate to them truly the account of Adam's two sons. When
the two of them offered an offering, it was accepted from one
of them and not accepted from the other. [One of them] said,
'Surely I will kill you.' [The other one] said, 'Allah accepts
only from the Godwary. Even if you extend your hand toward
me to kill me, I will not extend my hand toward you to kill
you. Indeed, I fear Allah, the Lord of all the worlds.* [2]

Envy continues to wreak havoc on the human race, even the
most pious amongst us. The moral can be seen in the parable
of Prophet Moses and al-Samiri. Our scholars tell us the al-
Samiri was a devout man and a scholar amongst the Israelites.
When Moses was given prophecy, al-Samiri grew envious and
decided to undermine God's chosen messenger. The Holy
Quran relays the story as follows,

---

[2] The Holy Quran, 5:27-28.

قَالَ فَإِنَّا قَدْ فَتَنَّا قَوْمَكَ مِن بَعْدِكَ وَأَضَلَّهُمُ السَّامِرِيُّ ﴿٨٥﴾

فَرَجَعَ مُوسَىٰ إِلَىٰ قَوْمِهِ غَضْبَانَ أَسِفًا ۚ قَالَ يَا قَوْمِ أَلَمْ يَعِدْكُمْ رَبُّكُمْ

وَعْدًا حَسَنًا ۚ أَفَطَالَ عَلَيْكُمُ الْعَهْدُ أَمْ أَرَدتُّمْ أَن يَحِلَّ عَلَيْكُمْ غَضَبٌ

مِّن رَّبِّكُمْ فَأَخْلَفْتُم مَّوْعِدِي ﴿٨٦﴾ قَالُوا مَا أَخْلَفْنَا مَوْعِدَكَ بِمَلْكِنَا

وَلَٰكِنَّا حُمِّلْنَا أَوْزَارًا مِّن زِينَةِ الْقَوْمِ فَقَذَفْنَاهَا فَكَذَٰلِكَ أَلْقَى

السَّامِرِيُّ ﴿٨٧﴾ فَأَخْرَجَ لَهُمْ عِجْلًا جَسَدًا لَّهُ خُوَارٌ فَقَالُوا هَٰذَا

إِلَٰهُكُمْ وَإِلَٰهُ مُوسَىٰ فَنَسِيَ ﴿٨٨﴾

*[God] said [to Moses], 'Indeed We tried your people in your
absence, and the al-Samiri has led them astray.' Thereupon
Moses returned to his people, indignant and grieved. He said,
'O my people! Did your Lord not give you a true promise?
Did the period [of my absence] seem too long to you? Or did
you desire that your Lord's wrath should descend on you and
so you failed your tryst with me?' They said, 'We did not fail
our tryst with you of our own accord, but we were laden with
the weight of those people's ornaments, and we cast them [into
the fire] and so did the al-Samiri.' Then he produced for them
a calf – a [lifeless] body with a low – and they said this is
your god and the god of Moses, so he forgot!*[3]

There are many similar stories in the Holy Quran, where
some of the prophets' communities turned against them out
of envy. We find that many people sacrifice their principles
and knowledge under the influence of this vile disease. The

---

[3] The Holy Quran, 20:85-88.

nation of the Holy Prophet (s) is no different from past nations. Human nature is one and the same, moral diseases that ravaged the ancient nations afflict all others throughout time.

When we look back at the history of Islam, we find that the Commander of the Faithful Ali (a) faced many great challenges due to adversaries who envied him. They saw that the Holy Prophet (s) would praise and favor Imam Ali (a) at every turn. The same was true for the remainder of the Holy Household. They were always the most excellent in terms of knowledge, bravery, benevolence, faith, and all other virtues. This is a truth that was mentioned in many of the traditions of the Holy Household.

Imam al-Sadiq (a) would say to his companions,

نحن قوم فرض الله طاعتنا لنا الأنفال ولنا صفو المال ونحن الراسخون في العلم ونحن المحسودون الذين قال الله في كتابه (أم يحسدون الناس)

We are a people who God has obligated obedience to us. To us belong the bounties and the [alms imposed on] surplus wealth. We are those who are 'firmly grounded in knowledge' and the objects of envy about whom God says in His Book, 'Do they envy those people for what Allah has given them out of His bounty?'[4]

Regarding this verse Imam al-Sadiq (a) would also say,

---

[4] Al-Saffar, *Basa'er al-Darajat*, 222. Citing: The Holy Quran, 4:54, 162.

نحن والله الناس الذين قالها فيهم الله تبارك وتعالى ونحن والله
المحسودون ونحن أهل هذا الملك الذي يعود إلينا

*By God, we are the people whom God said this about. By
God, we are the object of envy and the people of sovereignty to
whom it will return.*[5]

Envy played a role in many individuals' abandonment of the
Holy Household, therefore leading to the tragic massacre of
Karbala. The Holy Prophet (s) is God's greatest blessing, sent
as a mercy to all creation. He was sent to lead mankind from
the darkness towards light. Yet the Holy Household was envied for all the bounties they were given by God. The nation
thus repaid its Holy Prophet (s) with massacring his grandsons and humiliating his granddaughters.

HATRED

Another important factor in people's abandonment of the
Holy Household was the hatred some held for the family of
the Holy Prophet (s). This was especially true for the Umayyad clan who saw the Messenger of God (s) as someone who
took away their status and influence. They dealt with the Holy
Prophet (s) as an adversary, even after their superficial con-
version to Islam.

There are many historical indications to this fact. For exam-
ple, we see that Abu Sufyan would tell al-Abbas, the Holy
Prophet's (s) uncle, during the Muslim return to Mecca,
"Surely, the kingdom of your nephew had become great!" Al-

---

[5] Al-Saffar, *Basa'er al-Darajat*, 56.

Abbas would rebuke him and say, "Rather, it is prophethood."

In another instance, Abu Sufyan would approach Imam Ali (a) and offer his support if the Imam was willing to take political power by force. Imam Ali (a) would see through his tricks and say,

والله ما أردت بهذا الا فتنة وإنك والله طالما بغيت للإسلام

شرا لا حاجة لنا في نصيحتك

By God, you did not want anything out of this but to cause
mischief! By God, you have always sought ill for Islam! We
do not need your advice![6]

Abu Sufyan was the one who said when Othman became the caliph,

O' Banu Umayya! The caliphate came to the clans of Taim
and 'Adi, and I began to yearn for it. It has now come to
you. Snatch it like a boy snatching a ball! By God, there
shall be neither Paradise nor Hellfire!

When Othman heard these words, he reprimanded Abu Sufyan and dismissed him from the gathering.[7]

Yet the course of history was such that Islam's greatest enemies became its supposed guardians. How would such individual's act when given power and authority? How would they treat the family that challenged their power and took away their wealth during the life of the Holy Prophet (s)?

---

[6] Ibn Katheer, *al-Kamil*, 3:327.

[7] Al-'Askari, *Ahadeeth Um al-Mu'mineen*, 1:293.

They put all their efforts in distorting Islam's true teachings. They fabricated narrations that praised them while punishing anyone who spoke the true narrations that praised the Holy Household. They ensured that the holiest cities in Islam would be centers for sin and deviation.

The result was that a man like Yazid would take power and murder the Holy Prophet's (s) grandson. Yazid would declare his intentions when the severed head of Imam Hussain (a) was brought to his palace. He would say, "A day [of vengeance] for the day of Badr!"

Thus, it was the deep seeded hatred and a lust for vengeance that drove the Umayyad clan to lead the nation towards the vilest crime against the family of their Prophet (s).

WANTON DISREGARD

One of the most important factors that contributed to the occurrence of this grand tragedy was the wanton disregard of Muslims towards the case of the Holy Household. Even though not all Muslims envied or hated the family of the Holy Prophet (s), most did not act to support them against the continued oppression they faced. This has several clear causes, including:

First, when the Arabs first entered Islam, they did not all adopt its teachings with devotion and fervor. The mission of the Holy Prophet (s) was to spread the message as widely as possible while at the same time training a corps of individuals who understood and applied his teachings in intricate detail. After all, we cannot expect that everyone who enters Islam will overnight become a pious scholar. This issue is compounded by the fact that Islam was still a new religion and its teachings did not yet take hold of the generation. Thus, hypocrites like the Umayyad clan could easily influence the nation and steer it away from the Holy Household and the Immaculate Imams (a) chosen by God to be the guardians of this faith.

Second, following the passing of the Holy Prophet (s) the conquests of the first century compounded the issue. Conquest meant that the bounties of war and increased trade enriched the Arabian Peninsula. The people of this region were unaccustomed to many of the luxuries that they began to experience. They quickly forgot the Holy Prophet's (s) teachings of austerity. Additionally, wealth encumbers its holder, as people often avoid any confrontation for fear of their worldly interests. When many Muslims, including many of the companions of the Holy Prophet (s) and their children, became the holders of capital in a new economy, they became lethargic. They could no longer risk their monetary interests, let alone their lives, for the sake of truth and justice.

Third, the engrossment of the nation in vice also lead to their abandonment of Islam's message. Only thirty years after the passing of the Holy Prophet (s), the cities of Mecca and Medina became capitals of vice. There is no doubt that moral decay has a role in suppressing the spirit. This meant that people became lethargic and did not care whether or not they stood in defense of the truth. Therefore, a man like Imam Hussain (a) could be murdered in their midst with only a few Muslims rushing to his aid.

Finally, Umayyad authorities were not shy to persecute when their policy of bribery did not work. Thus, a large segment of the nation was either bought off or silenced forcefully by Umayyad governors. We see this vividly when Ubaydullah ibn Ziyad entered the city of Kufa, which was getting ready to support Imam Hussain (a). His ploys and bloodlust ensured that only few Muslims could rise against Umayyad rule.

These were some of the reasons that made the Muslim nation live in a state of wanton disregard towards the truth.

From this perspective, we see that one of Imam Hussain's (a) primary objectives was to awaken the conscience of the Muslim nation. His tragedy was the force that awakened the Muslims and reminded them of the sublime teachings of their faith. With his sacrifice, the religion of Islam was given new life after the death of many Muslims conscience.

SAFEGUARDING A NATION

In the Name of God, the Most Compassionate, the Most Merciful

وَمَا لَهُمْ أَلَّا يُعَذِّبَهُمُ اللَّهُ وَهُمْ يَصُدُّونَ عَنِ الْمَسْجِدِ الْحَرَامِ وَمَا
كَانُوا أَوْلِيَاءَهُ ۚ إِنْ أَوْلِيَاؤُهُ إِلَّا الْمُتَّقُونَ وَلَٰكِنَّ أَكْثَرَهُمْ لَا يَعْلَمُونَ
﴿٣٤﴾ ... وَالَّذِينَ كَفَرُوا إِلَىٰ جَهَنَّمَ يُحْشَرُونَ ﴿٣٦﴾ لِيَمِيزَ اللَّهُ
الْخَبِيثَ مِنَ الطَّيِّبِ وَيَجْعَلَ الْخَبِيثَ بَعْضَهُ عَلَىٰ بَعْضٍ فَيَرْكُمَهُ
جَمِيعًا فَيَجْعَلَهُ فِي جَهَنَّمَ ۚ أُولَٰئِكَ هُمُ الْخَاسِرُونَ ﴿٣٧﴾

What [excuse] have they that Allah should not punish them, when they bar [the faithful] from the Holy Mosque, and they are not its custodians? Its custodians are only the Godwary, but most of them do not know... The faithless will be gathered toward Hell, so that Allah may separate the bad ones from the good, and place the bad on one another, and pile them up together, and cast them into hell. It is they who are the losers.[1]

Imam Hussain's (a) stance is one of great importance in the struggle of virtue against evil. This is why our Immaculate

---

[1] The Holy Quran, 8:34-37.

Imams constantly reminded their followers of that tragedy and asked them to commemorate and remember it. The events of the battle of Karbala are more than just a tragic story in the history of the Holy Household. It is more than just a story that excites the passions and renews affection towards the progeny of the Messenger of God (s). It is in fact a pivotal point of our Immaculate Imams' struggle to advance the word of God and connect the nation to it.

We must therefore understand that Imam Hussain's (a) stance was a great achievement in this regard. Despite the tragedy that Imam Hussain (a) endured, his stance was a triumph that safeguarded the Muslim nation against the greatest of dangers. He endowed the nation with a heritage that preserved the most sublime virtues and the teachings of its faith.

The worst danger that a nation can face is that of misguidance – where it no longer can distinguish between truth and falsity. Such misguidance would lead people to misappropriate the teachings of their faith and to venerate evil as if it were good. We see an example of this in the verse above where God describes how the polytheists had taken control of the Grand Mosque built by Abraham and turned it into a temple for their idols. The Holy Quran promises the believers that one day the light of guidance will remove this confusion and that the straight path will be made clear.

If we read into the history of all previous messages sent to us by God, we see that there was always a degree by which misguidance was able to overtake the message. Each of the previous messages was either fundamentally altered or completely dismantled by deviant corruptors.

When our Holy Prophet Muhammad (s) received the revelation, God promised him that He will protect His last message from alteration or dismantlement. As with past nations, deviation and misguidance rose to overtake the nation and corrupt the message. There were many times during the life of our Holy Prophet (s) when misguidance launched its attacks on faith, yet God's Messenger (s) was there to foil those attacks and return his followers to the true message.

After the passing of the Holy Prophet (s), the Holy Household took on the mission of safeguarding the faith and sacrificed all that they had for this purpose. We cannot in this brief book detail all the dangers that faced the religion of Islam and how our Immaculate Imams (a) were able to avert every calamity. However, we will mention the greatest of these dangers and how Imam Hussain's (a) eternal stance safeguarded the nation from the ultimate catastrophe.

UMAYYAD DANGER

The greatest danger that the Muslim nation faced came when the Umayyad clan took the reins of the caliphate. It was a great catastrophe when the enemies of the Holy Prophet (s) claimed authority as his successors. Imam Ali (a) warned of this great travesty when he said,

أَلَا وَإِنَّ أَخْوَفَ الْفِتَنِ عِنْدِي عَلَيْكُمْ فِتْنَةُ بَنِي أُمَيَّةَ، فَإِنَّهَا فِتْنَةٌ عَمْيَاءُ مُظْلِمَةٌ: عَمَّتْ خُطَّتُهَا، وَخَصَّتْ بَلِيَّتُهَا، وَأَصَابَ الْبَلَاءُ مَنْ أَبْصَرَ فِيهَا، وَأَخْطَأَ الْبَلَاءُ مَنْ عَمِيَ عَنْهَا.

Surely, the worst mischief for you in my view is the mischief of Banu Umayya. It is blind and dark, with great sway and precise repercussions. Whoever remains clear-sighted in it will be tested, and he who remains blind in it would avoid the test.

وَايْمُ اللهِ لَتَجِدُنَّ بَنِي أُمَيَّةَ لَكُمْ أَرْبَابَ سُوءٍ بَعْدِي، كَالنَّابِ الضَّرُوسِ: تَعْذِمُ بِفِيهَا، وَتَخْبِطُ بِيَدِهَا، وَتَزِنُ بِرِجْلِهَا، وَتَمْنَعُ دَرَّهَا، لاَ يَزَالُونَ بِكُمْ حَتَّى لاَ يَتْرُكُوا مَنْكُمْ إلاَّ نَافِعاً لَهُمْ، أَوْ غَيْرَ ضَائِرٍ بِهِمْ

By God, you will find Banu Umayya to be wicked masters after me. They will be like the old unruly she-camel who bites with its mouth, beats with its fore-legs, kicks with its hind legs, and refuses to be milked. They would remain over you till they leave among you only those who benefit them or those who do not harm them.

وَلاَ يَزَالُ بَلاَؤُهُمْ حَتَّى لاَ يَكُونَ انْتِصَارُ أَحَدِكُمْ مِنْهُمْ إلاَّ مثل انْتِصَارِ الْعَبْدِ مِنْ رَبِّهِ، وَالصَّاحِبِ مِنْ مُسْتَصْحِبِهِ، تَرِدُ عَلَيْكُمْ فِتَنُهُمْ شَوْهَاءَ مَخْشِيَّةً، وَقِطَعاً جَاهِلِيَّةً، لَيْسَ فِيهَا مَنَارُ هُدىً، وَلاَ عَلَمٌ يُرَى.

Their mischief would continue till your seeking retribution from them would become like the seeking of retribution by the slave from his master or of the follower from the leader. Their mischief would come to you like horrid fears and clouds from the Age of Ignorance. Wherein there would be neither a min-aret of guidance nor any banner [of virtue] to be seen.[2]

Imam Ali (a) speaks of the Umayyad clan and its dangers not only as someone who experienced their wickedness firsthand throughout the lifetime and after the passing of the Holy Prophet (s), but also as an expert who knows the message and understands the dangers that they pose to it. Imam Ali's (a) warning are not just about the Umayyad rise to political authority. Their power grab does not change anything about the teachings of Islam and the sublime virtues it espouses. Rather, Imam Ali (a) warned of their efforts to alter the religion and decimate the high values that the Holy Prophet (s) taught.

This was nothing new to the Umayyad clan. When the message was first revealed to the Holy Prophet Muhammad (s), he was confronted by the larger Quraysh tribe – of which the Umayyad clan was a part. The Quraysh had been benefitting substantially from their proximity to the Ka'ba – the shrine built by Abraham as a place for worship for his monotheistic followers.

Yet, Mecca was barely habitable and would not become a prominent city in the Arabian Peninsula was it not for the Ka'ba. Abraham himself complained to God about this and said,

$$رَّبَّنَا إِنِّي أَسْكَنتُ مِن ذُرِّيَّتِي بِوَادٍ غَيْرِ ذِي زَرْعٍ عِندَ بَيْتِكَ الْمُحَرَّمِ رَبَّنَا لِيُقِيمُوا الصَّلَاةَ$$

---

[2] Al-Radi, *Nahj al-Balagha*, 1:184, Sermon 93.

*I have settled part of my descendants in a barren valley, by
Your sacred House, our Lord, that they may maintain the
prayer.*[3]

When the people of Arabia began to lose Abraham's true
message and turned to polytheism, they made the Ka'ba a
temple for their idols. Mecca thus became a religious center
for much of Arabia's tribes. With the rise of its religious significance, the city also became a trade hub for the peninsula.

The tribe of Quraysh benefitted tremendously from all of
this. They became the custodians of the Ka'ba, giving them
great social status and economic influence. They saw the
Ka'ba that housed the idols of the Arabian tribes as the
source of their wealth and status.

The message of our Holy Prophet (s) posed a significant risk
to Quraysh — of which he was a descendant. If monotheism
were to take hold of Mecca, Quraysh was going to lose the
source of its influence and wealth over the polytheistic tribes.
They became the worst enemies of the Holy Prophet (s), con-
spiring to kill him and his followers at every turn. However,
Islam continued to spread and prosper despite their attempts
to destroy it.

Quraysh continued to oppose the Holy Prophet (s) until the
lattermost years of his life. Amongst these last vestiges of polytheism were the leaders of the Umayyad clan — namely Abu
Sufyan and his son Muawiya — who were the most vehement
in their opposition to the Holy Prophet (s). They did not en-

---

[3] The Holy Quran, 14:37.

ter Islam until they saw its spread across the Arabian Peninsula and realized that adherence to polytheism would no longer be a source of wealth and influence.

This was the origin of the Umayyad dynasty – a clan accustomed to misappropriating faith for their own private benefit. Their danger laid in the fact that they did not respect the message of the Holy Prophet (s), seeing it only as a tool for power and wealth. Of course, if properly understood and applied, Islam would not allow them to claim supremacy over the nation. It was therefore a primary goal for them to distort Islam's teachings. They had to shift the nation towards prejudice, hierarchy, and submission, and away from its sublime values of brotherhood and equity.

UMAYYAD PLOYS

If we study the Umayyad phenomenon in detail, we will find that it posed a great danger to the nation on multiple levels. We cannot here list all the crimes of the Umayyad dynasty and analyze all their ploys to deviate Islam from its path. However, we can categorize some of the important facets of their attempts to deviate the nation. This should be enough to better understand the great danger they posed to the message and teachings of the Holy Prophet (s). Understanding this will in turn allow us to better understand Imam Hussain's (a) stance and why our Immaculate Imams (a) continually reminded us of his tragedy.

Rooted Deviance

Muslim history has been written by hands not very distant from Umayyad courts. Muawiya was especially cognizant of how we would be viewed historically. He perceived his legacy as the cornerstone of the dynasty he sought to create. He therefore put much effort in distorting history to reflect his image and the image of his clan positively. But even with this deliberate effort to create a hallowed image for Banu Umayya, God willed that their true beliefs and motives be reflected through the ages. We therefore see that historians recounted vital pieces of Umayyad thought, despite their great effort to cover up.

We see, for example, Abu Sufyan's revelatory statement regarding what he thought of the Holy Prophet's (s) message. Historians recount that when Othman ibn Affan – an Umayyad – became the third caliph Abu Sufyan declared to his kin,

> O' Banu Umayya! The caliphate came to the clans of Taim and 'Adi, and I began to yearn for it. It has now come to you. Snatch it like a boy snatching a ball! By God, there shall be neither Paradise nor Hellfire!

When Othman heard these words, he reprimanded Abu Sufyan and dismissed him from the gathering.[4]

Muawiya was of the same mindset as his father. Historians recount that he once said,

> Surely, the son of Abu Kabsha [i.e. the Prophet Muhammad (s)][5] has his name called five times a day [i.e. in the daily calls to prayer]. Nay by God! We will surly bury it![6]

---

[4] Al-'Askari, *Ahadeeth Um al-Mu'mineen*, 1:293.

[5] "Son of Abu Kabsha" was a derogatory title that Quraysh gave to the Holy Prophet Muhammad (s) –eds.

[6] Al-Mu'tazili, *Sharh Nahj al-Balagha*, 5:130.

Then came Yazid who would declare in a verse of poetry, "Hashim has played with power! Surely, there was neither a message delivered nor any revelation."

Similar instances recounted by historians are too many list here. Suffice it to say that Umayyad faith was clearly a sham and the roots of their deviance was evident to anyone who had the foresight to see.

Social Deviance

The Umayyad clan began to institute social policies that uprooted the social mores taught by the Holy Prophet (s). Islam established a system of equality amongst all regardless of race or gender. The sole measure of difference was that of piety. The Umayyad government, on the other hand, instituted policies of discrimination and prejudice amongst citizens of the Muslim nation. Imam Ali (a) had warned of this in a letter to one of his governors in which he said,

وَلَكِنَّنِي آسَى أَنْ يَلِيَ أَمْرَ هذِهِ الْأُمَّةِ سُفَهَاؤُهَا وَفُجَّارُهَا، فَيَتَّخِذُوا مَالَ اللهِ دُوَلاً، وَعِبَادَهُ خَوَلاً، وَالصَّالِحِينَ حَرْباً، وَالْفَاسِقِينَ حِزْباً

I worry that the affairs of this nation will be in the hands of its foolish and wicked people. They will take the wealth of God [i.e. the public treasury] as their own, make His servants their slaves, take the virtuous as enemies, and take the sinful as allies.[7]

---

[7] Al-Radi, *Nahj al-Balagha*, 3:120, Letter 63.

This was the example of the Commander of the Faithful (a). Conversely, the example of Muawiya would be to deliberately create a social hierarchy. Muawiya would write to his governor over Egypt that people were of three types, "Either human, human-like, or non-human. The first are the Arabs, the second the non-Arab [Muslims], and the latter are the non-Muslims [i.e. the Coptic Christians of Egypt]."[8]

The Umayyad preference for Arabs over all other races eventually led to their downfall, when the Abbasids took advantage of the existing social strife and began their revolution.

On the other hand, the Commander of the Faithful Imam Ali (a) writes to his governor over Egypt,

وَأَشْعِرْ قَلْبَكَ الرَّحْمَةَ لِلرَّعِيَّةِ، وَالْمَحَبَّةَ لَهُمْ، وَاللُّطْفَ بِهِمْ، وَلاَ تَكُونَنَّ عَلَيْهِمْ سَبُعاً ضَارِياً تَغْتَنِمُ أَكْلَهُمْ، فَإِنَّهُمْ صِنْفَانِ: إِمَّا أَخٌ لَكَ فِي الدِّينِ، وَإِمَّا نَظِيرٌ لَكَ فِي الْخَلْقِ،

Habituate your heart to mercy for the subjects and to affection and kindness for them. Do not stand over them like greedy beasts who feel it is enough to devour them, since they are of two kinds, either your brother in faith or your like in creation.[9]

Imam Ali (a) acted in accordance with the Holy Quran and commanded his followers and disciples to do the same. God Almighty says in the Holy Quran,

---

[8] Mutahari, *al-Malhama al-Hussainiya*, 3:66.

[9] Al-Radi, *Nahj al-Balagha*, 3:84, Letter 53.

يَا أَيُّهَا النَّاسُ إِنَّا خَلَقْنَاكُم مِّن ذَكَرٍ وَأُنثَىٰ وَجَعَلْنَاكُمْ شُعُوبًا وَقَبَائِلَ
لِتَعَارَفُوا ۚ إِنَّ أَكْرَمَكُمْ عِندَ اللَّهِ أَتْقَاكُمْ ۚ إِنَّ اللَّهَ عَلِيمٌ خَبِيرٌ

*O mankind! Indeed, We created you from a male and a fe-
male, and made you nations and tribes that you may identify
yourselves with one another. Indeed the noblest of you in the
sight of Allah is the most Godwary among you. Indeed Allah
is all-knowing, all-aware.*[10]

This is all in line with the actions of the Messenger of God
(s), who taught that there is no distinction between the races
and ethnicities except through piety. He would say,

يا أيها الناس ألا إن ربكم واحد وإن أباكم واحد ألا لا فضل

لعربي على عجمي ولا لعجمي على عربي ولا لأحمر على أسود

ولا لأسود على أحمر إلا بالتقوى

*O' people! Surely, your Lord is One and your father [i.e.
Adam] is one! Surely, there is no preference for an Arab over
a non-Arab, nor for a non-Arab over an Arab, nor for a
red-skin over a black-skin, nor for a black-skin over a red-
skin – except through piety!*[11]

Intellectual Deviance

The Umayyad dynasty was a curse to the nation, especially to
the scholars and intellectuals of the time. Imam Ali (a)
warned of this when he said,

---

[10] The Holy Quran, 49:13.

[11] Al-Shawkani, *Nayl al-Awtar*, 5:164.

أَلاَ وَإِنَّ أَخْوَفَ الْفِتَنِ عِنْدِي عَلَيْكُمْ فِتْنَةُ بَنِي أُمَيَّةَ، فَإِنَّهَا فِتْنَةٌ
عَمْيَاءُ مُظْلِمَةٌ: عَمَّتْ خُطَّتُهَا، وَخَصَّتْ بَلِيَّتُهَا، وَأَصَابَ الْبَلاَءُ مَنْ
أَبْصَرَ فِيهَا، وَأَخْطَأَ الْبَلاَءُ مَنْ عَمِيَ عَنْهَا.

Surely, the worst mischief for you in my view is the mischief of Banu Umayya. It is blind and dark, with great sway and precise repercussions. Whoever remains clear-sighted in it will be tested, and he who remains blind in it would avoid the test.[12]

The individuals of knowledge and foresight were the ones who faced the worst of tribulation during this era. The ignorant who blindly followed Umayyad directives and propaganda were spared the test. History verifies Imam Ali's (a) words. It was at the outset of this era that the most righteous companions of the Holy Prophet (s) and the Commander of the Faithful (a) were murdered and crucified – men like Hijr ibn 'Adi, Maytham al-Tammar, Rasheed al-Hijri, and Sa'eed ibn al-Musayyab, not to mention the tragedies of the Holy Household.

This is in addition to the concerted Umayyad effort to supplant the Holy Quran and the tradition of the Holy Prophet (s) as the primary sources of Muslim culture and education. We see, for example, that instead of spreading the traditions of the Messenger of God (s), Muawiya would appoint story tellers to tell fairy tales in the mosques. And instead of instilling a respect for the Holy Quran, Muawiya would place great emphasis on poetry. He would even say, "Make poetry the

---

[12] Al-Radi, *Nahj al-Balagha*, 1:184, Sermon 93.

greatest of your worries and your primary art. In it are the tales of your forefathers and the means of your guidance."[13]

This is in clear contradiction to the teachings of the Holy Prophet (s) which emphasized the Book of God as the primary source of teaching and guidance. In fact, the Holy Prophet (s) made teaching of the Quran an obligation of every parent towards their child. It is narrated that Ghalib ibn Sa'sa'a and his son Farazdaq once visited the Messenger of God (s). When the Holy Prophet (s) asked about Farazdaq the father said, "This is my son. He is poet." The Holy Prophet (s) replied, "Teach him the Quran. It is better for him than poetry." Farazdaq was moved by the statement and refused to write any poetry until he memorized the Holy Quran.[14] He later became one of the best-known poets of the era.

Ethical Deviance

The message of Islam is one of virtue and dignity. The Umayyad authorities came to supplant the high morals of Islamic teachings with deviance and corruption. They understood that with deviance, the nation's will was broken and its character was changed. Historians recount that the holiest of Islam's cities, Mecca and Medina, became the centers of corruption and sin in the nation.

In the face of all this deviance came the stance of Imam Hussain (a) who sacrificed everything he had to bring life to the tradition of the Holy Prophet (s). It revived the best of

---

[13] Ibn Khalkan, *Wafiyyat al-A'yan*, 5:241.

[14] Al-Mu'tazili, *Sharh Nahj al-Balagha*, 10:21.

virtues that the message of Islam had espoused. It was much broader than just a stance against injustice – it was a stance of all virtue against all vice.

Because the battle between vice and virtue is continuous and constantly evolving, our Immaculate Imams (a) emphasized the need to keep the memory of this tragedy alive. Our commemorations are not merely to remember the grave massacre – although such a massacre is worth remembering. Rather, it is for us to take back the morals and virtues that Imam Hussain (a) sacrificed for.

Every year, the tragedy of Karbala revives our passions and fills us with sorrow and grief. These passions move us to learn about Imam Hussain (a) and the values that he stood for. They drive us to attempt to emulate his Immaculate character.

Imam Hussain (a) safeguarded the message of Islam and the nation of Muslims by giving us this sublime legacy. Through remembering his stance, we bring ourselves closer to our Immaculate role models and the teachings of our faith. Through this heritage, our beloved Imams achieved their goal of rescuing mankind from vice and returning them to virtue. This heritage is the great triumph that Imam Hussain (a) set out to achieve, and which he did achieve.

REVOLUTION

In the Name of God, the Most Compassionate, the Most Merciful

وَلَمَّا رَأَى الْمُؤْمِنُونَ الْأَحْزَابَ قَالُوا هَـٰذَا مَا وَعَدَنَا اللَّهُ وَرَسُولُهُ
وَصَدَقَ اللَّهُ وَرَسُولُهُ ۚ وَمَا زَادَهُمْ إِلَّا إِيمَانًا وَتَسْلِيمًا ﴿٢٢﴾ مِّنَ
الْمُؤْمِنِينَ رِجَالٌ صَدَقُوا مَا عَاهَدُوا اللَّهَ عَلَيْهِ ۖ فَمِنْهُم مَّن قَضَىٰ
نَحْبَهُ وَمِنْهُم مَّن يَنتَظِرُ ۖ وَمَا بَدَّلُوا تَبْدِيلًا ﴿٢٣﴾ لِّيَجْزِيَ اللَّهُ
الصَّادِقِينَ بِصِدْقِهِمْ وَيُعَذِّبَ الْمُنَافِقِينَ إِن شَاءَ أَوْ يَتُوبَ عَلَيْهِمْ ۚ
إِنَّ اللَّهَ كَانَ غَفُورًا رَّحِيمًا ﴿٢٤﴾

*But when the faithful saw the confederates, they said, 'This is
what Allah and His Apostle had promised us, and Allah
and His Apostle were true.' And it only increased them in
faith and submission. Among the faithful are men who fulfill
what they have pledged to Allah: there are some among them
who have fulfilled their pledge, and some of them who still
wait, and they have not changed in the least, that Allah may*

*reward the true for their truthfulness, and punish the hypo-
crites, if He wishes, or accept their repentance. Indeed Allah
is all-forgiving, all-merciful.*[1]

These blessed verses speak of the Holy Prophet (s) and the
believing Muslims when they were besieged in Medina during
the Battle of the Trench. God describes those who did not
waver in these dire circumstances as individuals who kept
their promises to their Lord. They kept their promises despite
the massive armies gathered against them. For some, their
pledges were fulfilled when they sacrificed everything they
had in defense of their faith and their homes. Others waited
patiently under siege but did not change in the least.

God gives great praise for these individuals. They were the
faithful who were increased in faith and submission. They
were the truthful who will be rewarded for their honest stance
and sincere devotion.

Yet the verses of the Holy Quran cannot be restricted to a
certain event or point in history. Although the revelation is
always connected to a historical point, the words of God are
eternal and are applicable throughout the ages. Therefore,
this description and praise given by God to the close companions of the Holy Prophet (s) in the Battle of the Trench
is also applicable to other believers who were resolute in their
principled stance in complete devotion to the Almighty.

It should not surprise us that Imam Hussain (a) would use
these verses in praise of the companions who stood alongside

---

[1] The Holy Quran, 33:22-24.

him in Karbala. Imam Hussain (a) stood on the plains of Karbala with a small group of resolute and devoted followers. They endured thirst and heat, unwavering the face of a massive army. They sought to support the divinely appointed Immaculate leader whose goal was to safeguard all virtue against the threat of corruption. They sacrificed everything for that purpose. They were individuals who kept their promises to God, either fulfilling through martyrdom or remaining resolute in their stance.

Imam Hussain's (a) stance was unlike any other movement or revolution in Muslim history. Through his movement, Imam Hussain (a) was able to provide the nation with a heritage that allowed it to safeguard its faith and values. No other revolution was able to provide a heritage or achieve similar outcomes.

Muslim history saw many movements and revolutions which were undertaken in the name of justice and whose leaders had an aura of religious authority and devotion. The best example of this can be seen in the Kharijite movement. The Kharijites had many a stance in the face of oppression and chanted many slogans for the sake of justice. Yet none of their sacrifices in pursuit of their sincerely held beliefs had an impact on the nation like the stance of Imam Hussain (a). In fact, we are almost certain that their stances are remembered only by a few.

No one seems to sympathize with the Kharijite movement. This is even though they were revolutionaries who were widely known for their piety and worship. They were reciters of the Holy Quran, devout worshippers, and fierce soldiers.

They even called themselves the Sellers in reference to the Quranic verse,

وَمِنَ النَّاسِ مَن يَشْرِي نَفْسَهُ ابْتِغَاءَ مَرْضَاتِ اللَّهِ ۗ وَاللَّهُ رَءُوفٌ بِالْعِبَادِ

And among the people is he who sells his soul seeking the pleasure of Allah, and Allah is most kind to [His] serv-ants.[2]

On the other hand, we see Imam Hussain's (a) stance remembered by millions every year. His call resonates in the hearts of his followers as well as the rest of humanity.

What is the difference between the movement of Imam Hussain (a) and movements like that of the Kharijites? Did they not all seek justice and oppose oppression? Were not the revolutionaries in all these movements devout and pious Muslims? Were not all these revolutionaries resolute in their sacrifices for what they believed was right? A cursory look at all these movements shows that they had many similarities. What, then, is the secret behind the great and lasting impact that Imam Hussain (a) and his stance had on the Muslim nation?

There are a number of factors that create a real difference between Imam Hussain's (a) stance and the other movements that cropped up throughout Muslim history. In taking a closer look at the special qualities of Imam Hussain's (a)

---

[2] The Holy Quran, 2:207.

movement, we will refer to the Kharijites as the primary example for all the other movements which did not have the same effect.

LEADERSHIP

Leadership is one of the most important factors that distinguishes Imam Hussain's (a) movement from all others. The movement is led by an Immaculate Imam – a divinely appointed leadership with the Holy Quran as its guiding document. And even though some Muslims may reject his Immaculate nature, none can reject his high status within the Muslim nation. After all, he is an extension of his father the Commander of the Faithful (a) and his grandfather the Holy Prophet (s). None can deny that the Holy Prophet (s) praised him and said,

حسين مني وأنا من حسين، أحب الله من أحب حسينا

Hussain is of me and I am of Hussain. May God love whomever loves Hussain![3]

No one can deny that the Holy Prophet (s) said,

الحسن والحسين سيدا شباب أهل الجنة

Hassan (a) and Hussain (a) are the masters of the youth of Paradise.[4]

No one can deny the many narrations in which the Messenger of God (s) praised his Holy Household.

---

[3] Ibn Hanbal, *Musnad Ahmad*, 4:172.

[4] Ibn Hanbal, *Musnad Ahmad*, 3:3.

Imam Hussain's (a) Immaculate leadership gives absolute legitimacy to the movement. The greatness and status of such a leader ensures the greatness of the movement. This is in addition to the many narrations in which the Holy Prophet (s) would foretell of Imam Hussain's (a) movement and tragic martyrdom. In one of these narrations the Holy Prophet (s) says,

إنّ ابني هذا ـ يعني الحسين ـ يُقتل بأرض يُقال لها كربلاء ، فَمَنْ شهد ذلك منكم فلينصره

This son of mine [i.e. Hussain] will be killed in a land called Karbala. Whoever lives to see that day should endeavor to be his supporter.[5]

This is in complete opposition to the Kharijite movement. Although history tells us that its leaders were apparently devout and pious Muslims, there are also many historical accounts that stain this reputation. There are narrations from the Holy Prophet (s) that specifically deprive them of any legitimacy because of their deviance.

One example of leaders in this movement who were specifically disparaged by the Holy Prophet (s) is a man by the name of Harqous ibn Zuhair al-Sa'di.

One day while the Holy Prophet (s) was dividing some wealth amongst the Muslims, Harqous walked up and said, "O' Messenger of God (s)! Be just!" The Holy Prophet (s) replied,

ويلك ومن يعدل إذا لم أعدل قد خبت وخسرت ان لم اعدل

---

[5] Ibn Asakir, *Tareekh Dimashq*, 14:224.

Woe to you! Who will be just if I were not?! I would certainly have failed and lost if I were not just!

Omar ibn al-Khattab said, "O' Messenger of God (s), grant me permission to strike his neck!" The Holy Prophet (s) replied,

$$دعه فإن له أصحابًا يحقر أحدكم صلاته مع صلاتهم وصيامه مع صيامهم يقرأون القرآن لا يجاوز تراقيهم يمرقون من الإسلام كما يمرق السهم من الرمية ... يخرجون على خير فرقة من الناس$$

Let him be! Surely he has companions who you would belittle your prayers if you see their prayers and belittle your fasting if you see their fasting. They recite the Quran but it does not go beyond their throats. They shall slip away from Islam as an arrow slips through its target... They shall go out against the best group of people.[6]

Shabath ibn Rib'e is another example of the condemned Kharijites leaders. Shabath was known for his inconsistency and disloyalty. One historian says of him,

He was the muazin[7] of Sajah[8] before he entered Islam. He was amongst the killers of Othman, then accompanied Ali (a), then joined the Kharijites, then repented, then was [amongst the Umayyad army that] killed Hussain (a), then joined al-Mukhtar in seeking revenge for Hussain (a) and

---

[6] Al-Nisabouri, *Sahih Muslim*, 3:113.

[7] A *muazin* is an individual who recites the *azan*, or call to prayer. —eds.

[8] Sajah was a false prophetess who claimed to have received revelation after the passing of the Holy Prophet Muhammad (s). —eds.

was made the chief of police in Kufa, then was [amongst the Umayyad army that] killed al-Mukhtar.[9]

One historical account tells of an instance when Shabath cursed Imam Ali (a) in a public square in Medina. Um Salama, one of the widows of the Holy Prophet (s), stood and asked Shabath, "Will the Holy Prophet (s) be cursed in your gatherings?" Shabath said, "It is only a matter by which we seek the wares of this world." She replied,

سمعت رسول الله (ص) يقول: من سب عليا فقد سبني ومن سبني فقد سب الله

I heard the Messenger of God (s) say. 'Surely, whoever curses Ali (a) has cursed me, and whoever curses me has cursed God!'[10]

Movements like that of the Kharijites are seemingly righteous but are in fact wicked and deviant. They are worlds apart from the movement of Imam Hussain (a) who inherited the best of morals and highest of virtues from his grandfather the Holy Prophet (s). Imam Hussain's (a) leadership was one that felt responsibility for the nation. It was this sense of responsibility that drove Imam Hussain (a), his family, and a small group of companions to make that eternal stance.

GOALS

Another main difference between Imam Hussain's (a) movement and all other movements can be seen when analyzing

---

[9] Al-Adheem Abadi, *'Oun al-Ma'boud*, 13:273.

[10] Ibn Asakir, *Tareekh Dimashq*, 42:533.

their true goals. By this we do not mean the purported purpose of each movement or its outward slogans. We must understand each movement's goals by analyzing its general course of action and what these actions were meant to achieve.

From day one, Imam Hussain (a) led a movement of reform. His words and his actions always indicated that as his highest purpose. He wrote in a letter to his half-brother Muhammad ibn al-Hanafiyya,

إِنِّي لَمْ أَخْرُجْ أَشِرًا وَلا بَطَرًا ، وَلا مُفْسِدًا وَلا ظَالِمًا ، وَإِنَّمَا خَرَجْتُ لِطَلَبِ الإِصْلاحِ فِي أُمَّةِ جَدِّي ، أُرِيدُ أَنْ آمُرَ بِالْمَعْرُوفِ وَأَنْهَى عَنِ الْمُنْكَرِ ، وَأَسِيرَ بِسِيرَةِ جَدِّي وَأَبِي عَلِيّ بْنِ أَبِي طَالِبِ

I do not rise due to discontent [with God's blessings], nor out of arrogance, nor as a corruptor, nor as an oppressor. Rather, I wish to call for reform in the nation of my grandfather. I wish to call for what is good, and to forbid what is evil. [I wish to] follow the tradition of my grandfather [the Prophet] and my father Ali ibn Abu Talib.

فمن قبلني بقبول الحق فالله أولى بالحق ومن رد علي أصبر حتى يقضي الله بيني وبين القوم بالحق وهو خير الحاكمين

Whoever accepts me because I carry the truth, then God is the refuge of the honest. As for whoever rejects this call, I will be

patient until God judges between me and the rejecters with His justice. Surely, He is the best of judges.[11]

The Imam (a) never said that he was setting out to wage war or kill his enemies. His purpose was always reform – to guide people toward virtue and warn them of vice. He declared that people should follow him because his path was the path of truth. But if they did not, he will be patient so that God Almighty may be the judge. As the Immaculate Imam, his movement was dedicated to God with its major tenets being reform and piety.

Other movements were led by warmongers that declared reform but did not in fact care or act for it. A great example of this can be seen in the Kharijites after their assassination of the Commander of the Faithful (a). They initially paid allegiance to Imam Hassan (a) because they thought the Imam would lead them into battle against Muawiya, their mutual enemy. But when Imam Hassan (a) agreed to peace with Muawiya, the Kharijites began to sow the seeds of war elsewhere. They even tried to convince Imam Hussain (a) to break rank with his brother and set out against Muawiya. Imam Hussain (a) refused their offers and commanded them to follow the directives of Imam Hassan (a).

The Kharijites were therefore a group of warmongers that did not care for reform. Their movement was built on belligerence against anyone that did not agree with their ideology. This is seen throughout their history, from the birth of their movement and through their battles with the Umayyad and Abbasid caliphates. The extent of their adherence to this

---

[11] Ibn Shahrashoob, *al-Manaqib*, 3:241.

---

twisted ideology will be seen in the following discussion on methods.

METHODS

There are many ways in which the practices of Imam Hussain (a) and his companions differed from other revolutionaries, especially the Kharijites. Let us discuss a few of these differences.

Guidance

Imam Hussain's (a) method of leadership doubtlessly stemmed from his grandfather's legacy of guidance. Leadership in the Holy Household always had guidance as its primary goal and tenet. As such, war and military triumph was not a primary goal – it only mattered as a reaction to the belligerent military campaigns of the enemy.

That is why we see Imam Hussain (a) continuously reminding both his allies and his enemies about God Almighty. From the outset of his movement to his last breaths, he would reach out to the other side and attempt to show them the error of their ways. He would remind them of who he is and his closeness to his grandfather the Messenger of God (s). He would remind them who Yazid is and demonstrate to them the great catastrophe that befell the nation when Umayyad reign over the nation was solidified. Imam Hussain's (a) path was always a path of guidance, as was the path of his father and his grandfather.

The method of the Kharijites was the complete opposite. They were a group that did not understand reason or accept dialogue. The sword was their only method of achieving their goals.

For example, we see that when the Commander of the Faithful (a) met the Kharijite army at Nahrawan, he began to advise, admonish, and warn them. He said,

$$ فَأَنَا نَذِيرٌ لَكُمْ أَنْ تُصْبِحُوا صَرْعَى بِأَثْنَاءِ هَذَا النَّهَرِ، وَبِأَهْضَامِ $$
$$ هَذَا الْغَائِطِ عَلَى غَيْرِ بَيِّنَةٍ مِنْ رَبِّكُمْ، وَلاَ سُلْطَانٍ مُبِينٍ مَعَكُمْ $$

I warn you lest you be killed on the bend of this river and on the grounds of these lowlands while you will have no clear excuse before God nor any manifest authority on your side.

They could not reply but to say to one another, "Do not engage with them or speak to them! Be prepared to meet your Lord, for you will surely enter Paradise!"[12]

The difference between the two movements is clear. One wishes to warn and guide while averting bloodshed. The other refuses the language of reason and dialogue and accepts nothing but warfare.

On one hand, you have bloodthirsty warmonger who wish to corrupt the earth in the name of God. On the other hand, you have Imam Hussain (a) who would have mercy and compassion for his enemy even while he stood amid that tragic massacre. His heart filled with sorrow for his enemies as he realized that they will enter Hellfire because of their transgressions against him. He emulated his grandfather the Holy

---

[12] Al-Tabari, *Tareekh al-Tabari*, 4:62.

Prophet (s) who would say, "My Lord! Forgive my people, for they do not know!"[13]

Knowledge

Imam Hussain (a) and his family and companions set out with great certainty and knowledge. A number of the Imam Hussain's (a) companions were companions of the Holy Prophet (s) like Habib ibn Mudhahir and Muslim ibn 'Awsaja. Others were companions of Imam Ali (a) and Imam Hassan (a). This is not the place to fully analyze the biographies of the companions. Suffice it to say that many of the companions were known in their respective communities for their knowledge and piety.

While the Kharijites had maintained an image as worshippers, their worship was limited because it did not stem from any real knowledge and understanding. Worship was nothing to them more than a set of rituals to be habitually repeated. Many of their stances and positions show their ignorance and the pettiness of their worship.

To illustrate the point, take the example of the Kharijites murder of Abdullah ibn Khubab and his family. Historians say that Abdullah was on the road with his family when he was stopped by a band of Kharijites. They asked him of his opinion of Imam Ali (a). He replied, "Surely, Ali (a) is more knowledgeable of God, more cautious for his faith, and of greater foresight." Abdullah was beheaded for his reply. His

---

[13] Ibn Hanbal, *Musnad Ahmad*, 1:427.

pregnant wife was stabbed and left to die.[14] What piety or knowledge do men like these possess?

Resolve

Imam Hussain (a) and everyone in his camp made their stance with great resolve and determination. Many opportunities were presented to the companions where they could flee and save their lives. They refused to leave Imam Hussain (a) face his fate alone.

The Kharijites, on the other hand, were unprincipled individuals who swayed with the wind. The example of Shabath ibn Rib'e that we discussed earlier should be enough to illustrate this point. Historically, the Kharijites fought under any banner that allowed them to engage in battle. This shows the reality of their bloodlust. They are as the noble verses describe,

$$قُلْ هَلْ نُنَبِّئُكُمْ بِالْأَخْسَرِينَ أَعْمَالًا ﴿١٠٣﴾ الَّذِينَ ضَلَّ سَعْيُهُمْ$$
$$فِي الْحَيَاةِ الدُّنْيَا وَهُمْ يَحْسَبُونَ أَنَّهُمْ يُحْسِنُونَ صُنْعًا ﴿١٠٤﴾$$
$$أُولَٰئِكَ الَّذِينَ كَفَرُوا بِآيَاتِ رَبِّهِمْ وَلِقَائِهِ فَحَبِطَتْ أَعْمَالُهُمْ فَلَا نُقِيمُ$$
$$لَهُمْ يَوْمَ الْقِيَامَةِ وَزْنًا ﴿١٠٥﴾ ذَٰلِكَ جَزَاؤُهُمْ جَهَنَّمُ بِمَا كَفَرُوا$$
$$وَاتَّخَذُوا آيَاتِي وَرُسُلِي هُزُوًا ﴿١٠٦﴾$$

Say, 'Shall we inform you who are the biggest losers in their works? Those whose efforts are misguided in the life of the world, while they suppose they are doing good.' They are the ones who deny the signs of their Lord and encounter with Him. So their works have failed. On the Day of Resurrection

---

[14] Al-Tabari, *Tareekh al-Tabari*, 4:61.

We will not give them any weight. That is their requital —
hell — because of their unfaith and for deriding My signs and
apostles.[15]

This is why Imam Hussain's (a) stance is an eternal one. It was a stance driven by divine purpose, headed by an immaculate leader, supported by great men, and pursued with virtuous actions at every step of the way.

The Kharijites movement could not compare to Imam Hussain's (a) immaculate nature and stance. It was a worldly stance made by worldly men. It became a blemish on Muslim history and an example of corruption on the earth. This is why the Kharijite movement, and many similar ones, could not become an eternal model to be remembered throughout the ages. That honor was reserved for the stance of Imam Hussain (a).

---

[15] The Holy Quran, 18:103-06.

LADY ZAYNAB

When we think and reflect over Imam Hussain (a) there is an essential issue that is so inherent to this discussion – the stance of Lady Zaynab (a). She was Imam Hussain's (a) counterpart in his revolution. She was one of the intrinsic secrets to this grand mission that made Hussain's (a) revolution eternal in the hearts of every generation that followed. Zaynab (a) became like her mother Fatima (a) – a role model in illustrating the essential role of women in bearing responsibility and sacrifice for the Word of God. We note that even though Lady Fatima's (a) modesty prohibited her from ever entering the gatherings of men, when the greater good of Islam dictated that she stand boldly to call out the oppression done to her husband she did so courageously. She endured all that she endured, until she passed as an oppressed martyr who died for truth and principle. Lady Zaynab (a), the daughter of Fatima (a), took on a similar burden, responsibility, and sacrifice. She left her home and traveled from country to country, taken as a captive of war, all for the sake of principles she believed in. Those principles were more beloved to her than anything in this world.

Lady Zaynab (a) played a monumental role in her brother's revolution. She was an outspoken representative of Imam Hussain's (a) movement, spreading word of the events that took place, the blood that was shed, and the sacrifices that were made. She told the world the story of Ashura – the day that Hussain (a) and his seventy-some companions gave their lives for the principles of their faith. Without Lady Zaynab (a) we would not know of the greatest sacrifice and the most profound oppression experienced by the Holy Prophet's (a) household.

It is important to realize that Lady Zaynab's (a) role cannot be summarized by the generic role played by women mourning the men they sent off into battle. Though she undertook the responsibility of caring for the families that Imam Hussain (a) and the martyrs of Karbala left behind, her role was greater than that of a mere caretaker. Her role was no less than those warriors who fell as martyrs alongside her brother Hussain (a), if not greater. In her position she was able to realize the goals of the revolution and achieve the objectives her brother set out to accomplish. Her role can be understood through the following points:

LADY ZAYNAB THE ROLE-MODEL

Adamant Supporter

Lady Zaynab went with Imam Husain (a) knowingly and willingly. She had all the proper excuses to remain in Medina, having a family, a home, a husband, and children. Nonetheless, she took permission from her husband to go with Imam Hussain (a) and went on that journey.

Someone could say that maybe Lady Zaynab (a) did not know about her fate and what would transpire from her brother's revolution. And if she did know she would not have embarked on that journey.

History tells us that ibn Abbas came to Imam Husain (a) and urged him not to leave Medina for his journey to Iraq. Imam Husain responded that this is the will of God and reform must take place. Ibn Abbas then told him don't take your family and women with you. To that Imam Husain (a) replied by saying that his grandfather, the Messenger of God (s), ordered him to take them with him and that he would never go against an order by God's Messenger (s). During the conversation, ibn Abbas heard crying behind him in the other room. The crying turned into a voice that said,

يابن عباس تشير على شيخنا وسيدنا أن يخلفنا ها هنا ويمضي وحده؟ لا والله بل نحيا معه ونموت معه، وهل أبقى الزمان لنا غيره؟

Ibn Abbas, you want our Master and Imam to leave us here and go on alone by himself? No, I swear by God, that we live only with him and we will die with him, for has time left anyone for us but him?

Upon hearing those words Ibn Abbas could not hold his tears and began sobbing.[1] That voice was the voice of Lady Zaynab (a).

---

[1] Al-Naqdi, *Zaynab Al-Kubra*, 140

This short story tells us clearly that Lady Zaynab (a) was fully aware of what this journey with Hussain (a) entailed. She made her decision to support and join her brother with this awareness and eagerness to sacrifice for their cause. Lady Zaynab (a) became the exemplar of a purposeful, mature, and aware woman that moves through life with a mission and goal in mind. She did not embark on the journey with her brother out of necessity or a feeling of social responsibility that she was burdened with. She knew what role she was going to play and accepted the greatness that she would embody. She would come to be the one to stand before the tyrants and speak words of truth and justice. She would let the words of truth ring wherever she would go. It was Lady Zaynab (a) that silenced the oppressors as she spoke and had the masses waiting on her next word, as if she were the Commander of the Faithful (a) in the flesh.

History also tells us that it was as if Lady Zaynab's role in the revolution of Imam Hussain (a) was foreseen and planned. Some historians note that when Imam Ali (a) married his daughter to her husband Abdullah ibn Ja'far he ensured that a condition in the marriage contract included that Abdullah would never prohibit Lady Zaynab (a) from travelling with her brother Hussain (a) when she chose to. This points to the divine will that designed Lady Zaynab's (a) role in the revolution – a revolution that rejuvenated the spirit of Islam and restored its teachings and principles.

Lady Zaynab (a) and Sacrifice

Lady Zaynab (a) was not satisfied with her role in the revolution of Hussain (a) without offering as many sacrifices as she could. She gave her son Aoun as a martyr for the principles that Hussain (a) rose for. Sacrificing your son is surely not an easy task. A mother could possibly endure every hardship except seeing her son slaughtered and beheaded before her very eyes. But Lady Zaynab endured. With her deep conviction and faith she gave everything she had for the sake of God.

Let us not forget the contributions and sacrifice of Lady Zaynab's (a) husband Abdullah Ibn Ja'far (may God be pleased with him) in his solidarity and support of Imam Hussain (a). Abdullah ordered his sons to join Imam Hussain (a) in his journey and be at his side in representation of their father. Abdullah was later informed that his sons, Muhammad and Aoun, were killed. People began coming over to pay their respects and mourn the young men. Abdullah's servant, Abu Lislas, said, "This is what we received from Hussain." Abdullah scolded Abu Lislas and said,

> *You wretched man! To Hussain you say this?! By God, if I were with him I would not leave him until I was killed before him. By God, I would rather sacrifice my soul than theirs. Yet what soothes the anguish of their kiss is knowing that they were killed at the service of my brother and cousin, consoling him and persevering alongside him.*

Abdullah then turned to those present who had come to pay respects and said,

> *Praise be to God who honored me with the saga of Hussain. I was not able to support him with my own hands but I supported him with my children.*

Every household Lady Zaynab (a) lived in – as a daughter in her parent's home and as a wife in her husband's home – was a house of sacrifice. These are the homes of the family of Abu Talib – Imam Ali's father – who stood for Islam and its Prophet from the very beginning. Thus, it is not surprising that Lady Zaynab (a) and her husband would so willingly give their children to defend the principles of faith and protect the religion of the Prophet Muhammad (s). The family of Abu Talib made a covenant with God to water the tree of Islam with their own sacred blood.

LADY ZAYNAB (A) AND HER ROLE

Lady Zaynab's participation in the revolution of Imam Hussain (a) can be divided into two primary points:

Involvement Prior to the Battle. Lady Zaynab (a) was fully involved in the battle that came with Imam Hussain's (a) revolution. She was briefed on all the developments that took place and was sought for consultation on strategy, tactics, and the course of action moving forward. Imam Hussain (a) did not keep her in the dark on any single issue. She had her role, her opinion, and her say. Lady Zaynab (a) was in the events as they unfolded; thus, she was able to tell of all the details that took place in Karbala, especially from within the camp of Imam Hussain (a). The Imam (a) would give Lady Zaynab (a) his will and bid her the responsibility of being the caretaker for the all the orphans of Karbala. Most importantly he would assign her the responsibility of taking the verdicts and decrees of Imam Ali al-Sajjad (a), his son, and delivering them to the Shia – protecting him from the risk of persecution and oppression – according to some of our scholars.[2]

Her Role After the Battle. If we were to examine Lady Zaynab's (a) demeanor and conduct before the end of the battle of Karbala we would see her in a characteristic state of deep sorrow and sadness. The sight of the tragedy of her brother Hussain (a) was a cause of much grief for her. Lady Zaynab (a) embraced the bodies of her fallen family members – her brothers, her sons, her nephews – and wept and wailed over their tragedy. However, after the battle ended Lady Zaynab (a) was seen as a monument of patience – unbreakable like a rock. She would place her hands below the body of the most beloved of God's creation to her – Imam Hussain (a) – and look to the heavens and say,

$$اللهم تقبل منا هذا القربان$$

God accept this sacrifice from us.

Was it that Lady Zaynab (a) was not patient during the tragedies of the battle and that God bestowed upon her patience as soon as Imam Hussain (a) was finally killed?

When Lady Zaynab (a) was weeping and grieving over the fallen warriors of her family during the battle she was reacting in a perfectly natural way. Emotion and affection are manifestations of God's mercy. The Prophet (s) cried over his children, Imam Ali (a) cried over Lady Fatima's (a) tragedy, and Imam Hussain (a) and Lady Zaynab (a) cried over their brother Imam Hassan (a). However, when it came to Imam

---

[2] See: al-Muqarram, *Maqtal Al-Hussain*, 218

Hussain's (a) tragedy Lady Zaynab's (a) role shifted. When Imam Hussain (a) was killed the responsibility of leadership and strength became hers. Note that the expressions of grief and emotions from the Progeny (a) are directly connected to God. Their tears for the tragedies are only shed because it is what God approves of, and so long as Lady Zaynab's (a) patience was for the pleasure of God she would be patient. Lady Zaynab (a) embodied this connection and adherence to God in all of her actions. Thus, we see the shift to patience due to her acknowledgement and acceptance of her needed role after her brother to continue what he set out to do. That mountain of patience that was Lady Zaynab (a) continues to bewilder the world to this day. Her role can be understood in three dimensions:

Guardian to the Family. She had put protecting the family, the women, and the children as a priority above all. After the massacre they witnessed and the psychological and physical abuse they endured, they needed someone to be strong and support them in their fragile state. Lady Zaynab (a) was that strength. She would give individual attention to each child and every woman, especially on the night after the tragedy.

Protecting the Imam. Lady Zaynab (a) had to protect the life of Imam Ali al-Sajjad (a). She risked her life in numerous situations to make sure that the son of Imam Hussain (a) – the continuation of the line of the Prophet's (s) progeny – would remain alive. When Shimr saw that there was still a son of Imam Hussain (a) alive he went for the blood of Ali ibn al-Hussain (a). Lady Zaynab (a) stood before him and said,

لا تصل إليه حتى تقتلني

You won't get to him unless you kill me first.

Her bravery was then again displayed in the court of ibn Ziyad when the governor ordered for Ali ibn al-Hussain (a) to be taken and killed. She leaped and grabbed onto her nephew and did not let anyone near him. She knew who Ali ibn al-Hussain (a) was. She knew his role as the proof of God on earth – the next Imam for the people and protector of God's message. She wasn't defending Ali ibn al-Hussain (a) for the mere fact that he was her nephew. Lady Zaynab (a) risked her life time and time again because she was serving her Imam, the inheritor of the Prophet's (a) leadership and knowledge.

Spreading the Message. This was by far one of the most important roles that Lady Zaynab (a) played. Beyond letting the people know who she was in her own right, she had the role of telling the masses about the revolution and sacrifice of Imam Hussain (a). The Umayyads tried to paint the battle of Karbala as being a legitimate use of force by the government to crush a rebellion by a Kharajite force that had defied the religion and defied the state. Thus, many of the cities that Lady Zaynab (a) along with the women and the children were taken through as captives of war did not know who they were. Here came the role of Lady Zaynab (a). Wherever she went she would announce who she was and what family she belonged to. She would tell the people what happened to the grandsons of the Holy Prophet (s) and exposed the Umayyads for the criminals and killers they truly were. Through her brave speeches and outspoken advocacy she was able to ensure the failure of the Umayyads' plans to justify their oppression. That is why Yazid actually tried to make himself out to be innocent from the massacre of Karbala blaming it on Ubaydallah ibn Ziyad, his governor in Kufa. We are certain that if it were not for Lady Zaynab (a) and the women with her, the revolution of Imam Hussain (a) would not have been able to miraculously awaken the dead conscience of the nation and bring it back to life. The blood that was shed would have been lost without the nation knowing what tragedy took place, how Imam Hussain (a) and his companions were massacred so gruesomely, and the crimes that the Umayyads carried out against the Progeny of Revelation (a).

From this brief overview we can see more clearly the monumental role of Lady Zaynab (a) and the sacrifices she made. By this very right we speak of, the Holy Prophet (s) said,

من بكى على مصاب هذه البنت كان كمن بكى على أخويها
الحسن والحسين

Whoever cries over the tragedy of this girl, will be like the one who cries over her brothers Al-Hassan and Al-Hussain.

"Cries" here means to interact and be affected by her cause, not simply displaying emotion. Such an interaction would move us to take her as role model and an example we can live by.

Imam Sajjad

God Almighty chose the Holy Prophet Muhammad (s) as the seal of messengers, who was tasked with delivering the last revelation to mankind. The mission of our Immaculate Imams (a) is an extension of the mission of the Holy Prophet (s). They are his divinely appointed successors and therefore must fulfill every role that he was tasked with. Their mission was to guide mankind and lead them closer to their Lord. As the vicegerents of God on earth, they expended all their efforts in service of this cause.

The duties of our Immaculate Imams (a) do not change because they did not have political authority over the Muslim nation. Although having that political authority goes a long way in serving their mission, it is not itself the goal. Thus, we see our Imams always working to achieve that mission no matter the condition and despite the grim circumstances they faced. They never abandoned the nation. They never shirked from the responsibilities of leadership, even though there were many others that sought to usurp that position without the proper qualifications. Despite all this, our Imams dedicated their lives to the service of God and His message.

When we study the history of our Imams (a), we must also realize that the differences in their approaches does not stem from any difference in mission, philosophy, or character. As we discussed in a previous chapter, any difference in action between our Imams (a) only stems from the different circumstances that they lived in, and each Imam (a) acted in the most suitable manner within the circumstances.

CIRCUMSTANCES

Imam Sajjad (a) was fated to take over the duties of Imam directly after the martyrdom of his father – a difficult time in which the Muslim nation saw the compounding of a number of threats against its faith and values. Let us address some of these circumstances briefly.

External Threats

Imam Sajjad (a) lived at a time when the Muslim nation was rapidly expanding and many new believers were entering the faith. This rapid expansion allowed the Umayyad dynasty to be one of the leading political and military powers on the world stage. However, all this made the Muslim nation vulnerable to a number of external threats, including:

The Intellectual Threat. The Muslim nation was introduced to the other nations of the world with their divergent cultures, legal traditions, and the like. This newfound diversity meant that more efforts were needed in explaining the primacy of Islam, defending its tenets, and demonstrating its inclusiveness of all races and ethnicities. Thus, there was a greater need during that period of time for a corps of scholars who understood the faith and were able to spread and defend it.

The Moral Threat. This era was also one of increased wealth and prosperity for the Muslim nation. Greater wealth meant a greater risk for the nation to fall victim to materialism and worldly luxury and desire. This constituted a threat against the spiritual and moral tenets of Islam, which emphasize the primacy of the spiritual over the material.

The Social Threat. By opening up to the rest of the world, the Muslim nation was able to enrich its own culture and the cultures of surrounding nations. Yet this openness also meant that the vices of each nation could spread to the other. This became a reality for Muslims as they began to enjoy the luxuries, decadence, frivolity, and vices of other cultures.

Internal Threats

As we've discussed before, Umayyad rulers were enemies of the Holy Prophet (s) and the message of Islam. There were a few instances of individuals who wanted to change this general direction, such as Omar ibn Abdulaziz, but their reign did not last. The majority of Umayyad caliphs worked to destroy the true message of Islam. However, the stance of Imam Hussain (a) foiled their plans. It returned to the Muslim nation its confidence and its ability to stand up for its faith and values.

When the Umayyad rules realized that their attempts to destroy this religion will not take them anywhere, they shifted their strategy. Their main goal became to steer the nation as far away as possible from the true values and principles of

Islam – values and principles which were in direct opposition to Umayyad interests.

The strategy was to inundate the nation with vice. If people were to be held captive to their base desires, they would have no will to put the Umayyad rulers in check. If the nation was enamored with vice, it will find it easy to overlook Umayyad corruption and depravity.

Umayyad authorities made Mecca and Medina, the two most important cities in the history of Islam, the focus of this strategy. During this period, these two holy cities were known for harboring all places of vice and debauchery of all kinds. By supporting the spread of vice in these cities, they hoped to give it acceptance and allow it to spread throughout the nation.

These holy cities were also the centers of religious authority and legitimacy within the nation. These cities held the heritage of the Holy Prophet (s) and were home to many of his companions. No religious movement could spread without finding root in these cities. Umayyad authorities knew that any political movement against them would stem from this region. They hoped to douse the light of guidance that was emanating from these cities through the spread of vice.

This is all in addition to the years of Umayyad social policies that struck at the fabric of the Muslim nation. They created a social hierarchy that left many people poor and disgruntled. They played on tribal and ethnic loyalties to create division in the nation, and used that division to maintain control.

METHODS

Imam Sajjad (a) pursued the mission of protecting the Muslim nation against the dire threats of the time. He began to reinforce the nation on a number of levels in order to allow it to weather the storm. If we look at the Imam's (a) actions, we find that he sustained the nation intellectually, spiritually, and ethically.

Intellectually

Imam Sajjad (a) began to spread the teachings and knowledge of his fathers. He established a school where he trained some of the foremost jurists of the era. This was an essential part of the Imam's effort to breathe new life into the Muslim nation. The Imam (a) – in the words of our scholars –

> started study circles in the mosque of the Holy Prophet (s), where he taught people a variety of Islamic sciences including Quranic exegesis, narration, and jurisprudence. He would inundate his students with the knowledge of his pure fathers. He trained the attentive amongst this group in the sciences of jurisprudence and derivation of law. From this school graduated a number of jurists who became the leaders of the several jurisprudential schools...[1]

This preeminence amongst scholars was recognized even by the Imam's (a) contemporaries. We see, for example, that during the season of Hajj, the scholars of Medina would not leave the city before him out of respect. Saeed Ibn Al-Maseeb narrates, "The scholars did not leave towards Mecca until Ali

---

[1] Al-Sadr, Introduction to *Al-Saheefa Al-Sajjadiya Al-Kamila*, 10.

ibn Hussain (a) would. So when he went so did a thousand others…"[2]

Even the Umayyad authorities of the time could not but acquiesce to his primacy over the Muslim nation. The Umayyad caliph of the time would praise Imam Sajjad (a) by saying,

> *Knowledge is apparent from your aura. By God, the good that comes from you is overflowing, as you are part and parcel of the Messenger of God (s) and so close in his lineage. You are of an honorable purpose and of noble favor to both your family and your era. You have come with virtue, knowledge, faith, and wisdom that no one has come with before except from your family…*[3]

Spiritually

Supplication was by far one of the most important methods that the Imam (a) used in rebuilding the spiritual connection of the Muslims after they had been numbed by so much material indulging. In writing and teaching supplications, in addition to his unique dedication to worship, the Imam (a) became known and addressed as Sayyid Al-Sajideen (the Master of Prostrators) and Zayn Al-Abideen (the Best of Worshipers). Promoting the culture of supplication had a significant effect on the community. It was a way to oppose the socio-political corruption that was taking place as well as the new culture of disgraceful ideas that had become widespread, all without raising the ire of Umayyad authorities. The supplications that the Imam (a) taught educated people about

---

[2] Ibid, 83:226. Citing: Al-Kashi, *Rijal Al-Kashi*, 108.

[3] Al-Majlisi, *Bihar Al-Anwar*, 46:56. Citing: Ibn Tawoos, *Fath Al-Abwab*, 170.

their faith, connected them to their Lord, and refocused their priorities to the true message of Islam – ultimately bringing people closer to the Almighty.

The use of supplication as a method of steering the nation back to God was especially fitting for the threats of the era. Imam Sajjad (a) combatted corruption and deviance with spirituality. He fought the frivolity and corruption of song and drink with whispered supplications and poignant prayers. He fought moral degeneration with constant reminder of God's justice and mercy. He fought the new culture of corruption with a counterculture of piety.

A quick review of the supplications taught by Imam Sajjad (a) is enough to understand the nature of this spiritual school. The supplications are embedded with all kinds of theological, intellectual, social, and ethical teachings. They constitute a comprehensive and holistic method to spiritual nurturement. As such, they had a profound impact on the nation at the time. In fact, if we assess our current circumstances and understand the threats that we face, we will find these supplications can have a similar affect in this era. If we understand how entrenched the world has become in worldly pleasures and desires, we can learn to use the Imam's (a) supplications as a holistic tool of spiritual upliftment.

Imam Sajjad (a) did not suffice himself with teaching supplication as a means of combatting the spiritual corruption of the time. He was also a role model in all his virtues. He was the best of worshippers in every sense of the word. He would not only give charity to the poor, but would personally deliver food to the poor. His embodiment of the greatest moral qualities gave his teachings special meaning and everlasting value.

Socially

With the rise of the Umayyad dynasty and its expansion through conquest came a wide array of social threats to the Muslim nation. One of the most critical threats came with the sale of prisoners of war into slavery. This served to inflate the social hierarchy that the Umayyad clan created based on ethnic and tribal discrimination. It also created a class of individuals within the nation that could have easily labeled Muslims as conquerors and slave drivers.

Imam Sajjad (a) did not reserve himself to teaching and supplication as a means of addressing this problem. Instead, he tackled it with a novel and graceful strategy. He would personally purchase considerable quantities of servants, then inundate them with the knowledge and magnanimity that were characteristic of the Holy Household. Every year, he would gather all his servants and set the best among them free, giving him a sum of money that he could use to start a new life as a parting gift.

With that, Imam Sajjad (a) was able to address the festering problem. Instead of being a social and economic threat to the Muslim nation, these individuals became respected members of society. The Imam (a) achieved two primary goals through this strategy. First, he was able to educate a corps of individuals who understood the true meaning of Islam by virtue of their prolonged contact with the greatest role model and teacher in the nation. Second, he was able to reduce the social tensions that were building up throughout the nation as a result of Umayyad policies by creating a class of non-Arabs who contributed to the social and economic health of their communities.

These are some of the methods by which our beloved Imam (a) was able to safeguard the pure message of Islam. He was able to continue in pursuit of the sublime goals of the Holy Household (a) despite the great tragedy that befell him and his family. He was able to invest the tragedy of Karbala for the betterment of God's divine message.

THE ABBASIDS

In the Name of God, the Most Compassionate, the Most Merciful

فَلَمَّا جَاءَتْهُمْ آيَاتُنَا مُبْصِرَةً قَالُوا هَذَا سِحْرٌ مُبِينٌ ﴿١٣﴾ وَجَحَدُوا بِهَا وَاسْتَيْقَنَتْهَا أَنْفُسُهُمْ ظُلْمًا وَعُلُوًّا ۚ فَانْظُرْ كَيْفَ كَانَ عَاقِبَةُ الْمُفْسِدِينَ ﴿١٤﴾

But when Our signs came to them, as eye-openers, they said, 'This is plain magic.' They impugned them, wrongfully and out of arrogance, though they were convinced in their hearts [of their veracity]. So observe how the fate of the agents of corruption was![1]

Having studied the role of Imam Sajjad (a) in continuing the mission and legacy of his father, let us turn to another era in the lives of our Immaculate Imams. The tides of history began to turn against the Umayyads after their continued brazen crimes against everything that the Muslim nation revered. Imam Hussain's (a) movement ushered the way for revolution after revolution in the Muslim nation. Yet our Immaculate Imams continued to hold a consistent stance against all

---

[1] The Holy Quran, 27:13-14.

155

these revolutions. To better understand the stance of our Imams, let us turn to the Abbasid revolution and study how the Alid and Abasid households acted and interacted during that time frame.

BANU HASHIM AT THE TIME OF THE UMAYYADS

Following the tragedy of Karbala, the Muslim nation began to recognize the wretchedness of Banu Umayya. It began to recognize Umayyad oppression and rise against their rule. A number of these movements recognized the primacy of the Holy Household and sought to return sovereignty to their rightful hands. Some of the Shia felt that the time was ripe for such a revolution. After all, the Umayyads were losing their grasp over the nation and the Holy Household had many sympathizers.

At the outset, the Abbasids were considered followers of the Holy Household. They faced similar persecution and oppression as the family of the Holy Prophet (s). In fact, the Abbasids were historically some of the first supporters of the several Shia movements against Umayyad rule.

Yet, when we turn back to our Immaculate Imams (a), we find that they consistently refused to take part in any of these movements. Instead, they focused their efforts on the spiritual and intellectual growth of the nation. In other words, our Imams (a) saw it best to pursue a cultural movement rather than a political one. Even though they always declared that political authority is rightfully theirs, they did not see that the time was ripe for the rise of their just state. The reasons for this can be summarized as follows:

First, the intense movement against Umayyad rule was not based on true theological knowledge and belief. Rather, it was based on people's passions against the Umayyads. They were disgruntled with Umayyad policies of discrimination and persecution. They did not understand the rights and status of the Holy Household, seeing them only as a political alternative to Umayyad oppression.

Our Immaculate Imams (a) would remind their companions of this fact whenever there was a push towards uprising. One of the companions of Imam al-Sadiq (a) by the name of Sudayr al-Sayrafi was amongst those followers who attempted to convince the Imam (a) to rise in revolution. Sudayr narrates that he once told the Imam (a), "By God, you can no longer refrain [from revolution]!"

The Imam (a) asked,

ولم ياسدير؟

And why is that, Sudayr?

"Due to your many devotees, followers, and supporters," Sudayr replied.

يا سدير وكم عسى أن يكونوا؟

O' Sudayr, and how many could they be?

"A hundred thousand!" Sudayr exclaimed. The Imam (a) asked doubtfully,

مائة ألف؟

A hundred thousand?

"Yes. Even two hundred thousand!" Sudayr exclaimed again. The Imam (a) asked again,

مائتي ألف؟

Two hundred thousand?

"Yes. Maybe even half the world!" Sudayr could not contain his passion. He continued to implore the Imam (a) to rise up and lead the revolution against the Umayyad tyrants. Imam al-Sadiq (a) did not answer him but asked whether he wanted to accompany him on a short trip. The Imam (a) took Sudayr toward a village on the outskirts of Medina. When the time of prayer came the Imam (a) and his companion stopped to pray. Imam al-Sadiq (a) saw that a young boy was herding a group of lambs nearby. He pointed to them and said,

والله يا سدير لوكان لي شيعة بعدد هذه الجداء وما وسعني القعود

O' Sudayr! If I had as many followers as these lambs, then I would no longer refrain [from revolution]!

Sudayr says that he prayed behind the Imam (a) and when he was finished he turned to the young shepherd. He counted the flock to find that they were only seventeen.[2]

Our Immaculate Imams (a) were not deceived by the large quantities of their supposed supporters. They knew that this support was not of a quality that cannot be relied upon and trusted.

---

[2] Al-Kulayni, *al-Kafi*, 2:243.

Second, there were some individuals who sought to remove the Umayyad clan from power and give political authority to the Holy Household, but only as a front for their personal ambition. This issue was clear to our Immaculate Imams (a), and we will see an example in the following discussion.

Third, our Immaculate Imams (a) understood that complete devotion to their cause was hard to come by and that there were elements within the Hashimite clan that sought to take power for themselves. Yet some of the era's influential Alid personalities did not have the same foresight as our Imams (a).

A number of Alid personalities pledged allegiance to Muhammad ibn Abdullah al-Mahd, a descendant of Imam Hassan (a). The most notable Abbasid personalities – such as Abu al-Abbas al-Saffah and Abu Ja'far al-Mansour – also pledged allegiance to him. Yet the Abbasids had their own plans. They wished to use the name of the Holy Prophet's (s) descendants to remove their common enemy, then take the empire to themselves. They had already mobilized personalities like Abu Muslim al-Khorasani to solidify their hold on parts of the Muslim nation.

Imam al-Sadiq (a) saw through these ploys. He attempted to dissuade his cousins from falling for the Abbasid trap, but to no avail. As part of the Abbasid mobilization, Abu Salama al-Khallal sent a message to specific Alid personalities offering them leadership of the movement. The first personality visited by the messenger was Imam al-Sadiq. When the messenger gave the Imam (a) Abu Salama's letter, the Imam (a) said,

$$\text{وما لي ولأبي سلمة وهو شيعة لغيري؟}$$

What do I have to do with Abu Salama who is a follower of others [and not one of my followers]?

The messenger asked the Imam (a) to read the letter. The Imam (a) told one of his servants,

ادن السراج

Bring me the lamp.

He burnt the letter in front of the messenger without reading it. The messenger asked, "Will you not give an answer?" The Imam (a) replied,

قد رأيت الجواب

You have seen the answer!

The messenger then went towards Abdullah al-Mahd, the grandson of Imam Hassan (a), and gave him a similar letter. Abdullah read it and was overjoyed. That same night he rode towards Imam al-Sadiq (a) to deliver the good news. He told the Imam (a), "This is a letter from Abu Salama calling me to the caliphate. It reached me through a follower of ours from Khorasan."

Imam al-Sadiq (a) replied sternly,

ومتى صار اهل خراسان شيعتك؟ أأنت وجهت إليهم أبا
سلمة؟ هل تعرف أحدا منهم باسمه؟ فكيف يكونون شيعتك
وأنت لا تعرفهم وهم لا يعرفونك؟

And since when were the people of Khorasan your followers? Did you send Abu Salama to them? Do you know any of

*them by name? How can they be your followers when you do
not know them and they do not know you?*

"It seems that there is a reason behind this reply," Abdullah
said, insinuating that the Imam (a) might have a hidden motive in trying to deter him from taking the caliphate. Imam al-
Sadiq (a) replied,

قد علم الله أني أوجب النصح على نفسي لكل مسلم فكيف
أدخره عنك؟ فلا تمن نفسك ، فإن هذه الدولة ستتم لهولاء
[يعني بني العباس]

*God knows that I oblige myself to advise any Muslim. Why
would I keep it from you?! Surely, you should not give yourself
hope for this government will be for them [i.e. the Abbasids].³*

It was clear to Imam al-Sadiq (a) that this movement had its
set of personalities with their own conflicting ambitions.
They only wished to claim the banner of the Holy Household
to further those ambitions. The Imam (a) was not willing to
be part of their ploys. We see this most clearly with the Abbasids who as soon as they solidified their grasp on power
turned against their own and killed Abu Muslim al-Khorasani
and Abu Salama al-Khallal.

It was also clear to Imam al-Sadiq (a) that not all the Hash-
imites were of one mindset. 'Seeking the contentment of the
Household of Muhammad (s)' was the popular slogan of that
movement. Many claimed legitimacy by their relationship to
the Holy Prophet (s) no matter how distant, overlooking the

---

³ Haidar, *al-Imam al-Sadiq wa al-Mathahib al-Arba'a*, 1:375.

primacy of the Immaculate Imams (a) who were his direct descendants. This is seen most vividly in the Abbasid household which took power for itself and abandoned the children of Abdullah al-Mahd. Moreover, history would show that the Abbasids' envy of the Holy Prophet's (a) descendants would lead to the continued persecution of the Holy Household despite their kinship.

THE ABBASIDS AND THE ALIDS

When the Abbasids solidified their control over the Muslim nation, they did not fulfill any of their promises with respect to the Holy Household. In fact, they took their Alid cousins as primary enemies. The reasons were as follows:

Alid Popularity

A primary purpose for Abbasid aggression against the Alids was their popularity and status in the heart of the Muslim nation. People knew that the Alids were most deserving of the caliphate for their proximity to the Holy Prophet (s). The Alids were the only possible challengers to the Abbasids as they were held in higher esteem with the public. This is evident in some of the Abbasids' own words. Abu Muslim would write to al-Mansour saying, "Yet God has raised your status through me despite your obscurity, baseness, and meekness."[4] Al-Mansour would also say to his uncle,

> *Marwanid corpses have not yet rotten and Talibid swords have not yet been sheathed. We are amongst a people who saw us yesterday as subjects and today as caliphs. Our majesty*

---

[4] Ibn Katheer, *al-Bidaya*, 10:69.

will not be established except through forgetting mercy and utilizing punishment.[5]

The Abbasids knew well that the Immaculate Imams (a) would not revolt or mobilize the nation against them. Yet they realized that the Holy Household held the hearts of the people who saw them as their saviors from every tribulation. That is what made them fear the Holy Household even though Imam al-Sadiq (a) and the other Imams (a) were clear in their refusal to participate in any political movement.

Alid Rights

Additionally, we find that the Abbasids knew the rights of the Holy Household and would declare it on numerous occasions. After all, they were considered amongst the Shia and understood the status of the Immaculate Imams (a).

In fact, history tells us that al-Saffah and his brother al-Mansour would travel around to towns and villages and solicit gifts by relaying the virtues of the Holy Household. In the process, Abu Ja'far al-Mansour became one of the multitude of narrators who would relay the event of al-Ghadeer.[6]

On one occasion, the Abbasid Caliph al-Ma'moun would turn to some of his companions and say, "Do you know who taught me Shi'ism?" They would answer, "No, by God, we don't know." He replied, "My father, al-Rashid." Confused, his companions would ask, "How is that so when he ordered the killing of people from that household?" Al-Ma'moun replied,

---

[5] Al-'Amili, *Hayat al-Imam al-Rida (a)*, 88.

[6] Haidar, *al-Imam al-Sadiq wa al-Mathahib al-Arba'a*, 1:45.

He killed them over power because power is vain. I went to hajj with him one year and when we arrived in Medina we entered in the dwelling we were going to be staying in. He ordered the guards saying, 'No man is allowed in whether he be from Mecca, Medina, from the Muhajireen or the Ansar, or from Banu Hashim or any of the tribes of Quraysh, except that he introduces himself and shows his lineage.' Upon that al-Rashid would honor the guest with a generous gift. The time passed and al-Fadl ibn al-Rabee' comes in saying, 'Master, there is a man at the door saying he is Moussa ibn Ja'far ibn Muhammad ibn Ali ibn Hussain ibn Ali ibn Abi Talib (a).' We were all present – al-Ameen, al-Mu'taman, myself and the rest of the commanders with al-Rashid. When he came near we gazed upon him in awe of his prestige, his light, his immaculate aura. My father greeted him with open arms, embracing him and kissing his head and taking him by the hand to seat him next to him in the center of the gathering. He inquired about his state and seemed so genuinely engaged in discussing with al-Kadhim (a). Finally when he excused himself from the gathering, my father got up with him and walked him out bidding him farewell. He came back and told us, 'Follow your uncle and master and assist him with whatever he needs.[7]

In another narration, al-Ma'moun was confused by the way his father acted towards Imam al-Kadhim (a) and privately asked him why he honored and praised al-Kadhim (a) in such a way. To that al-Rashid would reply, "My son, he is the owner of the right [i.e. the caliphate or leadership]." Al-

---

[7] Al-Hassani, *Seerat al-A'imma al-Ithney Ashar*, 2:330.

Ma'moun then asked, "If you know that then why don't you return this right back to him?" Al-Rashid would say, "It is power. By God, if you were to contest with me over it I would have your head…"[8]

There are tens of other instances that demonstrate the Abbasids' knowledge of the Holy Household's rights and status. The Abbasids always felt insecure so long as the Immaculate Imams (a) were present, as they knew how much more deserving the Imams were of leadership.

Corrupt Viziers

The caliphs' corrupt advisors also played a role in the Abbasids' transgressions against the Holy Household. These advisors used to continuously feed the caliphs' fears of the Imams (a). This allowed them to: (1) show the caliphs that they were keen to protect the caliphate, (2) create a constant enemy that compelled the caliphs to be in constant need of their advice and services, and (3) distance the caliphs from the Imams (a) who were always giving advice that conflicted with the viziers' interests.

Thus, we find that much of the Abbasid caliphs' transgression against the Holy Household was due in part to the ill advice of those around them. For example, historians tell us that the cause behind al-Rashid's poisoning of Imam al-Kadhim's (a) was one of the caliph's advisors by the name of Yahya ibn Khalid al-Barmaki.

Of course, the Abbasid caliphs believed anything told to them about the Holy Household due to their own fears and

---

[8] Ibid.

insecurities. As discussed, they knew well the rights of the Imams (a) and understood their status in the hearts of the populace. Moreover, the Abbasids used their kinship to the Holy Prophet (s) as a source of legitimacy, so they could not bear the fact that there were individuals in the nation who had a closer relationship to him than them. In the end, these factors combined to ensure that the Abbasid caliphs were as much a menace to the Holy Household as the Umayyads. Despite this, our Immaculate Imams (a) continued their stance in absolute submission and devotion to the Almighty.

LEGACY OF KARBALA

As soon as we hear the name of Imam Hussain (a), images of a grand tragedy rush to our minds. We see men murdered, tents burnt, and women and children taken captive. We remember the stance of a small group of individuals who were persecuted merely for their relationship to Islam's Holy Prophet Muhammad (s).

Despite this tragic scene, we realize that this small group of individuals who sacrificed everything they had were able to achieve a grand triumph. It was a triumph over the course of deviance that the Muslim nation had taken. It was a victory for divine principles over the principles of corruption which paralyzed the nation.

The ascension of a wicked man like Yazid to the Umayyad throne was no trivial matter. It was not long ago that the Muslim nation was born out of the honorable stances, determination, and sacrifices of the Holy Prophet (s) and his devout followers. How could that same nation be led by someone like Yazid?

The nation's conscience needed to be shook so it can remember its honorable past and its promised future. That came through the stance of Imam Hussain (a) and the small group of family members and companions who followed him. These individuals embodied the best of the nation. They were the carriers of the Holy Quran, the foremost scholars, and the companions of the Messenger of God (s). They knew well the fate that was in store for them. They proceeded with un-shakable resolve. They were successful in shocking the Muslim conscience and awakening its dormant spirit.

In this we see the true meaning of the Holy Prophet's (s) words,

حسين مني وأنا من حسين، أحب الله من أحب حسينا

Hussain is of me and I am of Hussain.[1]

Imam Hussain's (a) stance ensured the survival of the message that his grandfather delivered and the morals that he taught. His legacy and memory ensured that the religion of Islam is not subverted by its enemies. It is a sublime example of the words of God,

يُرِيدُونَ لِيُطْفِئُوا نُورَ اللَّهِ بِأَفْوَاهِهِمْ وَاللَّهُ مُتِمُّ نُورِهِ وَلَوْ كَرِهَ الْكَافِرُونَ

They desire to put out the light of Allah with their mouths, but Allah will perfect His light though the faithless should be averse.[2]

[1] Ibn Hanbal, *Musnad Ahmad*, 4:172.
[2] The Holy Quran, 61:8.

In this chapter, we wish to study the lasting memory of the tragedy in the conscience of the Muslims in the face of Umayyad attempts to erase it. We will first look at the policies that the Umayyads put in place to combat the intellectual and emotional legacy of Imam Hussain (a). We will then turn to two specific commemorative seasons – *Ashura* and *Arbaeen* – and study their individual significance.

UMAYYAD POLICIES

It was a priority for the Umayyad authorities to limit the spread of knowledge of the Holy Household's virtues. Muawiya summarized the policy when he said, "Nay by God! We will surly bury [the mentioning of Prophet Muhammad (s)]!"[3] People's recognition of the true status of the Holy Household would surely have been detrimental to Muawiya and his efforts to establish a dynasty for his descendants. He established the following policies to limit this danger. His successors, both Umayyad and Abbasid, continued these policies in the same vain.

Erasing the Legacy of the Holy Household

The Umayyad authorities sought to erase any mention of the Holy Household and their virtues. This can be seen in Muawiya's orders to his governors stating, "There shall be no

---

[3] Al-Mu'tazili, *Sharh Nahj al-Balagha*, 5:130.

protection for anyone who narrates any virtue for Abu Tu-rab[4] or his family!"[5] When the Umayyads commissioned al-Zuhari to write the history of the Holy Prophet (s), they warned him against relaying anything about Imam Ali (a) unless it disparaged or vilified him.[6]

Fabricating Against the Holy Household

Muawiya also used fabrication as a tool against the Holy Household. He would commission supposed scholars to fabricate narrations and attribute them to the Holy Prophet (s). These fabrications would gain immediate legitimacy out of the attribution to the Messenger of God (s), especially in the minds of laypeople who cannot differentiate the true from the fictitious.

In this regard, ibn Abi al-Hadeed al-Mu'tazili relays the following historical account,

> *My teacher Abu Jaafar a-Iskafi mentioned that Muawiya employed a group of the companions and followers[7] [of companions]. He asked them to fabricate narrations that disparaged Ali and required that they criticize him and disclaim any affinity with him. For that, he provided them with a salary that anyone would envy. They began to fabricate whatever*

---

[4] "Abu Turab," or "the Man of Dust," was a nickname given to Imam Ali ibn Abi Talib due to his long prostration that would cause dust to cling to his face. Umayyad rulers would use the nickname thinking it an insult to call him a "Man of Dust." In fact, it is said that Abu Turab was one of Imam Ali's favorite nicknames. —Eds.

[5] Al-Tabari, *Bisharat al-Mustafa (s)*, 163.

[6] Ameen, *Duha al-Islam*, 2:326.

[7] "Followers," or Tabieen, was a name given to the first generation that followed the generation of the companions. They were called followers because they followed the companions and became their disciples. —Eds.

pleased him. Of them was Abu Hurayra, Amr ibn al-Aas, al-Mughira ibn Shuba, and Urwa ibn al-Zubayr.[8]

Historians mention that, for example, Muawiya spent four hundred thousand silver coins to misappropriate the following verses of the Holy Quran.

وَمِنَ النَّاسِ مَن يُعْجِبُكَ قَوْلُهُ فِي الْحَيَاةِ الدُّنْيَا وَيُشْهِدُ اللَّهَ عَلَىٰ مَا فِي قَلْبِهِ وَهُوَ أَلَدُّ الْخِصَامِ ﴿٢٠٤﴾ وَإِذَا تَوَلَّىٰ سَعَىٰ فِي الْأَرْضِ لِيُفْسِدَ فِيهَا وَيُهْلِكَ الْحَرْثَ وَالنَّسْلَ ۚ وَاللَّهُ لَا يُحِبُّ الْفَسَادَ ﴿٢٠٥﴾

Among the people is he whose talk about worldly life impresses you, and he holds Allah witness to what is in his heart, though he is the staunchest of enemies. If he were to wield authority, he would try to cause corruption in the land and to ruin the crop and the stock, and Allah does not like corruption…

وَمِنَ النَّاسِ مَن يَشْرِي نَفْسَهُ ابْتِغَاءَ مَرْضَاتِ اللَّهِ ۚ وَاللَّهُ رَءُوفٌ بِالْعِبَادِ ﴿٢٠٧﴾

And among the people is he who sells his soul seeking the pleasure of Allah, and Allah is most kind to [His] servants.[9]

---

[8] Al-Mu'tazili, *Sharh Nahj al-Balagha*, 4:61.
[9] The Holy Quran, 2:204-07.

Muawiya's subordinates would claim that first segment of these verses disparaged Imam Ali (a), while the latter praised his assassin Abdulrahman ibn Muljim.

In another instance, al-Zuhari was asked to spread the lie that the following verse was disparaging Imam Ali (a).

لِكُلِّ امْرِئٍ مِّنْهُم مَّا اكْتَسَبَ مِنَ الْإِثْمِ ۚ وَالَّذِي تَوَلَّىٰ كِبْرَهُ مِنْهُمْ لَهُ عَذَابٌ عَظِيمٌ

Each man among them bears [the onus for] his share in the sin, and as for him who assumed its major burden from among them, there is a great punishment for him.[10]

Al-Zuhari refused and narrated that the verse was actually disparaging a man by the name of Abdullah ibn Sulool.[11]

Fabricating in Favor of Others

Another of Muawiya's strategies was to take the narrations regarding the virtues and status of the Holy Household and generalize them to include all the companions of the Holy Prophet (s). That way, the Holy Household would have no claim to any favor or status above the rest of the companions. Muawiya would send a directive to his governors stating,

> *When this letter reaches you, call men to relate the virtues of the companions and the earliest of the caliphs. Do not leave any narration that is recounted in favor of Abu Turab except that you get me a counter to it relayed in favor of another*

---

[10] The Holy Quran, 24:11.

[11] Ameen, *Duha al-Islam*, 2:326.

companion. I would surely love this and rest at ease, as it
would refute the proofs of Abu Turab and his Shia.[12]

One prominent historian even said,

The majority of the narrations that praise the companions
were fabricated during the time of Umayyads in order to gain
favor with them through what they [i.e. the Umayyads]
thought would humiliate the Hashimids.[13]

THE MEMORY OF THE TRAGEDY

Ibrahim al-Nakha'e narrates the following incident. He says
that the Commander of the Faithful (a) was once sitting in
the mosque surrounded by his companions when Imam
Hussain (a) approached. Imam Ali (a) put his hand on his
son's head and said,

يا بني ان الله عير أقواما بالقرآن فقال: فَمَا بَكَتْ عَلَيْهِمُ السَّمَاءُ
وَالْأَرْضُ وَمَا كَانُوا مُنْظَرِينَ، وأيم الله ليقتلنك بعدي ثم تبكيك
السماء والأرض

My son! Surely God has derided some people in the Quran
saying, 'Neither the sky wept for them, nor the earth; nor
were they granted any respite.' By God, they will kill you after
me and the sky and earth will weep for you![14]

The tragedy of Imam Hussain (a) holds special significance
for the Holy Household, greater than all the other tragedies

---

[12] Al-Mu'tazili, *Sharh Nahj al-Balagha*, 11:46.

[13] Ibid.

[14] Al-Qummi, *Kamil al-Ziyarat*, 180. Citing: The Holy Quran, 44:29.

that befell them. The Holy Prophet (s) and the Commander of the Faithful (a) forewarned of the great calamity. For example, all Muslim schools of thought narrate that the Holy Prophet (s) gave a bottle of sand to Umm Salama and told her that his grandson will be martyred and that the sand will turn red on that day.

The Immaculate Imams (a) after Imam Hussain (a) would not pass on any opportunity to remember this tragedy and point to its significance in changing the course of Muslim history. They commanded their followers to remember the tragedy of Karbala and visit the blessed shrines of the martyrs. They marked specific days for the remembrance of the tragedy, with a special emphasis on the days of Ashura and Arbaeen.

Ashura

Ashura is the date on which the tragedy of Karbala is remembered every year. In Arabic, the word Ashura literally means the eve of the tenth day and is a reference to the date of the massacre – the tenth of the lunar month of Muharram. The significance of commemorating this day should therefore be evident.

Unfortunately, the Umayyad propaganda machine worked to cast doubt over this day's tragic history. In short, the Umayyads used lies and fabrications to establish the Day of Ashura as a festive public holiday. These lies can generally be divided into two groups. One set of fabrications claimed that Ashura was a day of fasting in pre-Islamic times. Another set claims that the Day of Ashura was a date in which several of God's promises were fulfilled, such as being the date of the Israelites' escape from the clutches of pharaoh.

As a refutation of these fictions, consider the following:

First, these claims are linguistically untenable. Linguists agree that the word came into use until the first century after Hiijra. Moreover, Ashura is a feminine noun and linguistically describes the eve of the tenth day and not the day itself. If it were a name given to a day, then it would have to be masculine. If it were a day of fasting, why would the Arabs give it the linguistically improper feminine noun?

Second, there is nothing in the history of the Arabs that indicates this day as a day of fasting and celebration in pre-Islamic times.

Third, the claim that Ashura was the day in which the Israelites were liberated from Egypt does not reflect Jewish tradition. This is especially important since the claim is that the Holy Prophet (s) saw that the Jews fasted on this day, so he commanded his followers to fast it as well.[15] However, Jews historically celebrated this event with the seven-day festival of Passover, and not a one day fast.

Jews do fast on the tenth day of the Hebrew month of Tishrei, also known as Yom Kippur. The holiday commemorates the day when Moses received the second set of Commandments from God, as well as atonement for the sin of the Golden Calf. Yet claiming that Ashura is Muslim continuation of the Jewish holiday of Yom Kippur is also highly improbable. The Hebrew calendar is lunisolar, meaning that months are determined in accordance with lunar cycles, while the new year is determined in accordance with the solar cycle.

---

[15] See: al-Bukhari, *Sahih al-Bukhari*, 4:126.

This means that Yom Kippur is always celebrated in the fall. On the other hand, the Muslim lunar calendar means that the Day of Ashura shifts every year, and can fall at any time of the year depending on the lunar year and cycle. Therefore, although both Ashura and Yom Kippur mark the tenth day of a month, the differences in the calendars makes it highly unlikely that the two events are related in any way.

All this makes it clear that the traditions claiming Ashura to be a day of celebration are lies fabricated by the Umayyads to erase the memory of their crimes on the Day of Ashura.

The Significance of Arbaeen

The day of Arbaeen is a special day in which the Immaculate Imams (a) commanded their followers to visit the tomb of Imam Hussain (a). Arbaeen – literally the fortieth – is the fortieth day after the Day of Ashura. It is narrated that Imam Hassan al-'Askari (a) described the five marks of the believer and listed visitation of Imam Hussain (a) on Arbaeen as one of those marks.[16]

We must therefore shed some light on this special occasion. What gives this day such great significance? There are several opinions in this regard. Let us address a few of them one by one.

Return to Karbala. Some contend that the fortieth day after the tragedy of Karbala marked the return of the Holy Household to the site of the massacre. They returned with the severed heads of the martyrs to give them a proper burial and visit the tombs of their loved ones. The day of Arbaeen is

---

[16] See: al-'Amili, *Wasa'el al-Shia*, 3:42.

therefore remembered for its significance in the journey of the Holy Household.

This rationale is highly unlikely and is disputed by scholars. Forty days would not be enough time for the journey from Karbala to Kufa and then to Damascus. The captives were paraded around the nation, passing through major cities like Aleppo. Some historical accounts say that they remained in Damascus for a month, where they were held in a place that did not shelter them from the heat of the sun or the cold of night. It is therefore highly unlikely that this entire journey, in addition to the trip back to Karbala, took only forty days' time.

There are some who even claimed that the day of Arbaeen marked the return of the captives back to Medina. This claim is even more farfetched. As Sayyid ibn Tawus said,

> I read in the book of Misbah that the family of al-Hussain (a) reached Medina with our master Ali ibn al-Hussain (a) on the twentieth of Safar. Books other than Misbah said that they reached Karbala on their return from Damascus on the twentieth of Safar. Both claims are improbable.[17]

Jabir al-Ansari. Another opinion is that Arbaeen marks the visit of Jabir ibn Abdullah al-Ansari, a companion of the Holy Prophet (s), to the grave of Imam Hussain (a). It is even said that Jabir was the first individual to visit the graves of the martyrs after their burial. Yet this rationale is also improbable. Although Jabir was a companion of high status and a confidant of the Holy Household (a), it is hard to believe that

---

[17] Al-Majlisi, *Bihar al-Anwar*, 98:335.

his actions were the basis for establishing this tradition. Jabir's actions and his visitation of the blessed graves was a great act that we praise and admire. Still, it is improbable that such value is given to the day of Arbaeen solely out of one companion's actions on that day.

Freed from Captivity. Allama al-Majlisi writes that one possible explanation behind the great significance given to this day is that it marked the freedom of the Holy Household from the bonds of Umayyad captivity. This opinion is also improbable. As discussed earlier, historical accounts are conflicting when relaying the specific dates of this journey. Moreover, why would freedom from captivity in Damascus mark the day of visiting Imam Hussain (a) in Karbala? The logic of this opinion is tenuous. That is why Allama al-Majlisi lists all these possibilities, but does not place enough confidence in any one of them as to draw a solid conclusion.

No Significance. There are some who claim that there is no significance for the day of Arbaeen. They provide a different interpretation to the narration of Imam al-'Askari (a) listing the 'visitation of the fortieth' as a mark of the believer. They claim that the Imam (a) meant the visitation of forty believers. Not only is this opinion improbable, some scholars believe it is untenable.[18] This interpretation of Imam al-'Askari (a) words does not have any basis in Arabic linguistics. Moreover, why would the Imam (a) limit visitation of believers to forty? The traditions of the Holy Household (a) are clear that there is a special significance to the fortieth day after the tragedy of Karbala.

---

[18] See: al-Muqarram, *Maqtal al-Hussein (a)*, 366.

The Significance of Forty Days. Commemorating the deceased for forty days is a tradition that dates back earlier than Imam Hussain's (a) stance in Karbala. It is not a Muslim tradition, but goes back to the earliest days of human history. There are several traditions that lead us to this conclusion.

For one, Imam al-Baqir (a) tells us that "Adam wept for Abel forty nights" after he was murdered by his brother Cain.[19] The ritual of mourning for forty days continues to this day. For example, in the Orthodox Christian Church, memorial services are held on the third, ninth, and fortieth days after death.[20]

The significance of forty days may be a result of the natural world's reaction to an individual's death. There are many narrations that speak of the earth and sky weeping for Imam Hussain (a) for forty days. In fact, Allama al-Majlisi narrates 48 traditions in this regard.

Imam al-Sadiq (a) is narrated to have said,

$$إن السماء بكت على الحسين بن علي ويحيى بن زكريا ولم تبك على أحد غيرهما$$

The sky wept for al-Hussain ibn Ali (a) and Yahya ibn Zakariya, and did not weep for anyone but them.

The Imam (a) was asked how it was that the sky wept. He replied,

[19] Al-Kulayni, *al-Kafi*, 8:114.

[20] See: "Prayers for the Departed," Orthodox Church in America, accessed October 2017, https://oca.org/questions/deathfunerals/prayers-for-the-departed.

مكثوا أربعين يوما تطلع الشمس بحمرة وتغرب بحمرة

It was forty days in which the sun rose with redness and set with redness.[21]

There are many similar narrations that speak of the earth and sky weeping for Imam Hussain (a) for forty days. This may be the reason behind the significance given to the fortieth day after his martyrdom, considering that the universe wept for him for forty days.

Supernatural Signs

If we consider the weeping of the earth and sky as the reason behind the significance of the forty days, a new question arises. What is the reasonability of claiming that such supernatural occurrences took place after the martyrdom of Imam Hussain (a)?

If we look at our religious texts, particularly the Holy Quran, we see that they deal with the natural world in a way different than our material understanding. Our faith teaches us that all creation has some form of sentience, even though we may not see or acknowledge it. For example, the Holy Quran says that everything in creation glorifies God in one way or another. However, humanity is unable to observe these glorifications due to the limitations of our senses. God says,

---

[21] Al-Majlisi, *Bihar al-Anwar*, 45:210.

$$تُسَبِّحُ لَهُ السَّمَاوَاتُ السَّبْعُ وَالْأَرْضُ وَمَن فِيهِنَّ ۚ وَإِن مِّن شَيْءٍ إِلَّا يُسَبِّحُ بِحَمْدِهِ وَلَٰكِن لَّا تَفْقَهُونَ تَسْبِيحَهُمْ ۗ إِنَّهُ كَانَ حَلِيمًا غَفُورًا$$

The seven heavens glorify Him, and the earth [too], and who-
ever is in them. There is not a thing but celebrates His praise,
but you do not understand their glorification. Indeed, He is
all-forbearing, all-forgiving.[22]

The Holy Quran also tells us that the natural world may react
to the death of an individual. We see this in the prayers of
Moses and God's drowning of the pharaoh and his army. The
blessed verses say,

$$فَدَعَا رَبَّهُ أَنَّ هَٰؤُلَاءِ قَوْمٌ مُّجْرِمُونَ ﴿٢٢﴾ فَأَسْرِ بِعِبَادِي لَيْلًا إِنَّكُم مُّتَّبَعُونَ ﴿٢٣﴾ وَاتْرُكِ الْبَحْرَ رَهْوًا ۖ إِنَّهُمْ جُندٌ مُّغْرَقُونَ ﴿٢٤﴾ كَمْ تَرَكُوا مِن جَنَّاتٍ وَعُيُونٍ ﴿٢٥﴾ وَزُرُوعٍ وَمَقَامٍ كَرِيمٍ ﴿٢٦﴾ وَنَعْمَةٍ كَانُوا فِيهَا فَاكِهِينَ ﴿٢٧﴾ كَذَٰلِكَ ۖ وَأَوْرَثْنَاهَا قَوْمًا آخَرِينَ ﴿٢٨﴾ فَمَا بَكَتْ عَلَيْهِمُ السَّمَاءُ وَالْأَرْضُ وَمَا كَانُوا مُنظَرِينَ ﴿٢٩﴾$$

Then [Moses] invoked his Lord, [saying,] 'These are indeed
a guilty lot.' [Allah told him,] 'Set out by night with My
servants; for you will be pursued. Leave behind the sea un-
moving; for they will be a drowned host.' How many gardens
and springs did they leave behind! Fields and splendid places,
and the affluence wherein they rejoiced! So it was; and We

---

bequeathed them to another people. So neither the sky wept for them, nor the earth; nor were they granted any respite.[23]

Some exegetes of the Holy Quran say that the sky and the earth do not actually weep, interpreting the blessed verse to mean that neither the denizens of the earth nor of the heavens wept for the pharaoh and his lot. Others concluded that the sky did weep, which meant that the sun emitted an unusual redness at sunrise and sunset. We saw this interpretation in the narration of Imam al-Sadiq (a) mentioned above.

We also see in some narrations that objects we consider to be inanimate responding to the spiritual atmosphere around them. In one famous tradition, a palm tree in the Prophet's Mosque was heard crying during the Holy Prophet's (s) life. The Holy Prophet (s) used to lean against this tree while propagating the message in the mosque. The companions built a pulpit for the Holy Prophet (s) so he could be seen and heard better by the mosque-goers. When he walked passed that tree and unto the pulpit, the tree began to cry. It did not stop until the Holy Prophet (s) came down from the pulpit, hugged it, and said,

اسكن فما تجاوزك رسول الله تهاونا بك ولا استخفافا بحرمتك،
ولكن ليتم لعباد الله مصلحتهم، ولك جلالك وفضلك إذ كنت
مستند محمد رسول الله

Be calm! Surely the Messenger of God (s) did not pass you up because he is neglecting you or out of disregard for your sanctity. Rather, it is so he can deliver to the servants of God

---

[23] The Holy Quran, 44:22-29.

*what benefits them. You have your honor and merit, as you
were the leaning place of Muhammad the Messenger of God
(s).*[24]

There are several other similar accounts in which objects we
consider inanimate spoke to the Holy Prophet (s) and
showed their sentience to the companions who observed.
Some might say that these are miracles that occur only at the
hands of prophets. While that may be true, the point here is
not to claim any miracle but to show that God created the
entire universe with the ability to sense and react in one form
or the other.

Therefore, the fact that the sky and the earth wept for Imam
Hussain (a) should not dismissed as improbable or unreasonable. There are numerous traditions which speak of this fact
and describe the details of the phenomena. In fact, Muslims
of all schools of thought relay this type of narration. Recall
the story of the bottle that the Holy Prophet (s) gave to Umm
Salama? The bottle contained sand from the plains of Karbala. The Holy Prophet (s) told Umm Salama that when that
sand turns red, she should know that Imam Hussain (a) was
martyred. The story is relayed by Muslims from all schools of
thought and is doubtlessly one form of weeping which our
Immaculate Imams (a) spoke of.

The Significance of Forty Days

One might ask, why does the number forty hold such a great
significance? Why would the world weep for Imam Hussain
(a) for forty days and not a day more or less? We cannot give

---

[24] Al-Majlisi, *Bihar al-Anwar*, 17:326.

a definite answer to this question. However, if we return to the narrations of the Holy Household, we find that the number comes up often, especially in narrations that speak of moral and spiritual consequences.

There are a great deal of narrations that mention forty days as the mark for achieving some type of spiritual excellence. For example, there are traditions that teach the believers supplications that should be recited for forty consecutive days to achieve some desired effect. Other narrations speak of forty days in a more general spiritual context. Imam al-Baqir (a) says,

ما اخلص العبد الإيمان بالله عز وجل أربعين يوما إلا زهده الله في الدنيا وبصره داءها ودواءها فأثبت الحكمة في قلبه وأنطق بها لسانه

No servant purifies his faith in God for forty days except that God shall make him austere in this world and open his eyes to its ills and remedies. God shall root wisdom in his heart and project it on his tongue.[25]

Just as forty days is the threshold for an individual's spiritual change, that time frame may also have its effect and meaning on the natural world. God created a system in which this time frame held great significance, whether or not we realize and acknowledge it. In any case, God made these forty days following the martyrdom of Imam Hussain (a) a season of

---

[25] Al-Kulayni, *al-Kafi*, 2:16.

morning and remembrance for all the believers who seek to
follow that role model.

TRIUMPH

In the Name of God, the Most Compassionate, the Most Merciful

إِنَّا فَتَحْنَا لَكَ فَتْحًا مُّبِينًا ﴿١﴾ لِّيَغْفِرَ لَكَ اللَّهُ مَا تَقَدَّمَ مِن ذَنبِكَ

وَمَا تَأَخَّرَ وَيُتِمَّ نِعْمَتَهُ عَلَيْكَ وَيَهْدِيَكَ صِرَاطًا مُّسْتَقِيمًا ﴿٢﴾

وَيَنصُرَكَ اللَّهُ نَصْرًا عَزِيزًا ﴿٣﴾ هُوَ الَّذِي أَنزَلَ السَّكِينَةَ فِي

قُلُوبِ الْمُؤْمِنِينَ لِيَزْدَادُوا إِيمَانًا مَّعَ إِيمَانِهِمْ ۗ وَلِلَّهِ جُنُودُ السَّمَاوَاتِ

وَالْأَرْضِ ۚ وَكَانَ اللَّهُ عَلِيمًا حَكِيمًا ﴿٤﴾

Indeed We have inaugurated for you a clear triumph, that Allah may forgive you what is past of your sin and what is to come, and that He may perfect His blessing upon you and guide you on a straight path, and Allah will help you with a mighty help. It is He who sent down composure into the hearts of the faithful that they might enhance in their faith. To Allah belong the hosts of the heavens and the earth, and Allah is all-knowing, all-wise.[1]

The message of Islam, the final divine message, was able to change the human mindset regarding a number of important

---

[1] The Holy Quran, 48:1-4.

issues. People normally think of triumph as synonymous to military victory over an enemy. They Holy Quran revealed to mankind that there is something greater than victory which it calls triumph. Whereas victory is understood as success in a competition, triumph gives a greater and more permanent meaning. A movement's triumph comes through achievement of all its goals and objectives.

The Holy Quran does not speak here of any triumph, but describes it as a great and 'clear' triumph. There is some disagreement between scholars over the exact incident described in the verse. Some said that it is in reference to the Battle of Khaybar, while others say that it was revealed after the Holy Prophet's (s) return to Mecca. However, a majority of scholars agree that this verse was revealed after the Holy Prophet (s) entered into the Treaty of Hudaibiya, and the verse is specifically describing this incident.

Many Muslims at the time saw the Treaty of Hudaibiya as a defeat. The treaty itself was skewed in favor of the Meccans. Its first provision was that the Muslims would not perform the Hajj in that year. Another provision obliged the Muslims to return any Meccans that enter Islam back to Mecca. All in all, many Muslims saw these provision as a sign of weakness and a defeat against the Meccans.

Yet this verse revealed that the truth of the matter was not as most people perceived. The treaty was a clear triumph – more than any military victory. That is because the Treaty of Hudaibiya was a pivotal moment in the history of Islam. It was the beginning of the fulfillment of God's divine promise.

Our purpose here is not detail this divine declaration. We mention it here so we can better understand the concept and how Imam Hussain (a) was able to apply it in his movement.

IMAM HUSSAIN'S (A) TRIUMPH

Imam al-Sadiq (a) relays that when his great-grandfather Imam Hussain (a) was leaving Medina, he sent a letter to his Hashimite kin saying,

إنه من لحق بي استشهد معي ومن تخلف لم يبلغ الفتح

Surely, whoever follows me will be martyred alongside me. Whoever does not follow me will not witness the triumph.[2]

The Imam (a) was unequivocal about the fact that his movement will lead to certain martyrdom. However, he did not hesitate to declare that military defeat a great triumph.

Imam Hussain (a) used triumph in its Quranic sense to describe the result of his movement. He declared to everyone that he had a set of goals that he wanted to achieve, and that he will doubtlessly achieve them despite his martyrdom. One should not misunderstand the Imam (a), thinking that the triumph he is alluding to is a metaphysical one to be reaped in the hereafter. If that was the case, martyrdom is enough of a triumph for the Imam (a). The Imam's words are clear that his movement achieved a triumph that we can observe and understand in this world before the hereafter.

To better understand Imam Hussain's (a) triumph, let us discuss a few points:

---

[2] Al-Saffar, *Basa'er al-Darajat*, 501.

Personal Triumph

Imam Hussain (a) was able to achieve a lasting legacy through his sacrifice on the plains of Karbala. Legacy here is not intended to mean the continued mentioning of his name across centuries – although he definitively achieved that. This type of remembrance is of no use to any one after their passing. Even though each nation remembers its heroes in its culture and history books, that mentioning is not of any benefit to the hero who has long departed this world.

The legacy that Imam Hussain (a) is much different than the legacy of any national hero. His memory does not live only on books and tongues, but in the hearts of the believers. This type of remembrance is a great reward for our beloved Imam (a), even after his martyrdom. His name brings believers together to practice their faith and grow closer to their Lord. Mosques, schools, orphanages, and community centers are built in Imam Hussain's (a) name. This legacy brings him a continuous flow of divine favors and rewards.

The Holy Prophet (s) said,

من سن سنة حسنة فله أجرها وأجر من عمل بها من غير أن ينتقص من أجورهم شيء

Whoever establishes a good tradition shall have its reward and the reward of whoever acts in accordance to it without diminishing any of their rewards.[3]

If God will give all this to someone who starts a good tradition, what is the reward of an individual whose memory is a

---

[3] Al-Sadouq, *al-Khisal*, 240.

cause for guidance and virtue? Imam Hussain (a) will continue to reap the rewards of every religious gathering and every good deed done in his name until the end of days.

As Imam Hussain (a) promised, that small number of companions that accompanied Imam Hussain (a) on that day achieved the same great triumph. They will continue to reap these rewards until the Day of Judgement, so long as there are believers who continue to learn from their stories.

Triumph Against the Enemy

When it comes to his struggle against the Umayyad enemy, Imam Hussain (a) was able to triumph through two major achievements.

Exposing Umayyad Corruption. Imam Hussain's (a) tragedy exposed the ruling Umayyads for their true corruption. Every image of that tragedy was a tear in the sanctified impression of the Umayyads that Muawiya tried so hard to instill. From the brutal massacre to the severed heads paraded across the nation. From the burning of the tents to the women and children taken captive and steered in chains from Karbala to Kufa to Damascus. From the children who were slaughtered in the arms of their parents to those who died of grief in captivity. The nation had never seen such gruesome images, even in the ages of ignorance before the message of Islam.

Add to all this the fact that the victims were the family and descendants of the nation's Holy Prophet (s).

All of this exposed the corrupt and bloodthirsty face of the Umayyads. It revealed the true motives of Muawiya and his kin for everyone to see. It exposed the wickedness of Yazid who joyously declared in those days, "The Banu Hashim have played with the throne! Surely, there was neither a message delivered, nor a revelation inspired!"[4] All this while claiming to be the 'prince of the believers' and the 'successor of the prophet.'

Yazid could not have been exposed like this without the movement and sacrifice of Imam Hussain (a). The tragedy of Karbala exposed the great hatred the Umayyads harbored for Islam, despite their attempts to portray piety. One of Imam Hussain's (a) goals was to expose this reality for all Muslims to see. That is why he declared in Medina,

يزيد رجل شارب الخمور قاتل النفس المحرمة معلن بالفسق
ومثلي لا يبايع مثله

Yazid is a deviant, a miscreant, a drunkard, and a murderer. He has publicly professed his impiety. Someone like me will never pay allegiance to the likes of him.[5]

Legitimizing Revolution. Imam Hussain's (a) revolution instantly became an established legal precedent in the field of Islamic jurisprudence. Muslim scholars from all schools of thought agreed that this movement embodied a legitimate stance in Islamic doctrine. Only few individuals disagree, and they are so rare and anomalous that their opinions cannot be seriously considered.

---

[4] Ibn Katheer, *al-Bidaya*, 209.

[5] Al-Muqarram, *Maqtal al-Hussein (a)*, 131.

In other words, Muslim scholars believe that the primary qualifications for a leader are knowledge and justice. This is true for the followers of the Holy Household who see that these attributes are perfected in the twelve Immaculate Imams (a). Most Muslim scholars who believe that the caliphate is a matter to be decided by the *Shura*[6] also believe that these are the primary qualifications.

Umayyad policies sought to remove consideration for any qualification. They sought to establish a dynasty where the throne was a birthright to the descendants of Umayya. Their failure cannot be attributed to anything but Imam Hussain's (a) stance. That stance became a legal precedent that Muslim jurists looked to in determining whether or not a revolution is legitimate. As the Hanbali scholar Muhammad ibn Muflih al-Maqdisi writes, "Ibn 'Aqeel and ibn al-Jawzi permitted rebellion against an unjust leader to establish justice, relying in their opinion on Hussain's (a) revolution against Yazid."[7]

Imam Hussain's (a) stance gave dissent against Umayyad rule the legitimacy and support that it needed. After the tragedy of Karbala, one revolution after the other began to crop up across the Muslim nation. In fact, the first revolution came from Medina, where Imam Hussain (a) was abandoned only a few years before. The brutal suppression of that revolution became known as the tragedy of al-Harra. Revolutions against Umayyad rule continued until the Abbasids were fi-

---

[6] *Shura* – literally, consultation – is what many Muslim scholars believe is the appropriate method for choosing a successor to the Holy Prophet (s). The details of this method are a matter of disagreement. –Eds.

[7] Al-Maqdisi, *al-Furu'*, 10:180.

nally able to supplant it. Many of these revolutions – including the Abbasids' – would point to Imam Hussain (a) as their role model and claim that they are avenging the tragedies of the Holy Household. Yet even the Abbasids could not claim absolute control and legitimacy, as revolutions against their newfound dynasty continued as well.

Triumph for the Holy Household

Imam Hussain's (a) movement achieved a number of significant victories for the Holy Household and their followers specifically. This can be summarized in the following points:

Emotional Bond. The great tragedies that befell the Holy Household made them the point of reference and role models for much of the Muslim nation, especially the oppressed and the meek. The Muslim nation held special love and affection for the progeny of the Holy Prophet (s), whether or not they believed in them as divinely chosen guardians of the faith. This love was especially solidified after Imam Hussain's (a) stance and the great massacre in Karbala. After that tragedy, many more Muslims were sympathetic to their cause and open to their teachings. Sayyid Murtada al-'Askari writes,

> As a result of all we have mentioned [about the tragedy of Karbala], the conscience of some Muslims awakened from its deep slumber. Their souls were disgusted by the current state of the caliphate. Love for the household of the Prophet (s) spread amongst all Muslims who did not benefit from the authorities. And while the Umayyads and the Abbasids wrestled for the caliphate, the opportunity came for the sensible amongst the Muslims to flock towards Imam al-Baqir and Imam al-Sadiq (a). The two Imams were able to spread

*the Islamic beliefs that were taught by the Messenger of God
(s), and to expose the falsity of distorted teachings.*[8]

Imam Hussain's (a) stance and tragedy created the emotional
connection that allowed many to be open to the teachings of
the Holy Household. It allowed the progeny of the Holy
Prophet (s) to spread the true and pure teachings of Islam.
This is the reform that Imam Hussain (a) achieved for the
Muslim nation – that they return to Islam's true teachings and
principles. What triumph can be greater than this?

Primacy of the Holy Household. There is no dispute
amongst the followers of the Holy Household that they are
the primary resource in terms of thought, theology, and jurisprudence. We believe that they are the leaders of the Muslim
nation, appointed by the Holy Prophet (s) as his successors
by divine command.

Other schools of thought did not give the same primacy to
the Holy Household. However, following the tragedy of Karbala, the entire nation recognized that the descendants of the
Holy Prophet (s) were foremost amongst the Muslims in piety and knowledge. Everyone flocked to have their opinion
in religious matters and seek their solutions to the most in-
tractable problems. Historians record that thousands of Muslims would come back to the Imams (a) to seek their guidance
and study in their circles. Even the caliphs would seek the
assistance of the Holy Household when faced with a significant and thorny problem.

---

[8] Al-'Askari, *Ma'alim al-Madrasatain*, 3:205.

Imam Hussain's (a) stance achieved this important goal for the Holy Household. After the tragedy of Karbala, none of the Immaculate Imams (a) rose like Imam Hussain (a) because he had already achieved this vital goal. Another revolution would not make the same significant shift in the course of the Muslim nation.

At the same time, the caliphs shifted their public position regarding the Holy Household after that tragedy. They became reluctant to challenge or confront them openly, and were especially careful not to repeat the bloody massacre. This allowed our Immaculate Imams (a) the opportunity to emerge as thought leaders for the Muslim nation. And although the caliphs were loath to allow them such leadership, it was a better alternative than confrontation and bloodshed. Thus, the recognition of the Holy Household as the primary source of religious learning was one of the grand achievements of Imam Hussain's (a) stance.

Distinguishing the Holy Household. The early caliphs were keen to ensure that all religious scholarship was monopolized by the state. Very few scholars were able to escape the sway of the authorities. In fact, many scholars at the time were dependent on the state. This was a point of distinction for the Holy Household, as they were fully independent from the ruling governments. This absolute separation was clear to the nation, giving greater legitimacy to the Immaculate Imams (a) and their movement.

There is no doubt that Imam Hussain's (a) stance played a significant role in this regard. The distinction between the

Holy Household and the scholars of the time became apparent during the time of the Umayyads and continued during the time of the Abbasids. The Immaculate Imams (a) made it clear that they will not be part of the political class's corrupt network. When the Abbasid caliph al-Mansour wrote to Imam al-Sadiq (a) asking him why he doesn't visit like all the other notables of the nation, Imam al-Sadiq (a) replied,

ليس لنا ما نخافك من أجله ولا عندك من أمر الآخرة ما
نرجوك له ولا أنت في نعمة فنهنئك ولا تراها نقمة فنعزيك بها،
فما نصنع عندك ؟

We have nothing for which we fear you. You have nothing of the hereafter for which we could seek you. You are not in a blessing for which we would congratulate you. You do not see it as a curse for which we can console you. What would we do if we were to visit you?

Al-Mansour wrote back, "You can accompany us and advise us." Imam al-Sadiq wrote in reply,

من أراد الدنيا لا ينصحك ومن أراد الآخرة لا يصحبك

Whoever seeks this world does not [sincerely] advise you. Whoever seeks the hereafter does not accompany you.[9]

Imam Hussain's (a) stance crystalized this distinction to the public, while at the same time giving the Holy Household (a) a degree of moral immunity in the public mind. Though the governing authorities despised and feared the Immaculate Imams' (a) stance, they could not directly confront them for

---

[9] Al-Majlisi, *Bihar al-Anwar*, 47:184.

fear of reaping the same ill consequences that befell Yazid. This does not mean that the Imams (a) were free of persecution, as they were continually harassed, plotted against, and assassinated by the ruling authorities. Yet the caliphs fear of direct confrontation meant that our Imams (a) had a degree of liberty to spread the true teachings of Islam without a replication of the tragedy of Karbala.

Triumph for the Nation

God willed that the nation of the Holy Prophet Muhammad (s) be the best of nations. He prescribed to us the means by which we can attain this. God says in the Holy Quran,

كُنتُمْ خَيْرَ أُمَّةٍ أُخْرِجَتْ لِلنَّاسِ تَأْمُرُونَ بِالْمَعْرُوفِ وَتَنْهَوْنَ عَنِ الْمُنكَرِ وَتُؤْمِنُونَ بِاللَّهِ ۗ وَلَوْ آمَنَ أَهْلُ الْكِتَابِ لَكَانَ خَيْرًا لَّهُم ۚ مِّنْهُمُ الْمُؤْمِنُونَ وَأَكْثَرُهُمُ الْفَاسِقُونَ

You are the best nation [ever] brought forth for mankind: you bid what is right and forbid what is wrong, and have faith in Allah. And if the People of the Book had believed, it would have been better for them. Among them [some] are faithful, but most of them are transgressors.[10]

It is this principle of 'bidding what is right and forbidding what is evil' that makes a nation greater when compared to others. Yet the Umayyads were bent on twisting and destroying this principle. It is a reflection of a nation's honor and resolve, two traits that the ruling authorities did not care to see in their subjects.

---

[10] The Holy Quran, 3:110.

It was Imam Hussain's (a) stance that returned to the nation its honor and free will. It awakened it from its slumber with tragic shock. Through his rejection to give allegiance, refusal to bend to humiliation, determination to walk the path of martyrdom, and willful acceptance of the greatest of tribulations, Imam Hussain (a) became a role model for the Muslim nation.

Through his stance, Imam Hussain (a) drew red lines which succeeding governments could not cross. If corruption ever reached a level that posed an existential threat to the religion of Islam, then revolution was in order. That is why the Umayyad plan to destroy Islam ended with Yazid, despite all the vices and faults of the caliphs that came after. This is how Imam Hussain (a) was able to safeguard Islam through his stance and sacrifice. What triumph could be greater than this?

This was what Imam al-Sajjad (a) told the people who doubted the wisdom of his father's stance. Historians say that Ibrahim ibn Talha bin Ubaydullah mockingly asked Imam al-Sajjad (a), "So who was the victor?" The Imam (a) replied with absolute faith and resolve,

إذا دخل وقت الصلاة فأذن وأقم تعرف من الغالب

When the time of prayer comes, recite the Athan and Iqama. Then you will know who the victor was![11]

This grand triumph was clear as day to the Holy Household (a). If there was any doubt that Imam Hussain's (a) sacrifice

---

[11] Al-Muqarram, *Maqtal al-Hussain (a)*, 375.

would achieve such a result, he would not have set out from Medina in the first place.

THE CHANGES BROUGHT BY IMAM HUSSAIN (A)

To understand the change that Imam Hussain (a) caused in nation, we must first study the state in which Muslims lived during the preceding period. We must understand how Muawiya and Yazid worked to destroy the will and honor of the nation and divert it away from its course. This nation was meant to be the greatest of all. God blessed it with His final messenger and most perfect message. He tasked it with being that middle nation which bids what is right and forbids what is wrong.

Umayyad Corruption

The Umayyads were bent on destroying this message and ridding the nation of all its values and principles. They wished to divert Muslims away from a Godwary people focused on the hereafter, to a materialistic people whose greatest worry is this world and all its embellishments. They attempted to do this through two main policies:

First, they used worldly temptations to divert the Muslim nation. Muawiya especially was adept at buying the consciences of Muslim notables and tribal chieftains with brazen bribes and lavish gifts. He knew that as people steep in luxury and wealth, their connection to the morals and principles of their faith weakens. Material interests begin to take hold of the nation and become the primary factors in decision making.

An example of this can clearly be seen during the brief months following the martyrdom of the Commander of the Faithful (a). Imam Hassan (a) readied his army and mobilized against Muawiya. Yet through bribery Muawiya was able to turn many in Imam Hassan's (a) camp against the Imam (a). Individuals as close as the Imam's (a) cousin, Ubaydullah ibn al-Abbas, turned against him. Historians record that there were individuals in the camp who corresponded with Muawiya and offered to capture the Imam (a) and hand him over to Umayyad hands. This incident illustrates how materialism seeped into the ranks of Imam Hassan's (a) army and caused a shift the nation's course.

Add to this the great moral corruption that the Umayyads spread in order to kill the nation's conscience. All this lead to the Muslim nation's submission to the rule of an individual like Yazid, despite knowing that it displeases God and His Messenger (s). Imam Hussain (a) declared this unequivocally to al-Hurr and his battalion when they met on the outskirts of Kufa. He said,

أيّها الناس إنّ رسول الله (ص) قال: من رأى سلطانا جائراً مستحلاً لحرم الله ناكثاً لعهد الله مخالفاً لسنة رسول الله صلى الله عليه وآله وسلم يعمل في عباد الله بالاثم والعدوان فلم يغيّر عليه بفعل ولا قول كان حقا على الله أن يدخله مدخله

O' people! The Messenger of God (s) said, 'Whoever sees an oppressive ruler who freely commits what God forbade, violates his oaths, acts contrary to the tradition of the Messenger of God (s), and treats the servants of God with offense and

transgression, but does not rebuke him by either word or deed,
God has obliged Himself to admit into the same abode.'

أَلَا وَإِنَّ هٰؤُلَاءِ قَدْ لَزِمُوا طَاعَةَ الشَّيْطَانِ وَتَرَكُوا طَاعَةَ الرَّحْمَنِ

وَأَظْهَرُوا الْفَسَادَ وَعَطَّلُوا الْحُدُودَ وَاسْتَأْثَرُوا بِالْفَيْءِ وَأَحَلُّوا حَرَامَ

اللهِ وَحَرَّمُوا حَلَالَهُ، وَأَنَا أَحَقُّ مِمَّنْ غَيَّرَ

Surely, they [i.e. the Umayyad clan] have attached themselves
to Satan, abandoned obedience to the All Merciful, professed
corruption, obstructed judgment, hoarded wealth, permitted
what God forbade, and forbade what God permitted. I am
more deserving [of being followed] then those who have
changed [God's message]![12]

Second, the Umayyads used force and oppression to enforce
their plans. This can be seen clearly through the actions and
personalities of their governors. Ziyab ibn Sumaya,[13]
Muawiya's governor over Iraq, was particularly gruesome in
his tactics of persecution and torture. He was the main cause
behind the murder of some of the notable companions of the
Holy Prophet (s) and Imam Ali (a), like Hijr ibn 'Adi, who
pledged their allegiance to the Holy Household (a). Ziyad
would execute citizens for mere suspicion that they may be

---

[12] Al-Hakeem, *Thawrat al-Hussain (a)*, 53.

[13] Otherwise known as Ziyad ibn Abeeh (literally, Ziyad "the son of his father" –
a reference to a bastard son whose father is un-known). Historians dispute the
identity of his father with some identifying him as Ubayd al-Thaqafi and others
identifying him as Abu Sufyan, which would make him a member of the Umayyad
clan. Muawiya had personally claimed Ziyad as his brother and appointed him as
governor of Kufa and Basra. –Eds.

followers of Imam Ali (a). These tactics ensured that the nation lived in terror of Umayyad persecution even for the smallest of offenses.

With these two tactics, Umayyad authorities were able to tighten their grasp on the Muslim nation and ensure that people's will and honor were broken beyond repair. People of the time were generally split into four groups. A group was paralyzed by the terror of the Umayyads and their gruesome tactics. Another group was under the influence of personal desires and Umayyad bribes. A third group was so submerged by Umayyad propaganda that they believed Muawiya was the rightful successor of the Holy Prophet (s). This group were unwittingly brainwashed such that they did not know of Imam Hussain (a) and thought that he was simply one of the Kharijites. A fourth group considered itself the nation's elites, waiting for the opportune time to rise against the Umayyads simply so they can grasp power for themselves. This group neither cared for the corruption and deviance instilled by the Umayyads, nor were willing to sacrifice anything for the religion of Islam. They were opportunists who were waiting for the tides to turn in their favor.

The nation was living in a state where it could not consciously take the appropriate stance. It lost sight of Islam's sublime teachings and principles which freed the nation from slavery to idols, wealth, and desires. It was shackled, unable to follow the path drawn by the Holy Prophet (s) towards the great honor of servitude and proximity to the Almighty.

Awakening the Conscience

Imam Hussain's (a) stance and tragedy shook the Muslim nation to its core. Although this immaculate stance did not result in an immediate and absolute change within the nation, it did achieve a grand triumph that allowed Muslims to return to the teachings and ethics of their Holy Prophet (s). As Muslims saw the greatest of morals embodied in Imam Hussain (a) and his companions on the plains of Karbala, they took them as role models and were reoriented to Islam's true teachings. We see this in the following principles which the tragedy of Karbala brought back to life in the Muslim nation.

The tragedy of Karbala reminded the nation of the meaning of sacrifice for the sake of truth and principle. It reminded them of how the Muslims only a few decades earlier sacrificed all they had for the sake of their faith and their Lord.

The tragedy of Karbala shattered the shackles of terror that the Umayyads had subdued the nation with. This can be seen clearly in the many revolts that began to emerge after Imam Hussain's (a) stance.

The tragedy of Karbala showcased the sublime values of Islam which were the primary focus of Imam Hussain's (a) movement. It showcased justice, loyalty, patience, honor, dignity, and reliance on God in all matters. Imam Hussain (a) etched these values into the conscience of the nation through the eternal memory of his stance.

The tragedy of Karbala solidified the principle of austerity in this world and certainty in the hereafter as the abode of blessings and happiness for the faithful. Imam Hussain (a) would say,

إني لا أرى الموت إلا سعادة والحياة مع الظالمين إلا برما

I do not see anything in death but satisfaction, while living with the oppressors is nothing but weariness.[14]

The tragedy of Karbala instilled the concept of absolute servitude and surrender to God. No matter what tragedy befell them, the Holy Household submitted to God's will and accepted His judgment. After the martyrdom of his children, family members, and companions, Imam Hussain (a) would stand on the plains of Karbala and say,

صبرا على قضائك يا رب، لا إله سواك، يا غياث المستغيثين. مالي ربّ سواك، و لا معبود غيرك. صبرا على حكمك.

[Grant us] patience with Your judgment. There is no God but You, O' aid of those who call [upon You] for aid. I have no Lord but You and I do not worship anyone beside You, [so grant me] patience with Your judgment.[15]

These statements – which are not made except by God's greatest servants – take hold of a believer's heart and ensure that its greatest role model is none but an Immaculate Imam (a).

This is how Imam Hussain (a) achieved his decisive triumph through his stance against corruption and deviance. It was a triumph that breathed life into the Muslim nation and safeguarded the last of God's messages to humanity.

---

[14] Al-Hilli, *Mutheer al-Ahzan*, 32.

[15] Al-Muqarram, *Maqtal al-Hussain (a)*, 356.

ETHICS IN IMAM HUSSAIN'S (A) MOVEMENT

The ethical dimension was an essential element in Imam Hussain's (a) movement. As we've discussed, the primary goal of the movement was to shock and reawaken the moral conscience of the Muslim nation. Probably one of the root causes of the absence or death of one's conscience is a defect in the ethics of the community. A community that is built on ethics and lives in accordance with ethics is a community that is alive in its conscience, and thus cannot be defeated. A community that has left its ethics, however, is a dead community no matter how large it becomes and how great its resources.

This ethical dimension is in fact one of the most important elements of all prophetic missions. The Holy Prophet (s) considered teaching ethics as a focal point of his mission,

$$ إنّا بعثت لأتمّم مكارم الأخلاق $$

Indeed, I have been sent to perfect the best of ethics.[16]

The most effective way to conquer and control a community is by killing its moral conscience. That does not happen except by ridding the community of its principles, values, and ethics. A community that lives by the principles of honesty, loyalty, sacrifice, courage, and generosity is one that cannot be dominated, controlled, or conquered. But when such a community loses these principles and values, its moral conscience dies along with any motivation to live a noble life. Such a community will accept anything in order to ensure its interests and desires.

---

[16] Al-Majlisi, *Bihar Al-Anwar*, 16:210.

The focus of the Umayyads was to destroy the morals and ethics of the Islamic community. This is evidenced by Yazid's first speech upon becoming Caliph after his father Muawiya, luring people in through time off, money, relaxation, and luxury:

> ...*Muawiya used to take you on expeditions through the seas... and I will not be taking you on such expeditions... and keep you in the lands of the Romans during the winter, and I will not keep any of you in such lands in such harsh times... and he would give you your payments in thirds, but I will give that to you in whole lump sums.*[17]

A clearer example is seen in the words of Ibn Ziyad, Yazid's governor in Kufa, as he stated the arguments to people to go out and fight Imam Hussain (a):

> *You found the Umayyads as your hearts please. This is Yazid, you know him as one with a good, solid, praiseworthy path... he honors people and makes them rich with wealth... he increased your sustenance hundreds-fold... he is now ordering me to give you all these riches and take you out to wage war on his enemy Hussain... so listen to him and obey this command.*[18]

Imam Hussain (a) would describe this painful reality that turned the Muslims from people who sought God and fought for His cause to people who are bought and sold with money. They lost their moral conscience and their will, selling their

---

[17] Al-Hakeem, *Thawrat Al-Hussain (a)*, 141. Citing: Ibn Katheer, *al-Bidaya*, 8:153.

[18] Ibid. Citing: Al-Muqarram, *Maqtal Al-Hussain (a)*, 198-199.

afterlife for their limited pleasures in this world. The Imam
(a) would tell his companions,

إن الناس عبيد الدنيا، والدين لعق على ألسنتهم، يحوطونه ما
درّت معايشهم، فإذا محّصوا بالبلاء قلّ الديّانون.

*People are slaves to this world and religion is only words on
their tongues. They hold on to it so long as their means of
living are se-cured. But if they are tested with tribulation the
true believers will be less.*

أما بعد، فقد نزل بنا من الأمر ما قد ترون. وإن الدنيا قد
تغيّرت وتنكّرت وأدبر معروفها،

*You see what has come upon us. This world has changed and
be-come corrupted. What was commonly known as right has
withered away.*

ولم يبق منها إلا صبابة كصبابة الإناء، وخسيس عيش كالمرعى
الوبيل. ألا ترون إلى الحق لا يعمل به، وإلى الباطل لا يتناهى
عنه،

*Nothing is left but a trace like the last few droplets of an
empty cup and a lowly life like a tainted unwholesome pas-
ture. Do you not see that truth [and righteousness] are not
being acted upon [and abided by]? And that falsehood is not
being discouraged?*

ليرغب المؤمن في لقاء ربه محقّا، فإني لا أرى الموت إلا سعادة،
والحياة مع الظالمين إلا برما.

So let the believer long for meeting his Lord. For I do not see death [for God's sake] except as happiness, and life with these oppressors except as weariness.[19]

The Imam (a) places his thumb on the wound. The corruption of ethics and the lack of moral values are the reasons that many Muslims stopped caring about religion and focused their attention only on matters of this world.

The Holy Quran and the noble narrations point to the importance of the ethical dimension of the life of the community, its advancement, and its happiness. The verses and narrations discuss the extent of harm that is brought to mankind by losing ethics. It moves people away from the grounds of nobility that God established for us. Furthermore, that loss changes individuals from servants of God to servants of this finite world, where pleasures are fleeting and all life ends with death.

Imam Hussain's (a) movement was focused on establishing a number of ethical principles. The goal was to broadcast these principles through the movement of Imam Hussain (a) and the effect it would have on the people in all of its dimensions. Similarly, these ethical principles were established in such a manner that they can be pointed to by humanity, across all generations, and benefit from the light that is the movement of Hussain (a).

---

[19] Al-Muqarram, *Maqtal Al-Hussain (a)*, Pg. 192-193. Citing: Al-Tabari, *Tareekh Al-Tabari*, 4:305; Al-Andalusi, *Al-'Uqd Al-Fareed*, 2:312; and Al-Asbahani, *Hulliyat Al-Awliya'*, 2:39.

PRACTICAL EXAMPLES IN HIS MOVEMENT

It is not possible to confine all of the ethical principles that Imam Hussain (a) practiced and established through his blessed movement. However, we can point to some of the most important principles that no community should neglect. By holding on to the following principles and values, our communities can advance, move forward, and work along the godly path that God wished for humanity.

Honesty and Transparency

Honesty in our dealing with one another is among the most significant ethical principles that Imam Hussain (a) established. From the beginning of his movement, the Imam (a) did not give people false hope in spoils of war, well-being, or victory. Instead, he went against the norm of most political leaders who only cared for rallying the masses without regard to the reality facing the people, their conscience, and their intentions. Imam Hussain (a) was clear from the very beginning in the first announcement of his movement before leaving Mecca,

الحمد لله وما شاء الله ولا قوة إلا بالله وصلى الله على رسوله،

خط الموت على ولد آدم مخط القلادة على جيد الفتاة

Praise be to God, everything is by His will, there is no strength save in God, and praise be upon His Messenger. Death is to the son of Adam like a necklace is to the neck of a young lady.

وما أولهني الى أسلافي اشتياق يعقوب الى يوسف وخير لي
مصرع أنا لاقيه... ألا ومن كان فينا باذلا مهجته موطنا على لقاء
الله نفسه، فليرحل معنا فإني راحل مصبحا إن شاء الله

O' how I long for my forefathers, like the longing of Jacob to Joseph. And I will meet the best of ends. Whoever would sacrifice his heart for us and is determined to meet God, let him journey with us for I am departing tomorrow morning God willing.[20]

Imam Hussain (a) did not trick or force anyone to go on his journey with him. He did not use the methods of the Umayyads in coercing people to fight or buying people's loyalty to mobilize them against the grandson of their Prophet (s). Honesty and transparency are the features that distinguished Imam Hussain (a) and his companions from the rest of people. Initially, there was a huge group of people that followed Imam Hussain (a) thinking that he was going to take over government, as many matters were established for him completely. But then came the news of Muslim Ibn Aqeel, the ambassador of Imam Hussain (a) who was betrayed and executed in Kufa. Imam Hussain (a) did not keep this news from the people; rather, he shared it with them. He gave them the choice to stay or leave. Those initial large numbers dwindled down to a small group of loyal companions.

Imam Hussain (a) could have used the tragic news to reinforce his position and gain recruits by promising them riches and wealth. But that was not his character – he was honest

---

[20] Ibid. 166.

with his men. As the heir of the Holy Prophet (s), there was no doubt he would establish these ethical principles and deal with reality instead of fraud and deception. This was the difference between the Holy Household and the forces that stood against them. Even on the eve of the tenth of Muharram, he would gather his companions and family members and say,

أما بعد، فإني لا أعلم أصحابا أولى ولا خيرا من أصحابي، ولا أهل بيت أبرّ ولا أوصل من أهل بيتي، فجزاكم الله عني جميعا.

Surely, I don't know of any companions more worthy than my companions, nor a family more pure and rooted than my own. May God reward you all on my behalf.

و قد أخبرني جدي رسول الله (ص) بأني سأساق إلى العراق فأنزل أرضا يقال لها عمورا وكربلاء وفيها أستشهد، وقد قرب الموعد.

My grandfather, the Messenger of God (s), had told me that I would be steered towards Iraq and camp in a land called Amora and Karbala, and that in it I will be martyred. Surely, that time has come.

ألا وإني أظنّ يومنا من هؤلاء الأعداء غدا، وإني قد أذنت لكم فانطلقوا جميعا في حل، ليس عليكم مني ذمام.

I see that the day they will transgress against us is tomorrow. I give you leave to take off in the night, there is no blame or fault on you if you leave.

و هذا اللّيل قد غشيكم فاتخذوه جملا، وليأخذ كل رجل منكم بيد رجل من أهل بيتي.

The night has shrouded you, so ride into it. Let each one of you take a member of my household [as a guardian].

فجزاكم الله جميعا خيرا، وتفرّقوا في سوادكم ومدائنكم، فإن القوم إنما يطلبوني، ولو أصابوني لذهلوا عن طلب غيري.

May God reward you all. Disperse in the lands and cities, for surely these people ask for me, and if they get to me they will be too preoccupied to go after anyone else.[21]

The Imam (a) relieved companions and family members of their duties towards him and gave them permission to leave. He did not coerce or compel anyone to stay by his side and face that tragic end. Yet despite that, we find that this small honorable group refused to leave the Imam (a) and was determined to live and die beside him. Through this honorable stand, Imam Hussain (a) proved to us the necessity of leaders to live with their populace in a state of honesty and transparency. Leaders must not take advantage of their followers and supporters or take them for granted. This is extremely important in the validity of the movement and its advancement.

Sacrifice

Islam has given great focus to sacrifice and considers it among the noblest of ethical principles. It is enough that we see the Holy Quran point to this ethical virtue when God

---

[21] Ibid. 513.

commends the Ansar for their stance with the Muhajireen and the sacrifices they made. God says,

وَالَّذِينَ تَبَوَّءُوا الدَّارَ وَالْإِيمَانَ مِن قَبْلِهِمْ يُحِبُّونَ مَنْ هَاجَرَ إِلَيْهِمْ وَلَا يَجِدُونَ فِي صُدُورِهِمْ حَاجَةً مِّمَّا أُوتُوا وَيُؤْثِرُونَ عَلَىٰ أَنفُسِهِمْ وَلَوْ كَانَ بِهِمْ خَصَاصَةٌ ۚ وَمَن يُوقَ شُحَّ نَفْسِهِ فَأُولَٰئِكَ هُمُ الْمُفْلِحُونَ

[They are as well] for those who were settled in the land and [abided] in faith before them, who love those who migrate toward them, and do not find in their breasts any privation for that which is given to them, but prefer [the Immigrants] to themselves, though poverty be their own lot. And those who are saved from their own greed—it is they who are the felicitous.[22]

The history of Islam is filled, from its very beginning, with wondrous stories that show that this particularity was present in the midst of the Muslims. Many of them espoused this honorable moral trait. However, the weakening of ethical principles came as a result of abandoning the teachings of Prophet Muhammad (s) and turning away from the righteous guardians of the faith – the Household of the Holy Prophet (s). The many conquests that were undertaken and the indulgence in wealth and worldly pleasures could not cover up the moral decay that had set in. Ethics were further weakened by the Umayyads' role in dissolving and ultimately eliminating the Muslims' adherence and identification with moral virtues. This specific trait was weakened just like many other ethical virtues.

---

[22] The Holy Quran, 59:9.

The school of Ashura came to reestablish this virtue. The Holy Household (a) struggled in this pursuit with Imam Hussain (a) and his companions at the forefront of this struggle. They sacrificed themselves for the sake of raising the word of God. This is in addition to some of the phenomena that human beings cannot fully comprehend and that can only be produced by that Holy Household (a). That household was the one that sacrificed for three consecutive days, as it fed the poor, the orphan, and the prisoner and remained hungry. This is the household that birthed the likes of al-Abbas, a hero who sacrificed for his brother and master Imam Hussain (a). He would head to the banks of the Euphrates River only to fill a satchel of water to quench the thirst of the women and children who had been without water for three days. Finally arriving, he kneeled down to take a sip of water. Despite his own thirst, he remembered the thirst of Imam Hussain (a) and the rest of the family. As he let the water go, it is reported that he said to himself,

يا نفس من بعد الحسين هوني *** و بعده لا كنت أن تكوني

هذا الحسين وارد المنون *** و تشربين بارد المعين

تالله ما هذا فعال ديني *** و لا فعال صادق اليقين

O' self, [be second] to al-Hussain (a)
As after him, it matters not whether you be or not
This is Hussain (a) approaching death
And you [dare] drink sweet, cold water?
By God, this is not an act of my faith
Nor an act of a man of true certainty

Al-Abbas did not drink in consolation of his brother al-Hussain (a) and his family. Who could compare to the sacrifice and consolation of al-Abbas (a) who would prevent himself from drinking because his brother did not drink? He put his brother before himself and proceeded to return to the camp to get him water. Unfortunately, he did not reach Hussain (a) or his family because he was killed by the treachery of Yazid's soldiers. This is one of many illustrations of sacrifice in the movement of Imam Hussain (a) and his companions.

Chivalry

Of the most noble and honorable virtues of Imam Hussain (a) was chivalry. He illustrated the highest forms of chivalry in his blessed revolution, which can be summarized in the following:

Imam Hussain (a) gave water to his enemies and their horses. The battalion of al-Hur al-Riyahi was ordered to stop the Imam (a) in Karbala before reaching Kufa. This battalion, loyal to Yazid, reached Imam Hussain (a) in a dire state of thirst and dehydration. They had come to stop the Imam (a). Nonetheless, when Imam Hussain (a) witnessed the thirst of his enemies, he ordered his companies to give water to the soldiers along with their horses. Who could compare to this show of chivalry? A man sees his enemies in such a weak state, knowing their plans against him, and despite that he chooses to quench their thirst.

Al-Hur al-Riyahi was responsible for much of the suffering that Imam Hussain (a), his companions, and family initially endured in Karbala. Regardless, the Imam (a) welcomed al-

Hur's repentance to God when he came forward on the Day of Ashura asking for forgiveness. On that day, al-Hur looked at the two camps and saw Heaven and Hell. Pacing back and forth, pale in the face, he made up his mind and made his way to the camp of Imam Hussain (a) – he chose Heaven. Coming down from his horse, with his head bowed in shame, he called out: "O' God to you I turn, so accept my repentance. I have frightened the hearts of your loved ones and the children of your Prophet. O' Abu Abdullah, I am repenting... is there repentance for me?" Imam Hussain (a) replied,

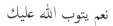

Yes. God will accept your repentance.[23]

This was the heart of Hussain (a). This was the heart so dear to the Messenger of God (s). A heart full of mercy, even to those who stopped him in Karbala. How could Hussain (a) be any other way, when God made him the spiritual heir to the one sent as a Mercy to all Mankind?

Imam Hussain (a) was adamant on not starting the battle. He did not permit any of his companions to launch any arrows or spears at the enemy until the enemy launched first. Omar ibn Saad released the first arrow saying, "Witness for me before the Prince [Yazid] that I was the first to cast his arrow!" At that point, Imam Hussain (a) permitted his companions to respond. This was a true stance of chivalry and honor. Imam Hussain (a) could have easily taken preemptive measures and killed a number of Omar ibn Saad's soldiers; however, he refused to do anything of the like. His objective

---

[23] Al-Muqarram, *Maqtal Al-Hussain (a)*, 182.

was to establish value and virtue and he made a point not to be the one who started the fight. Principle and virtue were victorious on that day.

The Imam (a) continues to establish and spread these moral values like loyalty, sacrifice, bravery, and nobility, amongst others. He is able to do so due to the eternal nature of his movement. As long as he is remembered, these virtues and values will also be remembered. The memory of Hussain (a) will remain as long as this world exists. Imam Hussain's (a) words ring true to this day. He said,

$$إنه من لحق بي استشهد معي ومن تخلف لم يبلغ الفتح$$

Surely, whoever follows me will be martyred alongside me. Whoever does not follow me will not witness the triumph.[24]

What triumph is greater than being eternal in memory and principle? These ethical virtues and godly principles will remain forever in his remembrance. Let every human being live in the love of Hussain (a) as he longs to follow his example of values and ethics.

---

[24] Al-Saffar, *Basa'er al-Darajat*, 501.

LET THE WEEPERS WEEP

Ibrahim ibn Abu Mahmood narrated that Imam al-Rida (a) said,

إن المحرم شهر كان أهل الجاهلية يحرمون فيه القتال،
فاستحلت فيه دماؤنا، وهتكت فيه حرمتنا، وسبي فيه ذرارينا
ونساؤنا، وأضرمت النيران في مضاربنا، وانتهب ما فيها من
ثقلنا، ولم ترع لرسول الله (صلى الله عليه وآله) حرمة في
أمرنا. إن يوم الحسين أقرح جفوننا، وأسبل دموعنا، وأذل
عزيزنا، بأرض كرب وبلاء، أورثتنا الكرب والبلاء، إلى يوم
الانقضاء

Muharram was a month in which the people of the Age of Ignorance forbade fighting. Still, in that month [the spilling of] our blood was permitted, our sanctity was desecrated, our women and children were taken captive, our camps were burned and plundered, and the sanctity of the Messenger of God (s) was not respected in regards to us [his family]. The day of al-Hussain (a) [and his martyrdom] has ulcerated our eyes, spilt our tears, and humiliated the honorable amongst

*us. It was in the land of karb [distress] and bala' [adversity]
that has endowed us with [enough] distress and adversity until the Day of [Judgment].*

فعلى مثل الحسين فليبك الباكون، فإن البكاء يحط الذنوب
العظام ...كان أبي (صلوات الله عليه) إذا دخل شهر المحرم لا
يرى ضاحكا، وكانت الكآبة تغلب عليه حتى يمضي منه عشرة
أيام، فإذا كان يوم العاشر كان ذلك اليوم يوم مصيبته وحزنه
وبكائه، ويقول: هو اليوم الذي قتل فيه الحسين (صلوات الله
عليه)

*So for the likes of al-Hussain (a) let the weepers weep! Surely,
weeping [for al-Hussain (a)] atones for the greater sins!...
My father [Imam al-Kadhim (a)] would not be seen laughing
once the month of Muharram begins. Grief would overcome
him for ten days. The tenth day would be his day of tragedy,
sorrow, and weeping. He would say, 'This is the day in which
al-Hussain (a) was murdered!'* [1]

Every year, we relive the tragedy of Imam Hussain (a) during
Ashura! We do not simply remember and commemorate.
Muharram is not a season of memories for us. Rather, we
relive those tragedies every year. Ashura is not a historical
event, but a living affair and principle.

This is seen in the despair that the pure hearted live during
this season, regardless of their faith or background. What
other tragedy can inspire so much emotion in mankind! No

---

[1] Al-Sadouq, *al-Amali*, 190.

matter how grief stricken we are at the loss of a loved one, no matter how much we may initially feel that life cannot continue without them, ultimately, over time, that sorrow begins to fade and life returns to a normal pace. It is rare that a deceased's memory and sorrow is carried for years.

However, when it comes to the tragedy of Imam Hussain (a), its sorrow has lived for centuries. We relive that tragedy every year as if it is occurring before our eyes for the first time. The sorrow of this tragedy has survived in the hearts of the millions who continue, despite its distant occurrence, to commemorate and relive the memory every year.. It is not an invented or shallow sorrow either. It is a deep and true sorrow.

Thus, we understand that there is a divine mystery in our sorrow for Imam Hussain (a). The closer an individual grows to God, the Messenger (s), and the Holy Household (a), the more this mystery becomes evident to them. This is the truth that Imam al-Sajjad (a) lived. One narration tells us that Imam al-Sadiq (a) said,

وأما علي بن الحسين فبكى على الحسين (عليهما السلام) عشرين سنة [أو أربعين سنة]، وما وضع بين يديه طعام إلا بكى، حتى قال له مولى له: جعلت فداك يا بن رسول الله، إني أخاف عليك أن تكون من الهالكين. قال: إنما أشكو بثي وحزني إلى الله، وأعلم من الله مالا تعلمون، إني لم أذكر مصرع بني فاطمة إلا خنقتني لذلك عبرة

As for Ali ibn al-Hussain (a), he wept for al-Hussain (a) for twenty years [or forty years, according to some traditions].

*Whenever a meal was placed before him, he wept. A servant
of his said to him, 'May I be sacrificed for you, O' son of the
Messenger of God (s)! I fear for you, lest you perish [out of
sorrow]!' He replied, "I complain of my anguish and grief
only to Allah. I know from Allah what you do not know."*
[2] *Surely, I never recalled the demise of the children of Fatima
(a) without being choked by tears for it.* [3]

The mystery lies in his statement, "I know from Allah what
you do not know." It signifies that there is a mystery. Not
everyone can know and understand the divine secret that was
rooted in Imam Hussain's (a) tragedy. There are other narrations that refer to this secret. As Imam Hussain (a) described
it himself,

أنا قتيل العبرة، لا يذكرني مؤمن إلا استعبر

*I am the martyr of tears. No believer will remember me with-
out shedding a tear.* [4]

Why is it that we shed our tears whenever we hear his name?
Why does his memory and sorrow not fade away like the
memory and sorrow of all the loved ones we have lost? Why
do we continue to live this tragedy that took place almost
fourteen centuries ago?

We will try to shed some light on this mystery but must acquiesce that no complete and exhaustive explanation can be
found. Divine mysteries are not so easily solved. We will lay
out some possibilities and provide some evidence that may

---

[2] The Holy Quran, 12:86.

[3] Al-Sadouq, *al-Amali*, 204.

[4] Al-Sadouq, *al-Amali*, 200.

bring this mystery closer to being unraveled in the mind of the reader. You will see that everything we will provide will be supported by Quranic verse and noble traditions. Again, truly unraveling this mystery requires the true devotion and faith that allows for divine inspiration.

WEEPING FOR AL-HUSSAIN (A)

Looking at the noble traditions, we see that weeping over Imam Hussain's (a) tragedy was not specific for one group or one era. Rather, his tragedy has been a cause of sorrow and weeping since ancient times and will be until the end of times.

The Weeping of the Holy Prophet (s)

The are many narrations that mention the weeping of the Holy Prophet Muhammad (s) over the tragedy of his grandson. He did so at Imam Hussain's (a) birth and on countless other occasions.

The Holy Prophet's (s) aunt Sophia narrated that when Imam Hussain (a) was born, she handed him to The Holy Prophet (s) who kissed him on his forehead and handed him back saying,

$$لعن الله قوما هم قاتلوك يا بني$$

May God curse the people who will murder you, my son!

Sophia asked, "May my mother and father be sacrificed for you! Who will kill him?" The Holy Prophet (s) replied,

$$بقية الفئة الباغية من بني أمية لعنهم الله$$

The remainder of the rebellious faction of the Banu Umayya, may God curse them.[5]

There are numerous other narrations that speak of the Holy Prophet's (s) foretelling and weeping over Imam Hussain's (a) tragedy.

At first glance, we may think that such an event is normal. The Holy Prophet (s) was told of the massacre of his grandson, to which he was undoubtedly moved emotionally. However, this cannot be the sole explanation for his weeping. After all, he was also told of the high status and rewards that Imam Hussain (a) would receive in reward for his sacrifice. That would have certainly alleviated some of the sorrow of the tragedy. And if that sorrow was purely emotional, it would have faded away like all other emotional sorrows we experience in our lives. However, the Holy Prophet (s) continuously recounted that tragedy and wept for it.

This all serves as evidence that there was something greater than a grandfather's sorrow for his grandson. This is especially true when we take into account the character of the Holy Prophet (s), a model of patience and strength who persevered through any hardship and acted only in accordance to divine will and command. There must therefore be a mystery beyond familial affection behind the Holy Prophet's (s) continuous remembrance and constant weeping for Imam Hussain (a).

---

[5] Al-Sadouq, *al-Amali*, 199.

The Weeping of Other Prophets (a)

Even if we explain the weeping of our Holy Prophet Muhammad (s) as an emotional reaction to the news of his grandson's tragedy, we must still find an explanation for the weeping of all the other prophets over the tragedy of Imam Hussain (a). There are numerous traditions, coming from credible sources that reference the weeping of these prophets over the tragedy. Why would they weep for a tragedy of an individual they have not met and who has not even been born yet? Why would they weep when they were countless centuries removed from the tragedy?

One narration tells us of the sorrow of Prophet Abraham over the tragedy of Imam Hussain (a). Abraham was tested by the divine command to slaughter his son Ishmael. When Abraham found the strength to obey God's command and have faith in God's judgment, God Almighty decreed that a great ram be sacrificed in Ishmael's place. After this incident, the following conversation took place between Abraham and God,

فأوحى الله عز وجل إليه: يا إبراهيم من أحب خلقي إليك؟

فقال: يا رب ما خلقت خلقا هو أحب إلى من حبيبك محمد

(ص) فأوحى الله عز وجل إليه: يا إبراهيم أفهو أحب إليك أو

نفسك؟ قال: بل هو أحب إلى من نفسي قال: فولده أحب

إليك أو ولدك؟ قال: بل ولده

God Almighty revealed to him, 'O' Abraham, who is the most beloved of My creation to you?' He responded, 'O' Lord,

You have not created a creation more beloved to me than Your beloved Muhammad (s).' God Almighty revealed to him, 'O' Abraham, is he more beloved to you or yourself?' He replied, 'Rather, he is more beloved to me than myself.' [God] said, 'Is his son more beloved to you or your son?' [Abraham] said, 'Rather, his son.'

قال: فذبح ولده ظلماً على أعدائه أوجع لقلبك أو ذبح ولدك بيدك في طاعتي؟ قال: يا رب بل ذبحه على أيدي أعدائه أوجع لقلبي

[God] said, 'So is the murder of his son unjustly at the hands of his enemies more painful to your heart, or the killing of your son by your hand in obedience to Me?' He said, 'O' Lord, his murder at the hands of his enemies is more painful to my heart.'

قال: يا إبراهيم فإن طائفة تزعم أنها من أمه محمد (ص) ستقتل الحسين عليه السلام ابنه من بعده ظلماً وعدواناً كما يذبح الكبش فيستوجبون بذلك سخطي

[God] said, 'O' Abraham, a group that claims to be from the nation of Muhammad (s) will kill his [grandson] al-Hussain (a) after [Muhammad's (s)] passing, unjustly and out of transgression, like the slaughtering of sheep. They will incur My wrath through this.'

فجزع إبراهيم عليه السلام لذلك وتوجع قلبه وأقبل يبكي فأوحى الله عز وجل إليه: يا إبراهيم قد فديت جزعك على ابنك

إسماعيل لو ذبحته بيدك بجزعك على الحسين عليه السلام وقتله

وأوجبت لك ارفع درجات أهل الثواب على المصائب فذلك

قول الله عز وجل: (وفديناه بذبح عظيم)

Abraham despaired for this, his heart was pained, and he begin to weep. God Almighty revealed to him, 'O' Abraham, you have ransomed your despair for your son Ishmael had you killed him with your hands, with your despair for al-Hussain (a) and his murder. You have earned the greatest levels of reward for that.' And those are the words of God Almighty, 'Then We ransomed him with a great sacrifice.' [6]

There are many similar narrations that speak of the prophets and their sorrow for Imam Hussain's (a) tragedy, all narrated from credible and authenticated sources. Many of these narrations can be found in the book *Kamil al-Ziyarat*, one of the most highly regarded books of tradition in our school of thought. The reader will find there the stories of weeping by Adam, Noah, Ishmael, Zacharias, and others.

What is the mystery that made all these pure individuals weep for Imam Hussain's (a) tragedy – a tragedy that had not yet occurred? What gives his tragedy more gravity and sorrow in their hearts than the trials that they experience themselves?

The Weeping of all Creation

We have seen that the purest of mankind wept for Imam Hussain (a) since the beginning of human history. Now, let

---

[6] Al-Sadouq, *'Uyun Akhbad al-Rida (a)*, 2:187.

us turn to the rest of creation and see how they too wept for that tragedy.

We find in our traditions countless narrations that speak of the weeping of creation for this tragedy. Again, such narrations come from credible sources and can be found in the books of all Muslim schools of thought. We can categorize these traditions as follows.

The Angels. Al-Fudayl ibn Yasar narrates that Imam al-Sadiq (a) said,

مالكم لا تأتونه - يعني قبر الحسين (عليه السلام) - فان أربعة
آلاف ملك يبكون عند قبره إلى يوم القيامة

Why do you not go to it [i.e. the grave of al-Hussain (a)]? Surely, four thousand angels weep over his grave until the Day of Resurrection. [7]

The Jinn. It is also narrated that the jinn wept for Imam Hussain (a) and recited in verse,

What would you say if the Prophet (s) asked you,
'What have you done, and you are the last of nations
With my family, brothers, and honored friends?
You have taken some prisoners while others laid soaked in blood!' [8]

---

[7] Al-Qummi, *Kamil al-Ziyarat*, 171.
[8] Ibid, 193.

The Heavens and Earth. It is narrated that Imam Ali (a) was sitting at the mosque one day with his companions surrounding him when his son Imam Hussain (a) walked in. Imam Ali (a) put his hand over his son's head and said,

يا بني ان الله عبر أقواما بالقران، فقال: (فما بكت عليهم السماء والأرض وما كانوا منظرين)، وأيم الله ليقتلنك بعدي ثم تبكيك السماء والأرض

My son, God disparaged communities in the Quran by saying, 'So neither the sky wept for them, nor the earth; nor were they granted any respite.' By God, they will kill you after [my passing], then the sky and the earth will weep for you! [9]

Some accounts explain how the heavens and earth wept. For example, the account of Ali ibn Mushir al-Qurashi states, "My grandma told me that she had lived when al-Hussain ibn Ali (a) was murdered. She said, 'It was a year and nine months where the sky was like a clot, like blood, and the sun could not be seen.'" [10]

There are additional accounts stating that the sky rained dark-red blood, and that whenever a stone was lifted off the earth, there was blood underneath it. Moreover, some traditions indicate that the heavens and the earth wept for Imam Hussain (a) even before he was born. As one supplication taught by Imam al-Askari (a) states,

---

[9] Al-Qummi, *Kamil al-Ziyarat*, 180.

[10] Al-Qummi, *Kamil al-Ziyarat*, 182.

اللهم إني أسألك بحق المولود في هذا اليوم الموعود بشهادته قبل
استهلاله وولادته، بكته السماء ومن فيها والأرض ومن عليها،
ولما يطأ لابتيها قتيل العبرة

O' God, I ask you by the right of the one born on this day;
the one whose martyrdom was promised before his birth or the
cries of his birth. He was wept for by the heavens and those
in it, and the earth and its inhabitants before he touched
them. He is the martyr of tears.... [11]

Some Conclusions

There are three important conclusions that we can draw from
the foregoing discussion.

First, the traditions regarding weeping for al-Hussain (a) are
so abundant and diverse that there can be no doubt as to their
authenticity. The fact that we may not be able to fully comprehend, or believe that the weeping took place does not
mean that it did not in fact occur. This is especially true
knowing that the source are the progeny of our Holy Prophet
(s), and that the narrators include individuals from all back-
grounds and schools of thought. Even if a few of these narrations were rejected, the great quantity and variety of traditions that laud weeping over Imam Hussain (a) places the issue at a level beyond doubt.

Second, weeping for Imam Hussain (a) is not a phenomena
limited to mankind. All creation wept for his tragedy, a trag-

---

[11] Al-Tusi, *Misbah al-Mutahajjid*, 826.

edy that forms a common ground for all creation. This highlights the link amongst all creation and the centrality of mankind amongst them – especially the greatest of mankind and all creation, the Holy Prophet (s) and his blessed household (a).

Third, weeping for Imam Hussain (a) is not limited to a certain place or time. The weeping we mentioned was not limited to the days, months, and years following the tragedy. Rather, it began countless centuries before the occurrence of the event and continues centuries after. This shows us that the tragedy of Imam Hussain (a) had an impact on all creation, irrespective of time and place. It was and continues to be a central event for all creation, inspiring grief without bound. This grief continues to be a divine mystery and will be so until the Day of Resurrection.

THE CREATIONAL CONNECTION

Perhaps one of the reasons as to why the tragedy of Imam Hussain (a) has such a great impact on creation is because of the general effect of human action on all creation. Mankind is the greatest of God's creation and is the one who carries God's trust. Thus, our actions and choices effect the entirety of existence. These effects vary based on the type and gravity of our actions. This can be best explained by studying a number of Quranic examples.

The Holy Quran speaks of how some natural phenomena can be linked directly to human choices, and the degree of our obedience or disobedience to God Almighty. For example, the Quran speaks of how mankind's obedience can be a cause for greater blessings and bounties in this world. God says,

$$\text{وَأَن لَّوِ اسْتَقَامُوا عَلَى الطَّرِيقَةِ لَأَسْقَيْنَاهُم مَّاءً غَدَقًا}$$

If they are steadfast on the path [of Allah], We shall provide them with abundant water. [12]

Being steadfast leads to the abundance of water, a divine blessing and mercy that allows for the growth and prosperity of all living things. The Holy Quran emphasizes in multiple verses that obedience to divine commands does not only lead to moral and spiritual gains, but also to worldly benefits. When it came to the people of prophet Hud, God tells us that Hud said to them,

$$\text{وَيَا قَوْمِ اسْتَغْفِرُوا رَبَّكُمْ ثُمَّ تُوبُوا إِلَيْهِ يُرْسِلِ السَّمَاءَ عَلَيْكُم مِّدْرَارًا}$$
$$\text{وَيَزِدْكُمْ قُوَّةً إِلَى قُوَّتِكُمْ وَلَا تَتَوَلَّوْا مُجْرِمِينَ}$$

O' my people! Plead with your Lord for forgiveness, then turn to Him penitently: He will send copious rains for you from the sky, and add power to your [present] power. So do not turn your backs [on Him] as guilty ones. [13]

There are countless other verses that convey to us the positive and negative effects that our actions can reap in this world before the next. There is no doubt that the gravity of these effects corresponds to the gravity of our actions. In fact, the verses lead us to conclude that our actions, no matter how big or small, have an effect on the rest of our world. This

---

[12] The Holy Quran, 72:16.

[13] The Holy Quran, 11:52.

is due to a direct creational link between humanity – the center of creation – and the rest of the world. We can also conclude that the effects of these actions are not constrained by time, just as this creational link is not limited by time. For example, the Holy Prophet (s) was a mercy and blessing to all creation. Yet this mercy was not limited to his lifetime. He was a mercy and blessing to those that lived before him and he continues to be a mercy and blessing to us presently.

We also find that the effects of our actions may be undone, although that depends on the action and its gravity. For example, there are sins whose effects can be erased by repenting and seeking forgiveness. On the other hand, some actions can be so grave that they lead to the demise of entire cities that were complicit in the act.

Let us take a few Quranic examples in this regard to better illustrate the point.

Salih's She-Camel

The Holy Quran tells us of Prophet Salih, who was asked by his people to give them an explicit sign from God. They asked him specifically for a she-camel to be created out of a mountain. Salih prayed to God, and God answered. A near mountain ruptured and gave birth to a pregnant she-camel, who immediately gave birth to a calf.

The she-camel was so bountiful with milk that the entire city could benefit from her produce. However, this sign and blessing came with a commandment. The people of Thamud were commanded to let the she-camel drink from the watering hole every other day, and that they and their cattle were forbidden from drinking on the days that the she-camel would drink. God gave them this sign and commanded them not to hurt it, or else they would meet their demise. God says in the Holy Quran,

وَإِلَىٰ ثَمُودَ أَخَاهُمْ صَالِحًا ۚ قَالَ يَا قَوْمِ اعْبُدُوا اللَّهَ مَا لَكُم مِّنْ إِلَٰهٍ غَيْرُهُ ۖ قَدْ جَاءَتْكُم بَيِّنَةٌ مِّن رَّبِّكُمْ ۖ هَٰذِهِ نَاقَةُ اللَّهِ لَكُمْ آيَةً ۖ فَذَرُوهَا تَأْكُلْ فِي أَرْضِ اللَّهِ ۖ وَلَا تَمَسُّوهَا بِسُوءٍ فَيَأْخُذَكُمْ عَذَابٌ أَلِيمٌ

And to [the people of] Thamud [We sent] Salih, their brother. He said, 'O my people, worship Allah! You have no other god besides Him. There has certainly come to you a manifest proof from your Lord. This she-camel of Allah is a sign for you. Let her alone to graze [freely] in Allah's land, and do not cause her any harm, for then you shall be seized by a painful punishment. [14]

Sadly, the people of Thamud did not heed God's commands. They hamstrung the she-camel, and thus met their demise for their transgression. God says,

فَعَقَرُوا النَّاقَةَ وَعَتَوْا عَنْ أَمْرِ رَبِّهِمْ وَقَالُوا يَا صَالِحُ ائْتِنَا بِمَا تَعِدُنَا إِن كُنتَ مِنَ الْمُرْسَلِينَ ﴿٧٧﴾ فَأَخَذَتْهُمُ الرَّجْفَةُ فَأَصْبَحُوا فِي دَارِهِمْ جَاثِمِينَ

So they hamstrung the She-camel and defied the command of their Lord, and they said, 'O Salih, bring us what you threaten us with, if you are one of the apostles.' Thereupon

---

[14] The Holy Quran, 7:73.

the earthquake seized them, and they lay lifeless prostrate in their homes. [15]

The Holy Quran tells us of the killing of a single camel, and how that brought down damnation on an entire city save the believers amongst them. Some may ask, what value does a she-camel have that its killing meant the demise of so many people? How does this make sense in light of the great value that the Holy Quran places on human life? How can God place so much importance on humanity and then punish so many for the sake of a camel?

These questions reflect a shortsighted view of the situation discussed in those verses. The crime in question was not a crime against a single camel. It was a crime against one of God's signs and in spite of God's direct commandment.

If an individual was to kill another's cattle, he would have to compensate the owner for damage to his property. But the killing of Salih's she-camel was not an issue of property damage. It was one of transgression against God's signs and commandments. God gave Thamud this sign on certain conditions and with specific commandments. When they willfully and wantonly disobeyed and transgressed, they became deserving of damnation.

The killing of an ordinary camel may have been a minor transgression that could be solved with repentance and compensation of its owner. But the transgression against God's signs and commands cannot so easily be undone.

---

[15] The Holy Quran, 7:77-78.

Repentance through Capital Punishment

We make look at some actions and judge them to be similar on face value, all the while they are greatly dissimilar in the divine view. This is because the actions may look similar, but their effects are greatly disparate. The Holy Quran illustrates this with the parable of the Golden Calf. God says,

$$ \text{وَإِذْ وَاعَدْنَا مُوسَىٰ أَرْبَعِينَ لَيْلَةً ثُمَّ اتَّخَذْتُمُ الْعِجْلَ مِن بَعْدِهِ وَأَنتُمْ} $$
$$ \text{ظَالِمُونَ ﴿٥١﴾ ثُمَّ عَفَوْنَا عَنكُم مِّن بَعْدِ ذَٰلِكَ لَعَلَّكُمْ تَشْكُرُونَ} $$
$$ \text{﴿٥٢﴾ وَإِذْ آتَيْنَا مُوسَى الْكِتَابَ وَالْفُرْقَانَ لَعَلَّكُمْ تَهْتَدُونَ ﴿٥٣﴾} $$
$$ \text{وَإِذْ قَالَ مُوسَىٰ لِقَوْمِهِ يَا قَوْمِ إِنَّكُمْ ظَلَمْتُمْ أَنفُسَكُم بِاتِّخَاذِكُمُ الْعِجْلَ} $$
$$ \text{فَتُوبُوا إِلَىٰ بَارِئِكُمْ فَاقْتُلُوا أَنفُسَكُمْ ذَٰلِكُمْ خَيْرٌ لَّكُمْ عِندَ بَارِئِكُمْ فَتَابَ} $$
$$ \text{عَلَيْكُمْ إِنَّهُ هُوَ التَّوَّابُ الرَّحِيمُ} $$

And when We made an appointment with Moses for forty nights, you took up the Calf [for worship] in his absence, and you were wrongdoers. Then We excused you after that so that you might give thanks. And when We gave Moses the Book and the Criterion so that you might be guided. And [recall] when Moses said to his people, 'O my people! You have indeed wronged yourselves by taking up the Calf [for worship]. Now turn penitently to your Maker, and slay [the guilty among] your folks. That will be better for you with your Maker.' Then He turned to you clemently. Indeed, He is the All-clement, the All-merciful. [16]

---

[16] The Holy Quran, 2:51-54.

When we compare this story to how God dealt with other nations, we find them to be greatly different. God accepts the repentance of a sinner who returns to Him, even when that sin was as great as disbelief and ingratitude to the Almighty.

Yet for Moses's followers, the effect of their sin could not be eradicated by mere repentance. Divine command thus required them to kill the sinners amongst them in order to eradicate the effects of their disobedience and disbelief.

Even though there were other nations that disbelieved, the disbelief of Moses's followers required an especially harsh penalty. This may be because they had witnesses so many amazing miracles and had just been saved from the evils of Pharaoh, yet continued to transgress. They tossed away their faith so quickly and disregarded all the magnificent favors of their Lord. As such, the proper means to erase the effects of this great transgression was through capital punishment.

Still, why would God impose such a great punishment in the parable of the Golden Calf when His punishments were not so severe on other nations that committed even worse transgressions?

The answer is that this event cannot be taken at face value and compared to others. In the case of Moses's followers and the Golden Calf, divine judgment was that the effects of this sin could not be eradicated without such a severe punishment. This takes into consideration all surrounding circumstances, as well as all possible future outcomes as known by our omniscient Lord.

In the same manner, we cannot compare the issue of Imam Hussain (a) to any other tragedy or massacre. Yes, there may be similarities on face value. However, the issue of Imam Hussain (a) has been shown, through noble traditions and through practical impact, to be completely different than other tragedy.

Sins and the Time Continuum

We must also speak of the continuation of the effects of sin, as there are some transgressions whose effects cannot be erased by any means. Some effects may continue so long as the sinners live, while other effects may continue until the Day of Resurrection. Let us address a few Quranic examples in this regard.

First, God speaks of the transgression of some Jews. He says,

وَقَالَتِ الْيَهُودُ يَدُ اللَّهِ مَغْلُولَةٌ ۚ غُلَّتْ أَيْدِيهِمْ وَلُعِنُوا بِمَا قَالُوا ۘ بَلْ يَدَاهُ مَبْسُوطَتَانِ يُنْفِقُ كَيْفَ يَشَاءُ ۚ وَلَيَزِيدَنَّ كَثِيرًا مِنْهُم مَّا أُنزِلَ إِلَيْكَ مِن رَّبِّكَ طُغْيَانًا وَكُفْرًا ۚ وَأَلْقَيْنَا بَيْنَهُمُ الْعَدَاوَةَ وَالْبَغْضَاءَ إِلَىٰ يَوْمِ الْقِيَامَةِ ۚ كُلَّمَا أَوْقَدُوا نَارًا لِّلْحَرْبِ أَطْفَأَهَا اللَّهُ ۚ وَيَسْعَوْنَ فِي الْأَرْضِ فَسَادًا ۚ وَاللَّهُ لَا يُحِبُّ الْمُفْسِدِينَ

The Jews say, 'Allah's hand is tied up.' Tied up be their hands, and cursed be they for what they say! No, His hands are wide open: He bestows as He wishes. Surely many of them will be increased in rebellion and unfaith by what has been sent to you from your Lord, and We have cast enmity and hatred amongst them until the Day of Resurrection. Every time they ignite the flames of war, Allah puts them out. They seek to cause corruption on the earth, and Allah does not like the agents of corruption. [17]

Their transgressive words and actions were cause for their increased deviance, and for the hatred and enmity that spread amongst them. This punishment did not stop at the perpetrators of those crimes, but continues through generations "until the Day of Resurrection."

Second, God speaks of some Christians and says,

$$\text{وَمِنَ الَّذِينَ قَالُوا إِنَّا نَصَارَىٰ أَخَذْنَا مِيثَاقَهُمْ فَنَسُوا حَظًّا مِّمَّا}$$

$$\text{ذُكِّرُوا بِهِ فَأَغْرَيْنَا بَيْنَهُمُ الْعَدَاوَةَ وَالْبَغْضَاءَ إِلَىٰ يَوْمِ الْقِيَامَةِ ۚ وَسَوْفَ}$$

$$\text{يُنَبِّئُهُمُ اللَّهُ بِمَا كَانُوا يَصْنَعُونَ}$$

Also from those who say, 'We are Christians,' We took their pledge; but they forgot a part of what they were reminded. So We stirred up enmity and hatred among them until the Day of Resurrection, and soon Allah will inform them concerning what they had been doing. [18]

This is another group of individuals whose actions resulted in enmity and hatred amongst them until the Day of Resurrection. The reason was their negligence of God's commands and transgression against His laws. Their actions led to an everlasting punishment from God.

When we study the verses of the Holy Quran, we find numerous other examples of how human actions can have disparate effects that could last throughout time and until the

---

[17] The Holy Quran, 5:64.

[18] The Holy Quran, 5:14.

Day of Resurrection. This highlights the creational link that runs through all existence and could cause such continuous effects.

This allows us to understand how the entirety of creation reacted to the tragedy of Imam Hussain (a), despite time and place. We can understand how this event can have an effect on creation that lasts until the Day of Resurrection. It is an extraordinary event, the gravity of which resonates throughout time. In fact, it may even be the gravest moment of creation's history, as we will address later.

Thus, it is easy to understand the reaction of humans, angels, jinn, and everything in the heavens and earth for that tragedy. As we have seen, the killing of a single she-camel could lead to the damnation of an entire people. The rejection of a group of Moses's followers after seeing God's most evident signs was cause for their damnation as well. The tragedy of Imam Hussain (a) is no less than the transgression of those groups. Thus, its effects will undoubtedly have an extraordinary effect on creation, lasting through space and time.

STATUS AND CENTRALITY

There is no doubt that the centrality of humankind in the framework of creation plays a great role in how our actions effect all other creations. This means that the greater an individual's status – the closer they are to God – the greater their effect on creation. It is enough to read a few Quranic verses and noble traditions to see the truth of this fact.

The Death of a Scholar

A scholar holds a great status within humanity. As such, the life and actions of a scholar have a great effect on creation. This translates into causing a specific effect when that scholar leaves this world. Imam al-Sadiq (a) tells us that his grandfather Imam Ali (a) used to say,

وإذا مات العالم ثلم في الاسلام ثلمة لا يسدها شئ إلى يوم القيامة

When a scholar dies, a piece is torn from Islam which will not be filled until the Day of Resurrection. [19]

The death of a scholar has such a great effect on creation that the void he leaves behind cannot be filled until the Day of Resurrection. Islam is the religion that God gave us and promised to safeguard. Still, the death of a scholar leaves a void that cannot be filled. Some scholars explain this as follows,

Because Islam is the collective of true and rational creeds, general rules and principles, then the godly jurist is the individual who knows and protects this collective through rational proofs and removes the misconceptions of the deniers. If such an individual passes away, a piece of this collective is torn and the delusions of the misguided deviators will attack without a deterrent or opponent. They will do as they please…. If you were to say that there could be a replacement when a jurist passes through another jurist that can fill the void, I respond

---

[19] Al-Barqi, *al-Mahasin*, 233.

that the void is in reality created by the death of that individual jurist as he was a fortress for Islam and its people. This void surely cannot ever be filled. Another jurist would constitute another fortress distinct form the one destroyed by the death of the former. [20]

Narrations also say that the angels, heavens, and earth weep for the passing of a scholar. This is despite the fact that a believer is freed of worldly pains and worries when he passes away, passing from the prison of this world to the gardens of paradise. Therefore, the weeping of the angels can possibly be explained through four points.

First, that they had spent time with this godly individual and grown fond of him. It is difficult for them to say goodbye.

Second, they miss recording all of his good deeds that raise his status amongst humanity.

Third, the fact that the deceased jurist can no longer be a servant and aid to the believers.

Fourth, that the jurist has to pass through the pains and trials of death.

As for the weeping of the heavens and earth, it can possibly be said that they will miss carrying his godly body that walked with grace and worshipped in devotion.[21]

Moreover, there are narrations that speak of such a creational reaction for the passing of any believer, and not just the scholar and jurist.

---

[20] Al-Mazandarani, *Sharh Usool al-Kafi*, 2:88.

[21] See: Al-Mazandarani, *Sharh Usool al-Kafi*, 2:90.

The Martyrdom of Prophet John

One of the important historical accounts that is narrated in the Holy Quran is that of the trials of Prophet John son of Prophet Zacharias. John set one of the greatest examples in his piety, purity, austerity, and God-consciousness. He was God's gift to his parents despite their old age due to their devotion to their Lord. However, Prophet John was gravely oppressed by his people, resulting in their eternal damnation. The accounts of that oppression are numerous and varied. However, Imam al-Sajjad (a) tells us that when his father Imam Hussain (a) was traveling on his final journey, he would recall the story of Prophet John at every stop. Imam Hussain (a) would say,

ومن هوان الدنيا على الله أن رأس يحيى بن زكريا عليه السلام
أهدي إلى بغي من بغايا بني إسرائيل

It is a sign of the insignificance of this world in the eyes of God that the head of John son of Zechariah was gifted to a harlot of the harlots of the Children of Israel. [22]

Prophet John had stood against the deviance of a tyrannical king. The king wished to marry his own illegitimate daughter, and Prophet John made a stance against such a grave sin. The daughter instigated against Prophet John and asked the king to kill him. The prophet was martyred, and his severed head was gifted to this harlot. [23]

---

[22] Al-Mufeed, *al-Irshad*, 2:132.

[23] See: Al-Majlisi, *Bihar al-Anwar*, 14:180.

Such an event may take place at any time, and there were many reformers and believers who were martyred for taking a stance. However, the martyrdom of Prophet John resulted in a grave punishment for his people, and an extraordinary effect on creation.

First, the sky wept for Prophet John's martyrdom – fact emphasized in many narrations. As Imam al-Sadiq (a) is reported to have said,

ان الحسين (عليه السلام) بكى لقتله السماء والأرض واحمرتا، ولم تبكيا على أحد قط الا على يحيى بن زكريا والحسين بن علي (عليهما السلام)

The heavens and the earth wept and reddened for the murder of al-Hussain (a). They never wept for anyone except for John son of Zechariah and al-Hussain son of Ali (a). [24]

The phenomenon of the sky's weeping was limited to only those two instances. This reveals the great similarity between the two events. This is despite the fact that there were so many prophets martyred before John.[25] However, there was something different about Prophet John and the circumstances of his martyrdom that lead to the sky's weeping.

Second, the narrations tell us that God took vengeance for the slaying of Prophet John by killing seventy thousand[26] men in that city. Of course, justice would demand retribution only

---

[24] Al-Qummi, *Kamil al-Ziyarat*, 181.

[25] See: The Holy Quran, 2:61.

[26] The reference to 'seventy thousand' in the Holy Quran and noble traditions seems to be metaphorical, indicating a great number and not a specific quantity.

from the killer and not from the entire city. However, divine vengeance reached everyone who was complicit in that murder, even though they may not have been the direct cause of death. This is due to the extraordinary character and status of Prophet John. To be content that such a crime be committed against such an individual is to be complicit in the crime. Thus, divine judgement saw seventy thousand punished for their heinous crime and conspiracy.

The creational reaction to Prophet John's martyrdom cannot be seen in many other crimes that we may judge to be similar at face value. These outcomes were due to the extraordinary status of the martyr and the circumstances of martyrdom.

Thus, we should not be surprised when we hear of a similar creational reaction for the martyrdom of Imam Hussain (a). Imam Hussain (a) has a special centrality in creation and a high status in the eyes of God that necessitated such effects. The circumstances of his martyrdom were also extraordinary, and even more heinous than the martyrdom of Prophet John. After all, Prophet John was martyred alone and not with his family. John's body was not trampled by horses, and the remainder of his family were not taken captive and paraded in glee.

The Sorrow of Jacob

The Holy Quran tells us the story of Prophet Jacob, one of God's select servants who suffered a great loss. God praises Jacob and the entirety of the family of Abraham, saying,

إِنَّ اللَّهَ اصْطَفَىٰ آدَمَ وَنُوحًا وَآلَ إِبْرَاهِيمَ وَآلَ عِمْرَانَ عَلَى الْعَالَمِينَ ﴿٣٣﴾ ذُرِّيَّةً بَعْضُهَا مِن بَعْضٍ ۗ وَاللَّهُ سَمِيعٌ عَلِيمٌ

*Indeed Allah chose Adam and Noah, and the progeny of
Abraham and the progeny of Imran above all the nations;
some of them are descendants of the others, and Allah is all-
hearing, all-knowing.* [27]

Thus, Prophet Jacob is an extraordinary individual whose actions are always in tune with divine will and command. He is an immaculate individual that does not make mistakes and does not fall into any error. He was a prophet, and he did not gain that status except through patience and devotion to God. As God says,

وَجَعَلْنَا مِنْهُمْ أَئِمَّةً يَهْدُونَ بِأَمْرِنَا لَمَّا صَبَرُوا ۖ وَكَانُوا بِآيَاتِنَا يُوقِنُونَ

*When they had been patient and had conviction in Our signs,
We appointed amongst them imams to guide [the people] by
Our command.* [28]

When we study the story of Prophet Jacob, we stand puzzled by many of his actions. Why would an immaculate prophet act in this way? The Holy Quran tells us of Prophet Jacob's love for his son Joseph and the other sons' envy of that love. The sons of Jacob were so envious that they determined to get rid of Joseph, eventually selling him as a slave and claiming that he was eaten by a wolf. Jacob was greatly saddened by this tragedy. This is where, at first glance, things begin to seem unreasonable.

---

[27] The Holy Quran, 3:33-34.
[28] The Holy Quran, 32:24.

Sorrow. The Holy Quran tells us of Prophet Jacob's extraordinary sorrow for the loss of his son. He wept so much that he lost his sight. God says,

$$وَتَوَلَّىٰ عَنْهُمْ وَقَالَ يَا أَسَفَىٰ عَلَىٰ يُوسُفَ وَابْيَضَّتْ عَيْنَاهُ مِنَ الْحُزْنِ فَهُوَ كَظِيمٌ$$

He turned away from them and said, 'Alas for Joseph!' His eyes had turned white with grief, and he choked with suppressed agony. [29]

This type of sorrow is unnatural and may even seem unreasonable. When has an individual ever wept so much for the loss of a loved one? When Imam al-Sadiq (a) was asked to quantify Jacob's sorrow for the loss of his son, he said,

$$حزن سبعين ثكلى بأولادها$$

The sorrow of seventy grieving mothers over their children. [30]

Why would an individual like Prophet Jacob — a descendent of Prophet Abraham, and a member of a greatly tried and tested family — deal with this incident with such sorrow? If these actions were not coming from an immaculate prophet, would we not consider them to be a type of despair coming from an individual who could not bear his trial? How can we explain this prophet's actions?

---

[29] The Holy Quran, 12:84.

[30] Al-Qummi, *Tafseer al-Qummi*, 1:350.

Patience. With all this sorrow and weeping for the loss of Joseph, Jacob never lost patience or hope in God. When Jacob's sons returned one day after losing another of their brothers, Benjamin, Jacob exclaimed,

$$بَلْ سَوَّلَتْ لَكُمْ أَنفُسُكُمْ أَمْرًا ۖ فَصَبْرٌ جَمِيلٌ ۖ عَسَى اللَّهُ أَن يَأْتِيَنِي بِهِمْ جَمِيعًا ۚ إِنَّهُ هُوَ الْعَلِيمُ الْحَكِيمُ$$

No, your souls have made a matter seem decorous to you. Yet patience is graceful. Maybe Allah will bring them all [back] to me. Indeed He is the All-knowing, the All-wise. [31]

The Holy Quran tells us that Jacob had great patience. In fact, had he not been patient, he surely would have been punished by God. After all, God had sent him as a prophet in order to be a role model in every way. How is the sorrow we have described compatible with being patient?

As an aside, we should note that the Holy Quran always mentions the prophets' great characteristics so that people do not fall for the illusion that they are ordinary people liable to err. For example, when the Holy Quran speaks of Prophet Joseph and the incident with the wife of the minister, it emphasizes his knowledge and wisdom. God says,

$$وَلَمَّا بَلَغَ أَشُدَّهُ آتَيْنَاهُ حُكْمًا وَعِلْمًا ۚ وَكَذَٰلِكَ نَجْزِي الْمُحْسِنِينَ$$

When he came of age, We gave him judgement and [sacred] knowledge, and thus do We reward the virtuous. [32]

---

[31] The Holy Quran, 12:83.
[32] The Holy Quran, 12:22.

Emphasizing these traits is important so that people do not read the story and think that Prophet Joseph may have fallen prey to sin in that moment.

This is the case with many Quranic accounts of the actions of prophets. Whenever a story could be misinterpreted as a fault or weakness in a prophet, the Holy Quran is quick to dismiss such thoughts with lauding of their high status and immaculate character. In the same way, the Holy Quran lauds Jacob's patience and wisdom before speaking of his sorrow.

Submission. What is even stranger than what we have already discussed is the fact that the Holy Quran emphasizes that Prophet Jacob had submitted his affairs to God. The Holy Quran relays the following conversation between Jacob and his sons,

قَالُوا تَاللَّهِ تَفْتَأُ تَذْكُرُ يُوسُفَ حَتَّى تَكُونَ حَرَضًا أَوْ تَكُونَ مِنَ الْهَالِكِينَ ﴿٨٥﴾ قَالَ إِنَّمَا أَشْكُو بَثِّي وَحُزْنِي إِلَى اللَّهِ وَأَعْلَمُ مِنَ اللَّهِ مَا لَا تَعْلَمُونَ

They said, 'By Allah! You will go on remembering Joseph until you wreck your health or perish.' He said, 'I complain of my anguish and grief only to Allah. I know from Allah what you do not know.' [33]

This is indeed strange. A man claims to be patient, that he has submitted to the will of God, and that he will only complain to his Lord. Still, he grieves and weeps so much that he

---

[33] The Holy Quran, 12:85-86.

loses his eyesight. How can we make sense of this and reach a true understanding of Prophet Jacob and his actions?

In this regard, Allama Tabatabaei makes an excellent point with respect to the connection between a prophet's internal state and the will of God. He says,

> *The prophets, who are guided by God's guidance, would never follow their whims. The psychological emotions and internal leanings – like desire, anger, love, hatred, happiness, or sorrow – in regards to worldly affairs like wealth, children, marriage, clothing, and the like, are all in reality for the sake of God. They seek nothing but God Almighty in all this. Afterall, there are only two roads to be followed – either the road of truth or the road of whim. In other words, the road of remembrance of God and the road of forgetfulness of Him. Prophets – who are divinely guided – do not follow whim. They are constantly in remembrance of their Lord, seeking none but Him in all their actions and inactions. When it comes to their worldly affairs, they do not knock on anyone's doors but His. Even if they grow attached to a creation, it does not lead them to forgetfulness of their Lord and that everything returns to Him....*
>
> *If they are as we have described in their true connection to God, then this allows them to always be cognizant of their Lord and vigilant of His stature of Lordship. They will not seek a thing except for the sake of God, and they will not let go of a thing except for the sake of God. They will not be attached to a creation except that they are attached to God before, alongside, and after it. He is their goal at all times.* [34]

---

[34] Al-Tabatabaei, *al-Mizan*, 1:274.

Thus, everything that Prophet Jacob did was within the realm of divine will and pleasure. When he favored Joseph over all his other sons, it was not out of an internal inclination or emotion. Rather, it was because Joseph was deserving of being favored because he was so dearly loved by God. Jacob's grief was not because he lost a beloved son, but because he lost someone who was chosen and favored by God.

In other words, the sorrow and weeping of Jacob was not for the loss of his son Joseph, but for the loss of God's divinely chosen Prophet Joseph. His grief was due to his sons' crimes against God's prophet, a transgression against God Himself. This is why despite the prophets' usual acceptance and patience when they are wronged personally, Jacob was still so greatly grieved. It is because Jacob was not enduring a crime against himself, but was witnessing a crime against his Lord.

Of course, we do not wish to say that Jacob was not grieved by the loss of his son. Feeling sorrow for the loss of a son does not fall outside God's commands and pleasure. Our Holy Prophet (s) also wept for a lost loved one when his son Abraham was stillborn. He said,

العين تدمع، والقلب يخشع، ولا نقول ما يسخط الرب

The eye may tear and the heart may chastened, but we shall not say anything that may enrage the Lord. [35]

Our Holy Prophet (s) never cared for the wrongs committed against his person or the pains that his people put him through. Even when he was rejected by some of the villages

---

[35] Al-Majlisi, *Bihar al-Anwar*, 12:327.

he visited and pelted with stones until he bled, he turned to
his Lord and prayed,

اللهم إني أشكو إليك غربتي وكربتي وهواني على الناس، يا أرحم
الراحمين، أنت رب المستضعفين، أنت رب المكروبين، اللهم إن
لم يكن لك علي غضب فلا أبالي، ولكن عافيتك أوسع لي،
أعوذ بك من سخطك، ومعافاتك من عقوبتك، وبك منك، لا
أحصي الثناء عليك أنت كما أثنيت على نفسك، لك الحمد حتى
ترضى، ولا حول ولا قوة إلا بالله العلي العظيم.

O' God, I complain to You of my solitude and distress, and
people's detachment from me. O' most merciful of the merciful!
You are the Lord of the oppressed! You are the Lord of the
distressed! O' God, so long as You are not angered at me, I
do not care! However, Your protection is encompassing of me.
I seek protection in You from Your wrath, and in Your pro-
tection from Your punishment, and in You from You. I can-
not enumerate praise to You [as You deserve]! You are as
You have praised Yourself! Praise be to You until You are
pleased! There is no might nor power save in God, the high
and glorious. [36]

Thus, our Holy Prophet (s) shows us his patience and his
submission to the will of God. God is the only thing he seeks
and cares for. This is the stance of prophets and imams. They
are not angered and grieved by wrongs committed against
their holy persons, but only by those committed against God.

---

[36] Al-Bahrani, *Hulyat al-Abrar*, 1:130.

This is what we see in the words of Imam Ali (a) when he commented on Muawiya's raids on some of the villages of Iraq. He said,

وَلَقَدْ بَلَغَنِي أَنَّ الرَّجُلَ مِنْهُمْ كَانَ يَدْخُلُ عَلَى الْمَرْأَةِ الْمُسْلِمَةِ،
وَالْأُخْرَى الْمُعَاهَدَةِ فَيَنْتَزِعُ حِجْلَهَا وَقُلْبَهَا وَقَلَائِدَهَا، وَرِعَاثَهَا مَا
تَمْتَنِعُ مِنْهُ إِلاَّ بِالِاسْتِرْجَاعِ وَالِاسْتِرْحَامِ ثُمَّ انْصَرَفُوا وَافِرِينَ مَا نَالَ
رَجُلاً مِنْهُمْ كَلْمٌ وَلاَ أُرِيقَ لَهُمْ دَمٌ، فَلَوْ أَنَّ امْرَأً مُسْلِماً مَاتَ مِن
بَعْدِ هَذَا أَسَفاً مَا كَانَ بِهِ مَلُوماً، بَلْ كَانَ بِهِ عِنْدِي جَدِيراً.

I have come to know that each of them entered upon Muslim women — and other women under the protection of Islam — and took away their anklets, bracelets, necklaces, and earrings. No woman could resist it except by pronouncing the verse, "We are of God and to Him we shall return," and seeking mercy. They left laden with wealth without any wound or loss of life. If any Muslim dies of grief after all this he is not to be blamed, but rather there is justification for him before me. [37]

If Imam Ali (a) thinks that transgression against a woman — whether Muslim or not — is such a grave transgression against God's commands that a person is justified to die of sorrow, then what about transgression against God's chosen servants and prophets? Was Prophet Jacob not justified in his sorrow? Was he not still patient in not allowing his sorrow to go further? This is the truth that the Holy Quran points to in the verse,

---

[37] Al-Radi, *Nahj al-Balagha*, Sermon 27.

$$\text{وَابْيَضَّتْ عَيْنَاهُ مِنَ الْحُزْنِ فَهُوَ كَظِيمٌ}$$

His eyes had turned white with grief, and he choked with suppressed agony. [38]

His eyes were blinded with grief, but he was still suppressing his agony!

The transgression against Joseph came out of his brothers' ignorance of his grand status. They thought that he was just like them, and that they were more deserving of their father's love because they could serve him better. The Holy Quran says,

$$\text{إِذْ قَالُوا لَيُوسُفُ وَأَخُوهُ أَحَبُّ إِلَى أَبِينَا مِنَّا وَنَحْنُ عُصْبَةٌ إِنَّ أَبَانَا}$$
$$\text{لَفِي ضَلَالٍ مُّبِينٍ}$$

When they said, 'Surely Joseph and his brother are dearer to our father than [the rest of] us, though we are a hardy band. Our father is indeed in manifest error.' [39]

They committed their transgression out of ignorance, and they later admitted their mistake. Jacob knew that his son was alive. Despite all this, their action caused this great grief in his heart. He suppressed a great deal of his agony, but whatever escaped him was enough to make him weep until he went blind.

So what sorrow and grief strikes all of creation for the great transgression against Imam Hussain (a)! His killers knew exactly who he was and his status in the eyes of God. They

---

[38] The Holy Quran, 12:84.

[39] The Holy Quran, 12:8.

slaughtered him along with his brothers and sons, and took his sisters and daughters captive. They did not hesitate or repent. Is the weeping of the heavens and earth and everyone between them so striking?!

In fact, what is striking is that some people are not moved by this tragedy.

IMAM HUSSAIN'S (A) STATURE

Having discussed the different dimensions that can compound and exacerbate the gravity of an event, we must now turn to the tragedy of Imam Hussain (a) and analyze how it was compounded by these dimensions. Of course, one cannot fully describe Imam Hussain's (a) person or his tragedy in a single sermon or book. What we wish to do is simply point to a number of significant points in this regard. This will allow us to better understand why he and his tragedy have taken such a significant role in believers' lives.

The Inheritor of Prophets

No one doubts that the Holy Prophet (s) was the inheritor of all prophets. He is their seal and leader, and the master of the entirety of creation. Thus, whatever capabilities, honors, and characteristics can be found in the prophets can also be found in their master Prophet Muhammad (s). In other words, the Holy Prophet (s) is a representation of all the prophets and the most perfect exemplar of the God's viceroys on earth.

Having understood this about our Holy Prophet (s), we then turn to look at the connection between him and Imam

Hussain (a). In the Holy Prophet's (s) own words and in the words of the Immaculate Household (a), we can see a number of points connecting the two.

First, Imam Hussain (a) is a representation of the two weighty things that the Holy Prophet (s) left for his nation before he passed away. This is documented in the widely narrated and authentic tradition of *al-Thaqalayn*. Thus, Imam Hussain (a) is the inheritor of the Holy Prophet (s) and his successor whom we were commanded to obey and hold fast to. The traditions that emphasize this point are too many to enumerate here. A prime example is the following words of our Holy Prophet (s),

قال النبي (صلى الله عليه وآله) :إن الله تبارك وتعالى اصطفاني
واختارني وجعلني رسولا، وأنزل علي سيد الكتب، فقلت:
إلهي وسيدي، إنك أرسلت موسى إلى فرعون، فسألك أن
تجعل معه أخاه هارون وزيرا، تشد به عضده، وتصدق به
قوله، وإني أسألك يا سيدي وإلهي أن تجعل لي من أهلي
وزيرا، تشد به عضدي.

God – blessed and high is He – favored and chose me, making me a messenger. He revealed to me the best of Books. I said [to Him], 'My God and master! When you sent Moses to Pharaoh, he asked you to send alongside him his brother Aaron as his minister – strengthening [Moses's] arm through [Aaron] and confirming by [Aaron Moses's] words. Thus, I ask You – my master and my God – to grant me a minister from my family, through whom You strengthen my arm.'

فجعل الله لي عليا وزيرا وأخا، وجعل الشجاعة في قلبه،
وألبسه الهيبة على عدوه، وهو أول من آمن بي وصدقني، وأول
من وحد الله معي، وإني سألت ذلك ربي عز وجل فأعطانيه.
فهو سيد الأوصياء، اللحوق به سعادة، والموت في طاعته
شهادة، واسمه في التوراة مقرون إلى اسمي، وزوجته الصديقة
الكبرى ابنتي، وابناه سيدا شباب أهل الجنة ابناي، وهو وهما
والأئمة بعدهم حجج الله على خلقه بعد النبيين، وهم أبواب العلم
في أمتي، من تبعهم نجا من النار، ومن اقتدى بهم هدي إلى
صراط مستقيم، لم يهب الله عز وجل محبتهم لعبد إلا أدخله
الله الجنة

Thus, God made Ali my minister and brother. He granted him courage in his heart and eminence over his enemies. He was the first to have faith and believe in me, and the first to pronounce God's unicity alongside me. I had asked that of my Lord, and He gave it to me. Thus, [Ali] is the master of guardians. Following him is felicity and dying in obedience to him is martyrdom. His name is coupled with my name in the Torah. His wife is the Most Righteous, my daughter. His two sons, the Masters of the Youth of Paradise, are my sons. He, the two of them, and the imams after them are the proofs of God over His creation after the prophets. They are the gates of knowledge within my nation. Whoever follows them is saved from hellfire, and whoever takes them as role models is guided to a straight path. God Almighty did not grant love of them to any servant except that He places that servant in Paradise. [40]

Thus, Imam Hussain (a) is a proof of God upon His creatures. This means that he is an inheritor of all the prophets and their knowledge, as is expressly stated in numerous traditions.

Second, the Holy Prophet (s) continuously emphasized that 'Hussain (a) is of him and he is of Hussain (a).' In one narration he says,

حسين مني وانا من حسين، أحب الله من أحب حسينا

Hussain (a) is of me and I am of Hussain (a). May God love those who love Hussain (a). [41]

The continuation of the Holy Prophet's (s) message was due to Imam Hussain (a) and his sacrifice. Imam Hussain (a) was of the Holy Prophet (s) in blood, upbringing, message, and principles. The Holy Prophet (s) is of Imam Hussain (a) in continuity of the eternal message. Imam Hussain (a) is thus the driver of continuity for the message of all prophets.

Third, the Holy Household (a) always emphasized that Imam Hussain (a) is the inheritor of the prophets. This can be seen in a great deal of visitations that they taught us to recite when we visit his grave and remember his tragedy. In fact, one such visitation taught by Imam al-Sadiq (a) is known as *Ziyarat Warith* – the Visitation of the Inheritor. It reads in part,

---

[40] Al-Sadouq, *al-Amali*, 73.

[41] Al-Qummi, *Kamil al-Ziyarat*, 116.

السلام عليك يا وارث آدم صفوة الله السلام عليك يا وارث

نوح نبي الله السلام عليك يا وارث إبراهيم خليل الله السلام

عليك يا وارث موسى كليم الله السلام عليك يا وارث عيسى

روح الله السلام عليك يا وارث محمد حبيب الله السلام عليك

يا وارث أمير المؤمنين عليه السلام

Peace be upon you, O' inheritor of Adam the choice of God. Peace be upon you, O' inheritor of Noah the prophet of God. Peace be upon you, O' inheritor of Abraham the friend of God. Peace be upon you, O' inheritor of Moses the speaker to God. Peace be upon you, O' inheritor of Jesus the spirit of God. Peace be upon you, O' inheritor of Muhammad the most beloved by God. Peace be upon you, O' inheritor of the Commander of the Faithful, peace be upon him. [42]

If Imam Hussain (a) is the inheritor of prophets, then transgressing against him is a transgression against all prophets. The creational reaction to his martyrdom can be no less than that of the martyrdom of Prophet John. How could it be any less when Imam Hussain (a) represented Prophet John and all other prophets and messengers?

The Best of His Time

No two Muslims will dispute the fact that Imam Hussain (a) was the greatest individual of his time. There was no individual at that time closer to God and His Messenger (s) than Imam Hussain (a). Neither was there any individual at that time who held such a great position of admiration and love

---

[42] Al-'Amili, *al-Mazar*, 123.

in the hearts and minds of the people. This was not the opinion of his admirers and followers alone, but that of the entirety of the Muslim nation. After all, he was the grandson of the Holy Prophet (s) and the last remaining member of the Five People of the Cloak.

To get a better understanding of his great stature, let us consider a few of the words of his enemies in his regard.

When Imam Hussain (a) began his journey towards Kufa, al-Walid ibn 'Utba, the Governor of Medina, wrote to Ubaydullah ibn Ziyad,

> *Al-Hussain ibn Ali is heading towards Iraq. He is the son of Fatima and Fatima is the daughter of the Messenger of God. So beware, O' ibn Ziyad, of harming him and inciting against yourself and your kin that which cannot be closed throughout this world, and that the masses the nobles will not forget so long as this world remains.*[43]

When Imam Hussain (a) was traveling from Medina to Mecca, he was met by a man named Abdullah ibn Muti' al-'Adawi. Abdullah suggested that Imam Hussain (a) should abandon the thought of going to Kufa, stating,

> *If you reach Mecca, beware of being deceived by the people of Kufa! In it was the murder of your father and the desertion of your brother. They stabbed him [i.e. Imam Hassan (a)] with a stab that almost killed him. Remain at the [Great Mosque of Mecca] for you are the master of Arabs in this*

---

[43] Al-Majlisi, *Bihar al-Anwar*, 44:368.

era. By God, if you were to perish, your household will surely perish alongside you. [44]

Even Shabath ibn Rib'i, a general in the Umayyad army that massacred Imam Hussain (a) and his family, would say before the battle,

> *May God never grant the people of this land any blessing or guide them towards prudence! Do you not wonder at how we fought alongside Ali ibn Abu Talib and his son [i.e. Imam Hassan (a)] after him against [the Umayyads] for five years, and now we turn against his son [i.e. Imam Hussain (a)] while he is the best of the people of earth, fighting him alongside the family of Muawiya and the son of Sumayya the adulteress?! Deviance! Oh, what deviance!* [45]

These accounts reflect the position of Imam Hussain's (a) enemies. His followers had no less to say about his stature. For example, Abdullah ibn Jafar wrote to Imam Hussain (a) saying,

> *I ask you by God to reconsider after reading my letter. Surely, I am concerned for you in the journey you are taking, lest you face your death and the eradication of your family. Surely, if you were killed today, the light of the earth would be dimmed as you are the model for the guided and the hope of the believers. Do not hurry on your journey, for I am on my way [to you] following my letter. Peace.* [46]

---

[44] Ibn A'tham, *al-Futuh*, 5:23.

[45] Al-Tabari, *Tareekh al-Tabari*, 4:332.

[46] Al-Mufeed, *al-Irshad*, 2:68.

There are numerous other historical accounts that show the great reverence and honor with which Imam Hussain (a) was held. Transgression against such a godly character cannot be considered normal, and its effects cannot be ordinary. If the killing of Salih's she-camel resulted in the destruction of an entire city, then no doubt the transgression against an individual like Imam Hussain (a) can bring about the creational effects that were witnessed at his martyrdom and that continue to this day.

THE GRAVITY OF THE TRAGEDY

The foregoing discussion was concerning Imam Hussain (a) and his stature. Let us now turn to the event and the gravity of the tragedy.

The Nature of the Conflict

The importance of the event of Ashura lies in part in the nature of the conflict between Imam Hussain (a) and his enemies. It was not a tribal, economic, or political struggle. It was truly a battle between good and evil. It was a struggle between Imam Hussain (a) who represented the principles and message of God and His prophets on one side, and those who wished to rebel against God's will and command. It was a struggle between the forces of God and the forces of Satan.

Imam Hussain (a) described the nature of this conflict from the outset. He wrote to his half-brother Muhammad,

إِنّي لَمْ أَخْرُجْ أَشِرًا وَلا بَطَرًا ، وَلا مُفْسِدًا وَلا ظالِمًا ، وَإِنَّما خَرَجْتُ لِطَلَبِ الإِصْلاحِ في أُمَّةِ جَدّي ، أُرِيدُ أَنْ آمُرَ

262

بِالْمَعْرُوفِ وَأَنْهى عَنِ الْمُنْكَرِ ، وَأَسِيرَ بِسِيرَةِ جَدّي وَأَبي عَليِّ
بْنِ أَبي طالِبٍ فمن قبلني بقبول الحق فالله أولى بالحق ومن رد
علي أصبر حتى يقضي الله بيني وبين القوم بالحق وهو خير
الحاكمين

*I do not revolt due to discontent [with God's blessings], nor
out of arrogance. I did not rise as a corruptor, nor as an oppressor. Rather, I wish to call for reform in the nation of my
grandfather. I wish to call for what is good, and to forbid
what is evil. [I wish to] follow the tradition of my grandfather
[the Prophet] and my father....* [47]

Lady Zainab also emphasized this truth in her sermon, saying,

ألا فالعجب كل العجب لقتل حزب الله النجباء بحزب الشيطان
الطلقاء

*Surely, what a great wonder it is to see the chosen party of
God being slaughtered by Satan's army of Tulaqa' [i.e. the
prisoners of war freed by the Prophet (s)]!* [48]

When we study the movement of Imam Hussain (a) and his
words, we find that all he did was for the sake of God and
His message. The complete opposite is found on the opposing side. They were individuals moved by tribal tendencies,
greed, and political aspirations. This is seen through the
words of Omar ibn Saad and the rest of the army. They all

---

[47] Ibn Shahrashoob, *al-Manaqib*, 3:241.

[48] Al-Majlisi, *Bihar al-Anwar*, 45:134.

knew who they were fighting – the grandson of the Holy Prophet (s) and the inheritor of God's message – but persisted for the sake of their worldly ambitions.

Thus, it is only normal that anyone and anything that has the slightest connection to God be moved by the tragedy that took place solely for the sake of God. It is no surprise that the angels, jinn, heavens, and earth all wept for the sake of Imam Hussain's (a) sacrifice on that day.

The Nature of the Tragedy

When we study the events that took place in the battlefield of Karbala and in the aftermath of the battle, we find it to be the most gruesome massacre in the history of humanity. The terror that Imam Hussain's (a) bloodthirsty enemies inflicted on the entire camp – including women, children, and elders – is indescribable. They continued to massacre every man in that camp, and even some women and children. In recalling the tragedy that befell Imam Hussain (a) and his family, Imam al-Rida (a) told one of his companions,

يا بن شبيب، إن كنت باكيًا لشئٍ، فابك للحسين بن علي بن أبي طالب (عليه السلام)، فإنه ذبح كما يذبح الكبش، وقتل معه من أهل بيته ثمانية عشر رجلًا ما لهم في الأرض شبيه

O' ibn Shabeeb! If you are to weep for anything, then weep for al-Hussain ibn Ali ibn Abu Talib (a)! Surely, he was slaughtered like the slaughtering of a ram. Eighteen members

of his family were murdered alongside him, the likes of whom could not be found on earth. [49]

The massacre was not just that of Imam Hussain (a), but of so many of the descendants of the Holy Prophet (s) who carried his message and characteristics. This is in addition to the group of righteous companions who stood by Imam Hussain's (a) side and were slaughtered without mercy. It is enough of an honor for that group to be described by Imam Hussain (a) as he did when he said,

فإني لا أعلم أصحابا أوفى ولا خيرا من أصحابي، ولا أهل بيت أبر ولا أوصل من أهل بيتي فجزاكم الله عني خيرا

Surely, I don't know of any companions more worthy than my companions, nor a family more pure and rooted than my own. May God reward you all on my behalf. [50]

The massacre did not stop at the able men within Imam Hussain's (a) camp, but even reached defenseless children. Imam Hussain's (a) infant child was slain with an arrow on his father's chest, without a drop of mercy to be seen in the enemies' camp. All this was while the camp was cut off from water and griped by thirst. And despite all this, none of them recanted their stance, and they persevered for the sake of the divine message and the pleasure of their Lord.

Is this not a horror that wrenches the heart of any living being?

---

[49] Al-Sadouq, *al-Amali*, 192.
[50] Al-Mufeed, *al-Irshad*, 2:91.

Perhaps the greatest tragedy in all this was the taking of the Holy Prophet's (s) daughters as captives, paraded from city to city with glee. The Holy Prophet (s) was a favor that God blessed this nation with. God says,

$$\text{لَقَدْ مَنَّ اللَّهُ عَلَى الْمُؤْمِنِينَ إِذْ بَعَثَ فِيهِمْ رَسُولًا مِّنْ أَنفُسِهِمْ يَتْلُو عَلَيْهِمْ آيَاتِهِ وَيُزَكِّيهِمْ وَيُعَلِّمُهُمُ الْكِتَابَ وَالْحِكْمَةَ وَإِن كَانُوا مِن قَبْلُ لَفِي ضَلَالٍ مُّبِينٍ}$$

Allah certainly favored the faithful when He raised up among them an apostle from among themselves to recite to them His signs and to purify them and teach them the Book and wisdom, and earlier they had indeed been in manifest error. [51]

How was this favor repaid? For everything that the Holy Prophet (s) did, there was only one thing that we were told to compensate him with – to have affection towards his kin. God says,

$$\text{قُل لَّا أَسْأَلُكُمْ عَلَيْهِ أَجْرًا إِلَّا الْمَوَدَّةَ فِي الْقُرْبَى}$$

Say, 'I do not ask you any reward for it except the love of [my] relatives.' [52]

Instead, this nation decided to turn its back on the Holy Prophet (s) and slaughter his grandson and take his daughters as captives. This nation decided to tie chains around the

---

[51] The Holy Quran, 3:164.

[52] The Holy Quran, 42:23.

hands and necks of the daughters of its Prophet (s), then parade them as captives in its cities. This left the greatest pain in the hearts of the Holy Household (a).

It is narrated that Abu Hamza al-Thamali, one of Imam al-Sajjad's (a) close companions, visited him one day and saw him sitting in sorrow. Abu Hamza tried to console the Imam and remind him of the great status that Imam Hussain (a) and his companions reached through martyrdom. He said, "Master, what is this weeping and despondency? Was your uncle al-Hamza not murdered? Was your grandfather Ali (a) not murdered by the sword? Surely, murder has become an expectancy for you, and martyrdom is an honor from God to you!" The Imam replied,

شكر الله سعيك يا أبا حمزة ، كما ذكرت ، القتل لنا عادة ،
وكرامتنا من الله الشهادة ولكن يا أبا حمزة ، هل سمعت أذناك
أم رأت عيناك أن امرأة منا أُسرت أو هُتكت قبل يوم
عاشوراء ؟ والله يا أبا حمزة ، ما نظرت إلى عمّاتي وأخواتي
إلاّ وذكرت فرارهن في البيداء من خيمة إلى خيمة ، ومن خباء
إلى خباء ، والمنادي ينادي أحرقوا بيوت الظالمين

May God reward your effort, O' Abu Hamza! Yes, it is as you mentioned. Murder has become an expectancy for us and martyrdom is an honor from God to us. However, O' Abu Hamza, have your ears heard or your eyes seen one of our women taken as captive or exposed before the Day of Ashura?! By God, O' Abu Hamza, whenever I look at my aunts and sisters, I remember their fleeing from one tent to

another and from one tent to another, all while a caller calls,
'Burn the homes of the oppressors!' [53]

This is only a small portion of the pain and suffering that this blessed family went through, despite being the purest and greatest of people on earth. It is not an exaggeration to say that this tragedy was the greatest in the history of humanity. This is why it deserved this reaction, becoming an eternal tragedy relived throughout the centuries.

UNDERSTANDING THE TRAGEDY

The foregoing discussion allowed us to shed some light on this tragedy and understand why it has become a living part of the human conscious for about fourteen hundred years. How could the world not be moved by this massacre when it was in direct transgression against one of God's greatest signs and blessings, and a household that is most connected to Him. This is how Imam Hussain (a) gained the nickname that we find etched in many of our noble traditions – 'the vengeance of God.' It is because the transgression against him was a transgression against God. This is a point emphasized time and again in the narrations of the Holy Household (a) and the visitations they taught us to recite at his grave. As one visitation taught by Imam al-Sadiq (a) states,

---

[53] We have not been able to locate an authentic primary source for this narration, although it is prevalent amongst the encyclopedias prepared by and for reciters of the elegies of the Ahlulbayt. There may be a primary resource that eluded us, or it may have been lost to history. Nonetheless, history describes in detail the tragedies of how the Holy Household was captured, terrorized, and paraded from city to city after witnessing the massacre at Karbala. Thus, it is not farfetched that this narration – although it lacks a proper primary source – accurately reflects the great sorrow that Imam al-Sajjad (a) endured.

السلام عليك يا حجة الله وابن حجته، السلام عليك يا قتيل

الله وابن قتيله، السلام عليك يا ثار الله وابن ثاره، السلام

عليك يا وتر الله الموتور في السماوات والأرض

Peace be upon you, O' proof of God and the son of His proof.
Peace be upon you, O' one murdered for the sake of God and
the son of the one murdered for His sake. Peace be upon you,
O' one whose vengeance is with God and the son of whose
vengeance is with Him. Peace be upon you, O' one whose
vengeance will be sought by God, and whose vengeance is
awaited by the heavens and the earth. [54]

The traditions of the Holy Prophet (s) also emphasize this.
The companion Jabir ibn Abdullah al-Ansari narrated that
the Holy Prophet (s) said,

يجئ يوم القيامة ثلاثة يشكون إلى الله عز وجل: المصحف،

والمسجد، والعترة. يقول المصحف: يا رب حرقوني ومزقوني،

ويقول المسجد: يا رب عطلوني وضيعوني، وتقول العترة: يا رب

قتلونا وطردونا وشردونا فأجثوا للركبتين للخصومة، فيقول الله

جل جلاله لي: أنا أولى بذلك.

Three will come forth on the Day of Resurrection and com-
plain to God Almighty; the Quran, the mosque, and [my]
Household. The Quran will say, 'O' Lord, they tore and
burned me.' The mosque will say, 'O' Lord, they neglected
and wasted me.' The Household will say, 'O' Lord, they

---

[54] Al-Qummi, *Kamil al-Ziyarat*, 364.

murdered us, exiled us, and displaced us.' They will sit on
their knees awaiting judgment. God Almighty will say to me,
'I am a more rightful [opponent than you, O' Messenger (s)]!'
[55]

God Almighty has a greater right than the Holy Prophet (s)
in demanding justice and seeking vengeance for those who
tore the Quran, neglected the mosque, and killed the Holy
Household! The tragedy of Ashura and the individuals massacred on the plains of Karbala are linked to God Almighty
and His signs and commands. Again, this makes it all the
more expected that there should be this creational reaction to
the tragedy. In fact, not being moved by the tragedy is a sign
of distance from God and a form of rebellion against Him.

Weeping for Imam Hussain (a) is not a political or sectarian
issue. It is the slogan of those who seek a stronger connection
to God. An individual who is moved to tears by the tragedy
is in complete harmony with the rest of God's creation. An
individual who is not moved is surely distant from God and
living in disharmony with the rest of creation.

This is why weeping for Imam Hussain (a) is so important,
especially for humankind who have decided to take on God's
divine trust. The fulfillment of this trust requires living in
complete harmony and obedience to God's will and commands. God says,

إِنَّا عَرَضْنَا الْأَمَانَةَ عَلَى السَّمَاوَاتِ وَالْأَرْضِ وَالْجِبَالِ فَأَبَيْنَ أَن
يَحْمِلْنَهَا وَأَشْفَقْنَ مِنْهَا وَحَمَلَهَا الْإِنْسَانُ ۖ إِنَّهُ كَانَ ظَلُومًا جَهُولًا

---

[55] Al-Sadouq, *al-Khisal*, 175.

Indeed We presented the Trust to the heavens and the earth and the mountains, but they refused to undertake it and were apprehensive of it; but man undertook it. Indeed he is most unjust and ignorant. [56]

What is strange is how some individuals – who God blessed with reason and raised above other creation – are not moved for this tragedy. Rather, they take a position in opposition of commemorating the event and bringing life and memory to its heroes.

There is no doubt that the existence of even a few individuals who weep for Imam Hussain (a) is a cause for mercy to all mankind. As is narrated from Imam al-Sadiq (a),

ولوأن باكيا بكى في امة لرحموا

If single individual weeps in a nation, they will be granted mercy. [57]

When we go back to the visitations that were taught to us by the Holy Household (a), we find several major focus points that they all share. Specifically, they call for us to take the following stance in regard to the tragedy.

First, they emphasize the position, stature, and character of Imam Hussain (a).

Second, disavowing the heinous crimes that took place and the criminals who transgressed against the Holy Household (a), whether by direct action, words, or mere complacency.

---

[56] The Holy Quran, 33:72.
[57] Al-Kulayni, *al-Kafi*, 2:481.

Third, vowing to stand by Imam Hussain (a) and being amongst the individuals who live and die with him as their master and role model.

The tragedy of Karbala was the greatest disaster in the history of humanity. Some individuals ask why this tragedy was greater than the tragedies of the Holy Prophet (s), Imam Ali (a), Lady Zahraa (a), and Imam Hassan (a). The answer is that they did not face crimes as heinous as those that Imam Hussain (a) faced. Moreover, whenever one of the other Five People of the Cloak passed away, there was someone remaining to remind mankind of those holy individuals. However, when Imam Hussain (a) was murdered in Karbala, the last of the Five People of the Cloak was gone. This is why Lady Zainab wept for Imam Hussain (a) and said,

اليوم ماتت أمي فاطمة وأبي علي وأخى الحسن يا خليفة
الماضين وثمال الباقين

Today, my mother Fatima, my father Ali, and my brother al-Hassan (a) have passed away! O' remainder of those who have passed! O' guardian of those who remain![58]

Imam Hussain (a) was a consolation to those who saw the passing and martyrdom of the Holy Prophet (s), Imam Ali (a), Lady Zahraa (a), and Imam Hassan (a). When Imam Hussain (a) was murdered, the Five People of the Cloak had all departed this world.

These are some of the points that allow us to better understand the tragedy of Imam Hussain (a) and why it continues

---

[58] Ibn Nama, *Mutheer al-Ahzan*, 35.

to live with us centuries on. They allow us to better understand why the entirety of creation wept and continues to
weep for that tragedy.

We hope that understanding these points will allow us to be
amongst those who weep for Imam Hussain's (a) tragedy,
thereby growing closer to our Almighty Lord for whom our
Imams sacrificed everything that they had.

REFERENCED WORKS

HOLY SCRIPTURES

The Holy Quran.

OTHER WORKS

Al-'Adheem Abadi, Muhammad. *'Oun al-Ma'boud*. Beirut: Daar al-Kutub al-'Ilmiyya, 1995.

Al-'Amili, Ja'far Murtada. *Hayat al-Imam al-Rida*. Daar al-Tableegh, 1978.

Al-'Askari, Murtada. *Ahadeeth Um al-Mu'mineen*. Al-Tawheed, 1994.

Al-'Askari, Murtada. *Ma'alim al-Madrasatain*. Beirut: Mu'assasat al-Nu'man.

Al-Amili, Muhammad ibn al-Hassan. *Wasa'el al-Shia*. Beirut: Daar Ihya al-Torath al-Arabi.

Al-Arbali, Ali. *Kashf al-Ghumma*. Beirut: Daar al-Adwa', 1985.

Al-Balathiri, Ahmad ibn Yahya. *Ansab al-Ashraaf*. Beirut: Daar al-Fikr, 1996.

Al-Bukhari, Muhammad ibn Ismael. *Sahih al-Bukhari*. Beirut: Daar al-Fikr, 1981.

Al-Daynouri, Ahmad ibn Dawoud. *Al-Akhbar al-Tiwal*. Cairo: Daar Ihya' al-Kitab al-Arabi, 1960.

275

Al-Hakeem, Muhammad Baqir. *Thawrat al-Hussain (a)*. Najaf, 2008.

Al-Hassani, Hashim Ma'roof. *Seerat Al-A'imma Al-Ithney Ashar*. Beirut: Daar Al-Ta'aruf, 1990.

Al-Hilli, Muhammad ibn Ja'far. *Mutheer al-Ahzaan*. Najaf: al-Matba'a al-Haydariya, 1950.

Al-Hindi, Ali al-Muttaqi. *Kanz al-'Ommal*. Muasasat al-Risala, 1989.

Al-Kulayni, Muhammad ibn Yaqoub. *Al-Kafi*. Tehran: Daar al-Kutub al-Islamiya, 1968.

Al-Majlisi, Muhammad Baqir. *Bihar al-Anwar*. Beirut: al-Wafaa, 1983.

Al-Maqdisi, Muhammad ibn Muflih. *Al-Furu'*. Beirut: al-Resalah Publishers, 2003.

Al-Mu'tazili, Abdulhameed ibn Hibatullah ibn Abi al-Hadeed. *Sharh Nahj al-Balagha*. Beirut: Daar Ihya al-Torath al-Arabi, 1965.

Al-Muqarram, Abdulrazzaq al-Mousawi. *Maqtal al-Hussain (a)*. Qum: Daar al-Thaqafa, 1990.

Al-Naqdi, Ja'far al-Rubei'i. *Zaynab al-Kubra*. Qum: Mu'assasat al-Imam al-Hussain, 1991.

Al-Nisa'i, Ahmad ibn Shu'ayb. *Al-Sunan al-Kubra*. Beirut: Daar al-Kutub al-Ilmiyya, 1991.

Al-Nisabouri, Muhammad ibn al-Fattal. *Rawdat al-Waa'ithein*. Qum: Manshoorat al-Radi.

Al-Nisabouri, Muslim ibn al-Hajjaj. *Sahih Muslim*. Beirut: Daar al-Fikr.

Al-Nu'man, Abu Hanifa. *Sharh al-Akhbar*. Qum: Jama'at al-Mudarriseen.

Al-Radi, Muhammad ibn al-Hussain. *Nahj al-Balagha*. Beirut: Daar al-Ma'rifa.

Al-Sadouq, Muhammad ibn Ali. *'Ilal al-Sharae'*. Najaf: al-Matbaa al-Haydaria, 1966.

Al-Sadouq, Muhammad ibn Ali. *'Oyoon Akhbar al-Rida*. Beirut: al-A'lami, 1984.

Al-Sadouq, Muhammad ibn Ali. *Al-Khisal*. Qum: Jama'at al-Mudarriseen, 1982.

Al-Sadouq, Muhammad ibn Ali. *Al-Tawheed*. Qum: Jama'at al-Mudariseen.

Al-Saffar, Muhammad ibn al-Hassan. *Basa'er al-Darajat*. Tehran: al-A'lami, 1983.

Al-Shawkani, Muhammad ibn Ali. *Nayl al-Awtar*. Beirut: Daar al-Jeel, 1973.

Al-Tabari, Muhammad ibn Jareer. *Tareekh al-Tabari*. Beirut, 1983.

Al-Tabatabaei, Muhammad Hussain. *Tafsir al-Mizan*. Qum: Jama'at al-Mudarriseen.

Al-Tousi, Muhammad ibn al-Hassan. *Tahtheeb al-Ahkam*. Tehran: Daar al-Kutub al-Islamiya, 1970.

Ameen, Ahmad. *Duha al-Islam*.

Haidar, Asad. *Al-Imam al-Sadiq wa al-Mathahib al-Arba'a*. Beirut: Daar al-Kitab, 1969.

Ibn 'Asakir, Ali ibn al-Hassan. *Tareekh Dimashq*. Beirut: Daar al-Fikr, 1995.

Ibn al-Atheer, Ali ibn Abu al-Karam. *Al-Kamil fi al-Tareekh*. Beirut: Daar Sadir, 1965.

Ibn Hanbal, Ahmad. *Musnad Ahmad*. Beirut: Daar Saadir.

Ibn Katheer, Ismail. *Al-Bidaya wa al-Nihaya*. Beirut: Daar Ihya al-Torath al-Arabi, 1988.

Ibn Khalkan, Ahmad ibn Muhammad ibn Ibrahim ibn Abu Bakr. *Wafiyyat al-A'yan*. Beirut: Daar al-Thaqafa.

Ibn Shahrashoob, Muhammad ibn Ali. *Al-Manaqib*. Najaf: Al-Matbaa Al-Haydaria, 1956.

Ibn Tawoos, Ali ibn Moussa. *Fath al-Abwab*. Maktab al-I'laam al-Islami, 1994.

Mutahari, Murtada. *Al-Malhama al-Hussainiya*. Qum: al-Markaz al-'Alami lil Dirasat al-Islamiyya, 1992.